Party, Parliament
and Personality

Hugh Berrington

Party, Parliament and Personality

Essays presented to
Hugh Berrington

Edited by Peter Jones

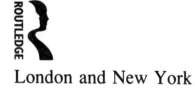

London and New York

First published 1995
by Routledge
11 New Fetter Lane, London EC4P 4EE

Simultaneously published in the USA and Canada
by Routledge
29 West 35th Street, New York, NY 10001

Typeset in Times by J&L Composition Ltd, Filey, North Yorkshire

Printed and bound in Great Britain by
Mackays of Chatham PLC, Chatham, Kent

British Library Cataloguing in Publication Data
A catalogue record for this book is available from the British Library.

Library of Congress Cataloguing in Publication Data

ISBN 0–415–11526–4

To Hugh Berrington

Contents

Notes on contributors

Ivor Crewe is Professor of Government and Pro-Vice Chancellor Academic at the University of Essex. He was co-director of the 1974 and 1979 British Elections Studies and is a former editor of the *British Journal of Political Science*. He has written widely on electoral behaviour, public opinion and political parties. His books include *Decade of Dealignment* and *British Parliamentary Constituencies*. He is currently completing, with Anthony King, a study of the Social Democratic Party.

Philip Daniels is Lecturer in Politics at the University of Newcastle. He has written widely on European politics with particular reference to Italy. He is currently preparing a book, with Ella Ritchie, on Britain's role in the European integration process.

Tim Gray is Senior Lecturer in Politics at the University of Newcastle. He is the author of *Freedom* and co-author of *Burke's Dramatic Theory of Politics* and *The Feminism of Flora Tristan*, and he has published several articles on the political thought of Herbert Spencer.

David Hine is an Official Student (i.e. Tutorial Fellow) at Christ Church, Oxford. He has written on Italian and comparative European politics and is the author of *Governing Italy: the Politics of Bargained Pluralism*.

Sir Bernard Ingham is Honorary Director of the Government–Enterprise Communication Unit at the University of Newcastle. He is a former civil servant who for eleven years was Prime Minister Margaret Thatcher's Chief Press Secretary. He is now a columnist and broadcaster and a public affairs consultant.

Peter Jones is Senior Lecturer in Politics at the University of Newcastle. He is the author of *Rights* and has also written on liberalism, toleration, democracy and social policy. He is currently working on political strategies for dealing with diversities of belief and culture.

Anthony King is Professor of Government at the University of Essex and a former editor of the *British Journal of Political Science*. He writes on American as well as British politics and was recently elected a foreign honorary member of the American Academy of Arts and Sciences. He is currently completing a book on the Social Democratic Party with Ivor Crewe and writing another book on the British prime ministership.

Michael Lessnoff is Reader in Politics at the University of Glasgow. He has published a number of articles on political philosophy and the philosophy of social science, and his books include *The Structure of Social Science* and *Social Contract*.

Iain McLean is Official Fellow in Politics, Nuffield College, Oxford, and co-editor of *Electoral Studies*. He is working on the history of social choice and has two volumes of translations of Condorcet in press. He has also written papers on rational choice and nineteenth-century politics.

Bill Miller is Edward Caird Professor of Politics at the University of Glasgow. He is the author or co-author of several books on elections, democracy and public opinion, most recently *Elections and Voters*, *Irrelevant Elections?*, *How Voters Change* and *Media and Voters*. He is currently engaged in survey studies of democratic values in Britain, Russia and Eastern Europe.

Ella Ritchie is Lecturer in Politics at the University of Newcastle. She is a specialist in contemporary French politics and in European politics. She has written widely on the French right and on *cabinets* in the French and European Union administrative systems. She is currently completing a co-authored book on France and the European Union.

Annis May Timpson is Lecturer in North American Politics at the University of Sussex. She has published a number of articles on electoral, constitutional and gender politics in Canada.

Albert Weale is Professor of Government at the University of Essex. He has written on political theory and public policy, and his work includes *Political Theory and Social Policy*, *The New Politics of Pollution* and a number of papers published in scholarly journals.

Vincent Wright is Official Fellow of Nuffield College, Oxford. He has written extensively on comparative European and, more especially, French government and administration. He has also been joint editor of *West European Politics* since its creation.

1 Introduction

Peter Jones

This collection of essays is presented by its authors to Hugh Berrington. It was prompted by Hugh's retirement from the Chair of Politics at the University of Newcastle, a post he held for twenty-four years. Hugh's career as a political scientist has spanned nearly forty years and this volume recognises and celebrates the many ways in which he has contributed to the study of politics during his long academic career.

In 1956, when Hugh started out as an assistant lecturer at the University College of North Staffordshire, political science was poorly represented in British universities. There were some prominent centres for the study of politics, such as Oxford, the LSE and Manchester, but those were exceptions. In many universities the teaching of politics was limited to two or three lecturers located in History or Economics departments who provided service teaching for students majoring in other subjects. Since those days the study of politics in Britain has been transformed. Most universities now have sizeable Politics departments, a vastly greater number of students read for degrees wholly or partly in Politics, and some of them go on to teach Politics in schools and colleges. The academic literature on politics has also grown immeasurably. Nor have these changes been merely ones of scale. In the 1950s the staple ingredients of Politics as an academic discipline were Public Administration and the History of Political Thought. Nowadays, the content of politics teaching is altogether more diverse and exciting and includes many subjects which barely existed forty years ago. Hugh's career has not merely coincided with this flowering of British political science. He has been a major contributor to its growth, both through his writings and through his role in developing the study of politics at Newcastle and nationally. His contribution to the development of political studies in Britain has won him respect, admiration and affection throughout the political science profession.

Hugh's own research and interests in politics encompass a wide portfolio of subjects. The essays in this collection cluster around just three of them: political parties, Parliament and the political significance of personality.

One of Hugh's favourite observations is that 'politics is about perceptions'. The behaviour of politicians and other decision-makers turns not upon the way the world is but upon the way they perceive it. The same applies to the political behaviour of ordinary citizens. How do people form their political perceptions? The answer is both complex and diverse, but nowadays most of what most people know about a government and its policies reaches them through the media. The relationship between government and media has therefore become extremely important in politics, and particularly in modern democratic politics. Sir Bernard Ingham is peculiarly well situated to comment upon that relationship, since he served as a press secretary in the civil service for twenty-three years, the last eleven of these as Chief Press Secretary to Prime Minister Margaret Thatcher.

In Britain, those formally charged with the task of communicating from government to the media are press secretaries. From the outside, the task of a press secretary may seem fairly straightforward – to communicate what the government or its individual Ministers want the media to hear. But Sir Bernard's essay makes clear that a press secretary's role is altogether more complicated and uncomfortable than that. For one thing, as a civil servant, a press secretary's task is to represent the government rather than the political party to which it belongs, but where the boundary between these two falls is not always clear, nor is it one for which the media has much regard. In addition, press secretaries find themselves having to satisfy and reconcile a number of different and often conflicting interests – those of Cabinet Ministers, Junior Ministers and senior officials, those of the government as a whole and of its MPs, those of television, radio, the press, and the public. These difficulties are compounded for the Prime Minister's press secretary, since he has responsibility for presenting in a coherent form the overall direction of government policy.

Before information can be communicated it has to be gathered, and a striking feature of Sir Bernard's account is how hard a press secretary may have to work to glean information from his own department and how contentious may be the form in which that information is presented to the outside world. Sir Bernard's essay provides a fascinating insight into the interstices of government and illustrates how necessary and exacting the art of reconciliation is not only in the public forum but also within the ranks of the government and the civil service themselves.

The title of Sir Bernard's essay – 'the awkward art of reconciliation' – might serve as a description of democratic politics in general and it is another aspect of that awkward art that Albert Weale examines. In his book *How Nations are Governed* (1964) Hugh Berrington stated his preference for a state that was both highly democratic and highly centralised and expressed his doubts about the alleged merits of 'checks and balances'. In other words, as a patriotic Englishman, he rated the British political system above the American. Yet, as Weale argues, the claim of the Westminster system to deliver clear majoritarian government holds only under special conditions. As long as people's policy preferences are spread along a single dimension, such as a left–right spectrum, a political system like Britain's is likely to deliver winning party programmes that command majority support. But people's policy preferences can be spread across many dimensions rather than just one. A person's preferred welfare policy need imply nothing about his preferred foreign policy and that, in turn, need imply nothing about his preferred policies on law and order and on environmental issues. Thus, when policies are bundled together into programmes, we should expect people's preferences to be spread across a variety of possible policy bundles rather than to be divided between just two of them. Hugh Berrington's work on backbench opinion has revealed how MPs' preferences have been divided in just this way in spite of their party loyalties.

Weale uses the concepts and methods of social choice theory to illustrate the problems that multi-dimensionality creates for the Westminster system. When people's preferences are divided amongst more than two options, no one option may be endorsed by an absolute majority of preferences. We then have to settle for the best analogue to majority preference. That may be either the Condorcet winner (that option which beats all other options in pairwise comparisons) or the issue-by-issue median (arrived at by disaggregating the elements of policy programmes and deciding upon them separately). Thus, under conditions of multi-dimensional policy preferences, the test of a political system's claim to be majoritarian becomes whether it succeeds in delivering programmes which are Condorcet winners or which embody issue-by-issue medians.

Weale argues that, judged by that standard, the Westminster system operated reasonably satisfactorily during the 1940s and 1950s. But by the 1980s its operation had been transformed by a combination of Labour factionalism, three-party competition and coherence on the right. These factors enabled Conservative governments to pursue a Thatcherite programme even though, amongst the electorate, that combination of policies was probably neither a Condorcet winner nor an issue-by-issue median. Indeed, given the likely distribution of policy preferences amongst MPs, including the Tory 'wets', the Thatcherite programme may not have constituted a 'winner' of either sort within Parliament itself, even though the imposition of party discipline enabled parliamentary majorities to be mobilised in its support. Thus the claims of the Westminster system to deliver strong government based upon majority support hold only under special conditions. In the absence of those conditions, he suggests, supporters of majoritarianism should turn their thoughts to constitutional reform.

The development which threatened to do most to upset the Westminster system and which exposed its inadequacies as a form of democracy was the founding of the SDP in 1981 and its subsequent alliance with the Liberal Party. The formation of the SDP represented the largest defection that a major British political party has experienced in this century. It also presented the most serious threat to the two-party system that there has been in post-war Britain. Yet the group of Labour MPs who broke away to form the SDP was actually quite small: roughly ten per cent of the Parliamentary Labour Party. So what distinguished the minority who left from the majority who stayed? Ivor Crewe and Anthony King answer that question by focusing upon 150 MPs who can be loosely identified with the Labour Party's right wing and who might therefore be thought of as potential recruits for the SDP. Why did only twenty-eight of that 150 defect to the SDP?

Despite impressions that developed once the SDP had been formed, Crewe and King show that the defectors had not formed a distinct ideological faction within the Labour right before their defection, nor had they been distinguished by their policy commitments. In particular, there was no clear correlation between defection and pro-European sympathies. Nor, for the most part, were the defectors distinguished by their fears of deselection or their pessimism about the Labour Party's long-term prospects. The factors which were critical to MPs' leaving or staying related much more to their individual political circumstances and to their background in the Labour Party. One such factor was their relationship with their constituency party: hostile constituency Labour Parties (CLPs) helped to push several MPs into the ranks of the SDP. But the most important factor was the character of an MP's relationship with the Labour movement. Those with deep roots in the Labour Party through trade union membership and service in local government, and who had strong personal ties with the community they represented, were much less likely to defect than those whose identities were less comprehensively absorbed by the party. It was these differences in the nature of MPs' relationships with the Labour movement, rather than divisions over policy, that were critical to most MPs' decision to leave or to stay. As Crewe and King conclude, 'the formation of the SDP is another reminder that the behaviour of MPs is often moved as much by the personal as by the political'.

During its short if optimistic life the SDP encountered a number of difficulties, not always of its own making, which led eventually to its disappearance as an independent party. But one matter which remained relatively trouble-free both for the SDP and for its Liberal Allies was Europe. For the SDP and the Liberals, and now the Liberal Democrats, the European issue has been a source of unity rather than division. That cannot be said for the Labour and Conservative Parties. Of all the policy issues that have arisen since the war, perhaps none has so disrupted the normal battle lines of political conflict as the European issue. There has, of course, been inter-party conflict over Europe; the adversarial nature of British politics ensures that parties will make the most of their differences. But the European issue has been more striking and more significant as a source of intra-party division. There is perhaps no clearer example in recent British politics of an issue that has divided politicians in ways which cut across other dimensions of political disagreement, nor one that better illustrates the inadequacies of the Westminster system described by Albert Weale.

Philip Daniels and Ella Ritchie chart the history of the European issue in British party politics. Until the mid-1980s intra-party divisions over Europe were most pronounced within the Labour Party, but since then conflicts between Euro-enthusiasts and Euro-sceptics have been more conspicuous and more damaging within the Conservative Party. Daniels and Ritchie indicate just how complex divisions over Europe have become amongst Conservative politicians: the European issue has itself become multi-dimensional. Nor are things much simpler in the Labour Party; at one time Labour divisions over Europe coincided roughly with the party's traditional left–right cleavage but that simple correlation has now disappeared.

Disagreements within the parliamentary parties have been accompanied by vacillations in their official policies. Daniels and Ritchie examine the changing mix of partisan and European factors that have motivated shifts in the parties' official stances on Europe. They also explain how Europe has injected into British politics not a single 'once and for all' issue but a succession of issues. European integration is a dynamic process which continually confronts member states with new issues. No single government can control the content or the timing of the changing European agenda. In addition, developments in integration inevitably bring with them greater intrusion of European issues into what were formerly matters of purely domestic policy. Europe will therefore continue to present both major parties with a 'poison'd chalice' and one from which they will be forced to drink not just once but many times and perhaps in ever deeper draughts.

One policy issue which may seem to remain very much a 'domestic' matter, uncomplicated by European concerns, is privatisation. Yet, Vincent Wright argues, European integration has been one of several factors which have encouraged the privatisation programmes of West European governments. Some aspects of economic integration, such as competition policy, have limited the ability of governments to use public enterprises as instruments of industrial policy; privatisation has also provided an escape from the constraints imposed by the European Commission on state-controlled enterprises. Other pressures that have converged to provide the impetus to privatisation have included disenchantment with state intervention, the changing nature of public-sector industries, financial constraints and the internationalisation of finance and ownership. But those general pressures alone do not explain why privatisation in Britain and France has been carried through to an extent and at a pace unmatched by the more modest measures of other West European governments. What has distinguished Britain and France, Wright argues, is that their governing parties have been resolutely committed to privatisation and have taken full advantage of favourable political and economic environments to engage in radical policy-making. 'Their privatisation programmes perfectly illustrate the capacity of determined governments to exploit those environments. The preconditions, the resources and the will have all been present.'

Yet, despite those common features, the French and British programmes have exhibited some significant differences. French governments have done more than British governments to shield their newly privatised companies; French privatisation has been less extensive than British and has not included the country's major public monopolies; and in Britain, but not in France, industrial privatisation has formed part of a wider programme of privatisation that has included an array of other market-oriented measures. How are we to explain these differences? Wright indicates that the answer is not simple. In part the explanation lies in the different financial environments and the different detailed aims of French and British governments. But, Wright argues, a more general and more significant explanation is that French governments have been inhibited by a variety of mutually reinforcing constraints – constitutional, political, legal and cultural – which have ensured that their privatisation programmes have been more limited in scope than their British counterparts. Thus both international pressures and national institutional environments have been important determinants of the privatisation programmes of Britain and France, but so too have been the ideological commitment and political will of their governing parties.

Much of Hugh Berrington's research has focused on political parties in their parliamentary contexts and, in particular, upon patterns of backbench opinion that have been obscured by MPs' party allegiances. Iain McLean argues that scholars of parliamentary behaviour have learned less than they might have done from Hugh's pioneering work in this area. What they have failed to notice sufficiently is not Hugh's detailed findings but the model provided by his research programme. This is all the more remarkable given that developments in computer technology have made possible an increasingly sophisticated analysis of the voting patterns, opinions and sociological characteristics of MPs. Nor is it just twentieth-century politics that remains to be fully investigated in this way. McLean insists that we still have much to learn about Victorian politics from an imaginative application of statistical techniques to nineteenth-century Parliaments. He himself argues that multi-dimensional analyses should supplant the dominant unidimensional approach to understanding parliamentary behaviour. Rather than supposing that we can satisfactorily interpret MPs' political behaviour across all issues as so many expressions of a single left–right or radical–conservative spectrum of opinion, we should recognise that their behaviour may be organised along many different and cross-cutting dimensions, and that those dimensions may include different interest group allegiances as well as different dimensions of opinion and ideology.

For much of the last century the pattern of MPs' voting genuinely revealed the pattern of their opinions. During this century, by contrast, party conformity has made the division lists poor indicators of the diversity of opinion to be found amongst MPs, even though in recent years MPs have become somewhat more willing to translate their dissenting views into dissenting votes. Yet there are still some parliamentary occasions when the whips are taken off and MPs are left free to vote in ways which genuinely express their individual opinions.

Perhaps the most celebrated occasions for free votes are parliamentary decisions on moral issues or 'issues of conscience', such as capital punishment, abortion and the regulation of sexual conduct. Something approaching a convention has developed in British politics that, on these issues, MPs are entitled to a free vote. In my own essay I examine that convention and question whether there really is a set of issues which can be distinguished from other political issues merely by their conscientious character and whether political parties, out of deference to the consciences of their MPs, should regard moral issues as beyond the reach of their authority. Sometimes, when MPs invoke their consciences, they do so to claim independence from the public rather than from their party. On issues of conscience, it is often supposed, the Burkean doctrine of the representative comes into its own. Yet that supposition, I suggest, also rests upon a mistake. The more MPs insist that certain issues are *merely* issues of conscience the harder it becomes to justify their resolving those issues in ways which conflict with public opinion.

Of course, the British political system is not designed to make Parliament responsive in any finely tuned way to public opinion. Indeed, there is a long-standing British political tradition which celebrates Parliament's sovereign status within the constitution, including its freedom to act independently of any formal popular constraint other than that exercised through elections. That tradition has attracted increasing opposition in recent years and many of its critics have been persuaded of the virtues of a Bill of Rights which would set limits on the power of Parliament.

So far the most audible voices in the argument over a Bill of Rights have been those of politicians, lawyers and academics. Much less attention has been paid to the views of those upon whom such a Bill would bestow its rights – the British people. William Miller, Annis Timpson and Michael Lessnoff have made good that omission by gathering opinion poll data on a number of issues that figure in the Bill of Rights debate. Amongst many significant findings that they report in their essay are the following: only half the public would feel morally bound to obey an unjust law passed by Parliament; two-thirds of the public believe that important issues should be decided by referendum rather than by Parliament; amongst various devices that might be used to safeguard citizens' rights and liberties, people rate a Bill of Rights the most highly; and rather more of the public would prefer that the power to overrule Parliament should be wielded by the European Court of Human Rights than by a British court. Thus Miller, Timpson and Lessnoff conclude that popular support for the doctrine of parliamentary sovereignty is now weak and that, with the further development of supranational institutions, it will probably continue to weaken.

A standard riposte to proponents of a Bill of Rights is that such Bills are either unnecessary or useless. If a society's political culture embodies the values and principles that a Bill of Rights would attempt to enshrine, that culture together with ordinary political processes should be enough to fend off abuses of power; if, on the other hand, the relevant values and principles are absent from a society's political culture, the deficiency cannot be made good by mere constitutional instruments such as formal declarations of rights. That simple dismissal of the case for a Bill of Rights is much too simple. Abuses can take many forms, and different sorts of protection may be effective for different forms of abuse. However, there are some misuses of power which are difficult to root out by institutional reform alone and one such is corruption.

The Western liberal democracy that has proved most vulnerable to corruption is Italy. Moreover, contrary to the pattern that maturing liberal democracies are supposed to display, political corruption in Italy seems to have *increased* during the last forty years. Why? David Hine describes the intricate and systematic nature of corruption in Italy and argues that a full explanation of its incidence cannot be simple. Part of that explanation lies in the way that sub-national styles of politics, particularly those of the south, have gradually come to infect national party politics. A range of structural features of the Italian political system have also facilitated corruption, such as the blocked and polarised nature of party competition, lack of turnover in government, the nature of relations between the public and the private sectors of the economy, and difficulties faced by the judiciary in prosecuting corruption. But, Hine argues, the explanation lies in cultural as well as structural features of Italian society, particularly in the low status its citizens accord the state and the public sector and in their widespead disrespect for law and legality. These have weakened the normative sanctions that check corruption in other liberal democracies. To that extent, efforts to eradicate corruption in Italy must aim to change the attitudes of politicians and the public as well as to reform the country's institutional structures.

A theme which runs through several of the essays in this collection, and which has formed the nucleus of some of Hugh Berrington's more recent work, is the significance of personality in political life. If we attempt to understand political events entirely without reference to the personalities active in those events we risk misunderstanding them. Can the same be said of political thought? If political theories are shaped in part by the psychologies of those who contrive them, can we fully understand those theories while ignoring the personalities of their authors? Taking Hobbes and Rousseau as his two prime examples, Tim Gray illustrates how certain aspects of their psychologies seem to have shaped their perceptions of the world and to have motivated their social and political prescriptions. Of course, if our concern is with the content and merit of notions such as sovereignty and the general will only as 'free-standing' ideas, the psychology of those who have proposed or entertained them need not detain us. But if our concern is with *Hobbes's* thought or with *Rousseau's* thought – with how they saw the world, with why they saw it in that way, with why they proposed what they proposed, with how their ideas do, or do not, hang together – we may not be able to furnish ourselves with adequate understandings by attending only to their historical circumstances or to the internal logic of their writings. Thus students of political thought, like students of political behaviour, may have to grapple with difficult and often speculative matters of psychology if they are fully to understand their subject. The study of political psychology, which Hugh has promoted so keenly, may help us to understand political thinkers as well as political actors.

2 Hugh Berrington: a profile and an appreciation

Peter Jones

The activity of politics centres upon power, and to be a student of politics is, therefore, to be a student of power. Power takes many forms and has many dimensions, and those engaged in its study can investigate it in different ways and for different reasons. Much of Hugh Berrington's work has focused upon the acquisition and the use of power through the institutions of the modern democratic state; but, in more recent years, he has also turned his attention to those who operate the levers of power – the politicians. What it is that drives their pursuit of power? In trying to answer that question Hugh, like many students of political psychology, has been greatly influenced by Karen Horney's thesis that the quest for power and prestige is a way of obtaining protection and of gaining reassurance against anxiety. According to Horney, the quest for power is, *inter alia*, a striving for two forms of protection: against helplessness ('If I have power no one can hurt me') and against the danger of feeling or being insignificant.

Might Horney's analysis tell us something about political scientists as well as about politicians? Do those who study politicians share something in common with their subjects? Hugh himself has some sympathy with Avner Falk's suggestion that

> political scientists and political biographers themselves have a certain need for (and a certain preoccupation with) power. . . . In other words, in writing a political biography [or, Falk implies, in writing about politics] the biographer [or writer] not only seeks to tell the story of his or her own life, his or her innermost feelings and conflicts, but also to work through early feelings of power-lessness and the quest for power (or fame, or fortune) as an antidote to such painful feelings.
>
> (Falk 1985: 612–13)

Those who choose to study politics may be themselves engaged in a *vicarious* pursuit of power.

However, politics is not concerned wholly or even primarily with 'raw' power. It is also concerned with authority, with what makes power legitimate. To someone with Hugh's acute moral sense, problems of authority were bound to be pressing and troublesome. How can those who wield power claim to do so legitimately and therefore have authority? How do those of us who are required to submit to authority incur that obligation of obedience? When are we entitled to defy, and to rebel against, those who claim authority over us? Hugh's early religious beliefs ensured that his fascination with power was accompanied by an absorption with these disconcerting questions about its legitimacy.

Given the roots of Hugh's interest in politics, it is not surprising that his academic interests have focused on those areas of the subject which relate to the winning and the legitimation of power. Elections, for example, confer legitimacy upon those who win them and, in a mature democratic society such as Britain, power as well. A society's electoral system is a critical determinant of who can claim the right, and who will gain the capacity, to wield power in the name of the people. Political parties have become the principal organisations through which political power is acquired and exercised in modern democracies, particularly in Britain, with its highly disciplined party system, its sovereign Parliament and its centralised form of government. To his study of these institutions and processes Hugh has added an 'internal' dimension. Power is wielded in and through institutions but it is won and used by people – not by bloodless ciphers, but by men and women with richly complex personalities. For Hugh it has become clear that we cannot fully understand the phenomenon of power without investigating the personalities of those who seek it.

The route by which Hugh entered the academic world of political science was far from conventional. He left school virtually on his fifteenth birthday, having failed in his ambition to leave when he was fourteen. University education did not figure in the aspirations of either his family or his school. So, despite being the only pupil in his class to pass the School Certificate, he drew a line under his formal education and went off to work as a junior clerk for Barclay's Bank for a wage of 29s per week plus 6s war bonus. (The bank adjoined Rutlish School, an establishment which spawned another 'school drop-out' – John Major.) Hugh soon discovered that his future did not lie in banking; he found neither the work nor the environment to his liking and was 'liberated' from both by his call-up for national service in 1947.

He spent the next two and a quarter years in the RAF, where he rose to the rank of acting corporal (paid). Although he was stationed in Gloucestershire, the RAF provided him with his first contact with the North East – at his recruit centre he was the only southerner billeted amongst thirty-two Geordies. Forty years later he was to find himself personal tutor to the son of an NCO in charge of his billet at RAF Innsworth. After his release from the RAF, Hugh drifted into local government and became a clerk for Surrey County Council. It was in that role that he took his first hesitant step towards the academic study of politics by entering for the intermediate examination of the new Diploma in Municipal Administration; at the first examination he was awarded the Sir James Aitken Prize for the best performance in the country.

Hugh discovered politics long before his encounter with local government. By the age of eleven he had already adopted and discarded ambitions to be a monk and an historian and had resolved instead to become an MP and eventually Prime Minister. At the politically precocious age of fourteen he joined the wartime Common Wealth Party, an organisation which provided, he recalls sardonically, 'the ideal combination of left-wing socialist aims and middle-class composition'. At the same age he read John Strachey's *Why You Should be a Socialist* (then priced 2*d*) and was totally convinced by it. He also read Conrad Noel's *Life of Jesus* and found in Noel's Christian socialism a compelling synthesis of his own religious beliefs and political convictions.

In 1945, with the virtual demise of Common Wealth, he joined the Labour Party and set about establishing a branch of the Labour League of Youth in the Tory heartland of Epsom and Ewell. It was in the league that he gained his first insights into political behaviour and political psychology, particularly at heavily charged meetings of the Surrey Federation of Labour Leagues of Youth held in a small back room near Clapham Junction Station. In 1952 his talents as an orator (and future lecturer) were spotted when he was awarded the prize for the best individual speaker in the National Labour League of Youth public speaking championship. The previous year's winner had been Betty Boothroyd, the current Speaker of the House of Commons, and, like her, Hugh might have pursued his ambition to sit in the House of Commons had not the academic study of politics diverted him from a political career.

Still lacking sufficient self-confidence to apply for a university place, Hugh decided in 1951 to study part-time for an external B.Sc.(Econ.) of London University. Feeling he was not good enough to do things in the normal way, he chose the hard route instead. For the next three years he spent his evenings attending classes at Kingston Technical College and exploiting the resources of Wimbledon Public Library and its Inter-Library Loans service. In later years, when he was asked where he had read for his degree, Hugh would reply, 'Wimbledon Public Library.' In 1954 his efforts were rewarded, much to his own surprise, with a first-class honours degree – a rare achievement for an external London student.

Hugh's interest in the academic study of politics had already begun to displace his enthusiasm for its practice, and his transition from the idealism and moralism of youth to the gentle scepticism of middle age was under way. His degree result had been noticed by K. B. Smellie, then Professor of Government at the LSE, and 'K.B.', with his redoubtable wife, Stephanie, became Hugh's patrons and steered him towards Nuffield College, where Norman Chester had just become Warden. Hugh has always remained sensible of the kindness and encouragement he received from the Smellies and Norman Chester. He was awarded a studentship by Nuffield and spent two years at Oxford researching the growth of party discipline in Parliament during the late nineteenth century, under the supervision of David Butler and the historian, Pat Thompson. In 1956 he was appointed assistant lecturer in Politics at the University College of North Staffordshire (later Keele University) and became one of the team headed by Sammy Finer from whose ranks so many of the leading figures of contemporary British political science have been drawn. In 1965 he was appointed Reader and Head of the Department of Politics at the University of Newcastle and in 1970 he was appointed to a personal Chair, which the university established on a permanent basis in 1988.

While he was at Keele, Hugh met Catherine Llewellyn Smith, who was then an administrator at the university. They were married just a few weeks before Hugh took up his post at Newcastle. Hugh and Catherine have had four children – Andrew, Lucy, Sarah and Mary – all of whom, unlike their father but like their mother, have taken the normal route into university education.

Hugh's two greatest academic loves have been political behaviour and political psychology. He was an early convert to the quantitative study of political behaviour, and his analysis, with Sammy Finer and David Bartholomew, of parliamentary opinion between 1955 and

1959 was an innovative application of statistical methods to British political institutions (Finer, Berrington and Bartholomew 1961). The book was original in two ways: first in its use of early day motions as indicators of parliamentary opinion and second in its statistical analysis of these. The British are constitutionally suspicious of both innovation and statistics and it is not surprising that a combination of the two provoked scepticism and hostility amongst some of the book's readers. Conspicuous amongst these were journalists, some of whom at that time regarded political scientists as remote and unworldly rivals, and politicians, who often resented the attentions of political scientists in much the same way that ordinary people resent those of psychologists and sociologists. Undeterred, Hugh went on to publish a second masterly study of backbench opinion, this time for the earlier period 1945–55 (Berrington 1973). The objections to the use of quantitative techniques in political science that Hugh and his co-authors confronted thirty years ago now seem as dated and as faded as the pages in which they first appeared.

Hugh subjected nineteenth as well as twentieth-century Parliaments to the rigours of statistical inquiry. His study of voting behaviour in the late nineteenth-century House of Commons (1968) disposed of a number of long-held myths about the nature and influence of the independent MP during the 'golden age' of Parliament that was commonly supposed to have preceded its dominance by the party system. Contrary to the conventional wisdom, Hugh showed that parliamentary dissidents were less of a force for moderation than their party leaders and that the relative independence of back-benchers contributed little to control of the executive. He also exposed fundamental errors in Ostrogorski's (1902) celebrated account of the growth of party government.

Hugh's many other writings have ranged over a wide variety of subjects, including electoral behaviour, electoral reform, political parties and party systems, centre–periphery relations, public opinion, the psychology of politics, the character of the British political system and the nature of politics in general. While he has been fascinated by what quantitative techniques can tell us about several of these, he has never been a fanatic of the quantitative revolution. He has always been acutely aware of the complexities of historical circumstance and of the inescapable significance of the individual political actor. What he has insisted upon is the need for evidence and rigorously sustained argument. He has set his face against the 'arm-chair' school of political science whose members believe that they can understand and explain the political world without leaving the comfort of their firesides. When confronted with the casual but confident generalisations that politics so often attracts, Hugh's favourite ploy is to ask, 'How do we know that?' Anecdote, personal experience and common sense have their place but they are no substitute for the systematic collection of reliable data and, if there is one thing to which Hugh's tolerance does not extend it is intellectual sloppiness.

Yet, in spite of his enthusiasm for hard data, Hugh has never supposed that something exists only if it can be measured, or that the truth must lie where the data are most accessible. Political processes are prey to an indefinite range of contingencies, and the significance of the individual actor is something that can never be excluded from a proper understanding of political activity.

Hugh's sensitivity to these features of the study of politics is no more manifest than in his commitment to the study of personality in politics. This is a difficult subject in which data are not easily gathered and hypotheses not easily tested. It also goes against the grain of most social science, which generally subsumes the study of the individual in the study of the group. But in a century that has witnessed the critical role of figures such as Woodrow Wilson, Lenin, Mao, Hitler, De Gaulle, Churchill and Gorbachev it should not be necessary to insist upon the crucial importance to politics of the personalities of its practitioners. Nor is it only the great and the bad that need the attentions of the political psychologist. Even 'ordinary' politicians are unusual in that most people neither aspire to nor achieve political office. So what is it that drives some members of the population to become politicians and why do those individuals pursue such different paths once they have gained political office?

So far the main beneficiaries of Hugh's work on these fascinating but testing questions have been the students who have signed up in large numbers for his course in the Psychology of Politics, which seems to be unique amongst British universities. They have been initiated in the mysteries of Hi Machs and Lo Machs, of Active-Negatives and Passive-Positives, of dissonance reduction and of groupthink. The wider world has been given only selected but significant tasters of Hugh's highly original work in this area.

Of these, perhaps the most striking is his study of 'British Prime Ministers and the search for love' (1974), prompted by Lucille Iremonger's book, *The Fiery Chariot*. What sort of people turn to careers in politics and succeed in gaining high office? Common sense suggests that they will be individuals distinguished by extrovert, sociable, self-confident and robust personalities, psychologically well equipped for the demands and the rebuffs of political life. Yet Hugh, following the lead of Iremonger, and drawing upon his extensive knowledge of political biography, observed something quite different. So far from fitting the commonsense stereotype, British Prime Ministers have more frequently been introspective, sensitive and reserved. A disproportionate number suffered bereavement in childhood and were unhappy at school. 'To go to Eton is an undoubted advantage for any boy with ambition to become prime minister; to be unhappy at Eton, it seems, is an even bigger one' (p. 357). Most disliked team games and many were lonely and sensitive in adulthood. How are we to account for this inversion of the popular image of the successful politician? Hugh suggests that an explanation can be found in Karen Horney's account of the neurotic personality; those who are deprived of love in childhood develop 'basic anxiety' which drives them to seek protection through the acquisition of power and prestige, including political power, with the eminence and recognition that it brings. 'If it is lonely at the top, it is because it is the lonely who seek to climb there' (p. 369).

It is the spirit of Karen Horney, much more than the shadow of Freud, which looms over the literature of political psychology. To this Hugh adds the work of the American psychologist, O. H. Mowrer, which, he believes, offers a more coherent explanation of the psychological roots of certain kinds of political radicalism than Freud's Oedipus complex. Indeed, it was the work of Mowrer, Hugh confesses, that finally revealed to him the roots of his own former libertarian radicalism and enabled him to see the world in other terms. Hugh has long held that individualism and socialism can derive from a common emotional root – resentment of authority. 'Socialism and individualism are ideologically distant but they can be psychologically akin.' If we wish to understand why ideologues profess the beliefs they do, we must investigate more than their own protestations.

Hobbes's advice to those who sought to understand the 'thoughts and passions' of others was 'Read thyself,' and that is advice that Hugh has followed. He has had first-hand experience of several of the conditions that he and Iremonger observed in the early lives of Prime Ministers. Like many of them, he was bereaved in childhood (his mother died when he was two), he disliked team games and he was unhappy at school. He also claims, with disarming frankness, that his ambition, like that of some politicians, springs from low self-esteem, itself a result of his childhood experience. Horney, Mowrer and the psychology of politics have enlightened more than his professional life.

Although Hugh has been very much one of the 'new school' in his approach to the study of politics, he is very much one of the 'old school' in the breadth of his interests and in his knowledge of the subject. He is as happy to swap thoughts on Hobbes or John Stuart Mill as he is to talk about the ecological fallacy or the latest opinion poll findings. His detailed knowledge of history enables him to turn to the past as readily as to the present for an understanding of political life and, in making his case, he is as likely to call upon the experiences of Ethelred the Unready or the penetrating cynicism of Lord Salisbury or the moral integrity of Sir Henry Campbell-Bannerman as he is to cite the Suez crisis or the presidency of Richard Nixon. His intimate knowledge of the Bible (the Authorised Version, of course) and of the 'greats' of English poetry, particularly the works of Shakespeare, Milton and Shelley, provides him with another rich source of wisdom, circumstance and character which he mines to great effect. That knowledge, combined with his prodigious memory (which so impressed the playwright John Osborne in their boyhood days) enables him to recite verse upon verse from the Gospels or *Julius Caesar* or *Samson Agonistes* or *Adonais* or, indeed, the *oeuvre* of Hilaire Belloc, as befits each personal circumstance or political occasion, tragic or comic.

Hugh's contribution to British political science has been institutional as well as academic. His shrewd judgement, practical wisdom, penetrating insight, fastidious attention to detail and willingness to work unstintingly have placed him much in demand as a committee member and as a chairman. He has served the UK Political Studies Association as successively its secretary, treasurer, chairman and president and, since 1983, as one of its vice-presidents. For many years he chaired the SSRC's and ESRC's advisory committees on Election Studies, a role in which he has exercised an important influence on the shaping of British election studies. Many scholars whose research proposals have passed through his hands have been grateful for the perceptive advice they have received from him. He has also been much sought after as a member of editorial boards, as an external examiner, and as an assessor for research proposals and for senior posts in the profession.

The qualities that have made Hugh such a valued member of the political science profession have also made him a much favoured candidate for office at the University of Newcastle. For twenty-one of his twenty-nine years he was a member of Newcastle's relatively small university senate. He also acted as the university's public orator, and served on its council and on innumerable committees, many of which he chaired. Prominent amongst these was the university's Library Committee, which he chaired for eighteen years. The excellence of the university's current library owes much to Hugh's assiduous promotion of its interests, as successive Librarians have been keen to acknowledge. In particular, his partnership with the university's innovative Librarian Brian Enright was one of the most rewarding and fruitful of his career.

Hugh also served several periods of office as Dean of the Faculty, often at times when the faculty was most in need of his resourceful and skilful handling of difficult problems (and sometimes difficult people). He has frequently been turned to as the only person able and willing to perform some important and difficult task. His ability to hold thirty things in his head simultaneously, his capacity to anticipate a dozen possible consequences of a course of action, and the adroitness with which he handles potentially fraught situations have made him the obvious choice. Perhaps his most outstanding contribution to the University of Newcastle, however, has been his development of the Department of Politics itself.

In 1965, when Hugh was appointed Reader in Politics at Newcastle, the department was said to consist of 'a man and a boy'. The man was Hugh and the boy was Tim Gray. They were soon joined by a youthful Vincent Wright. The department had narrowly escaped closure, and Hugh realised that closure would remain a threat as long as the department was so small. During the twenty-nine years that followed he worked tirelessly to develop the department. The task was not easy. Politics was not amongst the subjects that the university had planned to develop, and Hugh was able to expand the department only by a policy of 'enlargement by stealth' – by carrying abnormally high student–staff ratios and by repeatedly demonstrating to the university the acute need for another post in Politics. (In 1965 the department's student–staff ratio was 22 : 1; in 1994 it was still 22 : 1.) It is a measure of Hugh's success that, in the year of his retirement, the Newcastle Politics Department consists of some twenty members of staff, nearly 400 undergraduate students reading either for honours in Politics or for one of the department's five joint honours degrees, and over 100 postgraduate students working for either M.A.s or research degrees in Politics.

Hugh's commitment to his department has, in part, reflected his commitment to its students. He has always believed that a university's obligation to educate its students should not be sacrificed or allowed to take second place to its other purposes. He has also led by example. Despite the demands placed upon him by the headship of the department, deanship of the faculty and service on a plethora of committees, and despite the department's high student numbers, he has borne a teaching load equal to, and often greater than, those of his colleagues. His teaching has been inspirational. Generations of his former students, some of whom have gone on to become academics themselves, testify to the lasting impact upon them of Hugh's lectures and tutorials. But it is not only his undergraduates and postgraduates who number amongst his students. It is impossible to work alongside Hugh without being educated by him, and all those contributors to this volume who are either past or present members of the Newcastle department will readily admit to the impact Hugh has had upon their own intellectual development.

Hugh has remained head of department throughout his twenty-nine years at Newcastle. The department is so much his creation and is so marked by his presence that it is difficult to imagine what it will be like without him. But different it certainly will be. Who can match his capacity to anticipate quite so many ways in which decisions might adversely affect the department and worry about them with quite so much angst? Who can emulate the way he masterminds and negotiates his way through marathon departmental meetings – and emerges fit and feisty at their conclusion when exhausted bodies lie all around him? Can anyone else be quite so hungry for 'gossip' and retail it with such benign delight? Can anyone rival his dedication to the telephone? Will we ever discover how he manages to find the right document amidst the scattered mounds of paper that cover every available surface in his office, including the floor, and which constitute his special contribution to the art of filing?

In many ways Hugh has been the victim of his own virtues. His skill as an administrator and his Protestant sense of duty have made him easily put upon. That has benefited his departmental and university colleagues enormously but it has exacted a heavy price from Hugh himself, both personally and as a scholar. He has produced a continuous stream of publications throughout his career but there is no doubt that the constant demands of teaching and administration have deprived political science of the full benefits of his fertile intellect. Ironically, 'retirement' will give him opportunities to write which he has not enjoyed for many years.

Many projects await him. He is already engaged in a comprehensive study of British political parties. He is also under pressure from both publishers and colleagues to pass on to the world his insights into the psychology of politics. Then there is the continuing study of backbench opinion, a project that was stalled some years ago by the many other demands upon Hugh's energies and by the untimely death of his collaborator, John Leece. Much remains to be revealed about the make-up of backbench opinion during the last three decades and, in particular, about the shifts in parliamentary opinion that so altered the characters of both major political parties during the 1980s. This volume of essays is a tribute to Hugh's past achievements and to the contribution that he has made to political science; but its authors also hope it will encourage him to continue enlarging our knowledge of politics and our understanding of politicians.

REFERENCES

Berrington, H. B. (1968) 'Partisanship and dissidence in the nineteenth-century House of Commons', *Parliamentary Affairs* 21: 338–74.
—— (1973) *Backbench Opinion in the House of Commons 1945–55*, Oxford: Pergamon.
—— (1974) 'The fiery chariot: British Prime Ministers and the search for love', *British Journal of Political Science* 4: 345–69.
Falk, Avner (1985) 'Aspects of political psychobiography', *Political Psychology* 6: 605–19.
Finer, S. E., Berrington, H. B., and Bartholomew, D. J. (1961) *Backbench Opinion in the House of Commons 1955–59*, Oxford: Pergamon.
Ostrogorski, M. (1902) *Democracy and the Organisation of Political Parties*, trans. F. Clarke, London: Macmillan.

3 Democracy and disagreement

Albert Weale

Hugh Berrington's *How Nations are Governed* (1964) was a splendid book. Within the 107 pages of its main text it provided a lucid and knowledgeable introduction to the study of politics. Its Hobbesian account of the orgins of government was complemented by a series of chapters covering a wide range of topics, including constitutional issues, the role of political parties, electoral systems, varieties of executive and legislative relations in liberal democracies, government in non-democratic states and international government. It was theoretically clear, empirically informed, comparative in scope and written with Hugh Berrington's typical verve and conciseness. As far as I can see, there are only two – characteristically English – reasons why it has not become one of the standard texts put into the hands of all students of politics: the failure of the publishers properly to market it and the backward-looking nature of the British political science profession, for whom the behavioural revolution was (and in some cases still is) a thing of the future.

Of course it is unfair to take any author's textbook as the starting point of an extended discussion. Even if one thinks that the book contains the beginning of wisdom on the topics it discusses, authors are likely to feel that the genre compresses the exposition of their thoughts about a subject to the point of distortion. On the other hand, like those giving public lectures or broadcast talks, authors of textbooks often find themselves expressing succinctly thoughts that they can develop at length only elsewhere and perhaps then in a somewhat fragmentary and partial form. Such is true in this case. I am inclined to think that in the introduction to *How Nations are Governed* Hugh Berrington touched on a theme that has recurred throughout his research and writing. Here is the passage in question:

> my preference is for a state which is highly democratic, and in which authority is, at the same time, highly centralized. This

prescription may at first sight seem contradictory but in fact it corresponds closely to government in Britain. I am sceptical of the value of traditional 'checks and balances,' embodied in such devices as second chambers, federalism, and the separation of powers. The British Constitution is no longer 'a thing of checks and balances' and it is most unlikely, if it were, that any modern British Government could perform the tasks expected of it.

(Berrington 1964: viii–ix)

There is in part an echo here of an older controversy arising in the wake of the French Revolution about the relative merits of complex government, as favoured by Burke, and simple government, as favoured by Mackintosh, Paine and Godwin (Halévy 1928: 181–4), but there is also, as I shall try to show, a series of issues on which contemporary social choice theory has some interesting light to shed. Before passing on to these broader issues, however, I think it will be useful to see how the theme of democratically accountable, but authoritative, government arises in other parts of Hugh Berrington's work.

One of the clearest places at which this theme resurfaces is, perhaps unsurprisingly given the context, in the *Festschrift* for Sammy Finer edited by Kavanagh and Peele in a paper entitled 'British government: the paradox of strength' (Berrington 1984). This paper begins by noting the division of opinion among commentators and political scientists over whether the British central executive is to be regarded as weak or strong. Taking the traditional view of the Westminster system, expressed in the preface to *How Nations are Governed*, that the British system of disciplined two-party government provides a strong and stable executive, Berrington subjects it to analysis in terms of the development of post-war British policy-making. The main argument is that, in so centralising authority, British government has become vulnerable to the malign influence of pressure groups, seeking their own sectional interest, their own piece of the pork from the communal barrel. Whereas the multiple points of entry to government decision-making in the United States provide a check upon the influence of particular groups, at least rendering their activities visible, the concentration of political power in Britain within the central executive means that decision-making takes place behind closed doors (Berrington 1984: 27).

Much of the paper is concerned to document the extent and mode of influence of pressure groups upon decision-making in British government since the Second World War. However, the analysis takes place within a broader context of concern about constitutional and institutional redesign. The paper builds upon Finer's use of Calhoun's concept of concurrent majorities. In this view the influence of pressure groups is seen to be a form of decision-making based upon the principle of concurrent majorities, and Berrington agrees with Finer that the task of constitutional reform is to replace the system of concurrent majorities with one of numerical majorities (Berrington 1984: 25). The particular institutional prescriptions that emerge from this analysis are less distinctive than the reasons that are used to support them. In particular, Berrington's preference for proportional representation rests upon the interesting observation that, under the present system of voting, governments that alienate a particular section of the population incur a special electoral cost. Whereas with proportional representation the loss of seats in the Commons would be proportionate to the loss of the electorate that had been alienated, under the British system of 'first past the post' the electoral costs are normally multiplied by a factor of two or three (Berrington 1984: 36). The overall institutional prescription that emerges from the analysis is that British governments need the sphere of their competence constitutionally limited and prescribed, so that decision-making can be more effective within these prescribed limits. It is better to be an effective representative of the numerical majority over a limited range of issues than to be ineffective over an unidentifiably wide range of issues.

I have already noted that the traditional doctrine that is being attacked in 'British government: the paradox of strength' appears to be the doctrine that was being upheld in *How Nations are Governed*. Note, however, that in both cases there is a commitment to majoritarianism in principle, so that the evolution of view here is in line with the Burkean observation that the intellectually honest man changes his opinions but not his principles. But what has led to this change of opinion? One obvious source is the problem of overload much discussed in the 1970s (e.g. Brittan 1975; King 1976). However, another key influence, I conjecture, is to be found in Berrington's work on political parties, in particular in his work on backbench opinion in the House of Commons.

Towards the end of *Backbench Opinion in the House of Commons 1945–55* there is an interesting passage in which the function of the nation state in aggregating preferences and opinions is compared to that of political parties. Just as, according to Lipset's (1963: 83–90) famous analysis, cross-cutting cleavages reduce the level of intensity involved in political choice, so non-cumulative cleavages within a political party will increase its ability to make make a unified choice (Berrington 1973: 224). The argument here is both specific and general. In its specific form it relates to the differences between the Labour Party and the Conservative Party in the Parliaments between 1945 and 1955. In its general form it relates to the ability of any political institution to engage in successful preference aggregation. To understand this dual argument, we can use the specific example to explain the general proposition.

One of the main burdens of *Backbench Opinion in the House of Commons* is to describe and analyse the complexity of ideological divisions within the Labour Party, and in particular to scotch the misconception that the divisions within the party are to be understood as a conflict between an intellectual middle-class left and a working-class right. The analyses clearly show, to my untutored eye at least, that the divisions were more complex than this simple dichotomy presupposes and that not only did the social composition of the Labour left change over the ten-year period but also that on a number of issues coalitions were shifting and fluid. Thus the core of what was to become in the 1950s the Bevanite left did not share the same opposition to conscription and to NATO that the strongly pacifist and communist-inclined left did in the late 1940s. Nevertheless, despite these complexities, it is clear that the divisions that existed within the Labour Party did reflect certain structural differences both of occupation and of ideology. There were stable factions within the Labour Party and they were associated statistically with clearly defined social groups. Working-class, trade union-sponsored MPs were more concerned with material bread-and-butter issues and supported the Labour government on matters of foreign policy, whereas those from middle-class professional and miscellaneous occupations showed more concern with libertarian issues and formed the core of the consistent opposition to Labour's post-war foreign policy.

On Berrington's analysis there was a marked contrast here with the Conservative Party in the same period. Particularly after 1951 dissent within the Conservative Party became more difficult to manage, especially on law and order and colonial affairs. But the striking thing about this dissent was that it never took the rigid form that was manifest in the Labour Party. It was not possible from the scrutiny of early day motions or the analysis of floor revolts to find a factional core of opposition to the Conservative leadership. Nor were there any occupational correlates of those who rebelled. Instead, the picture that emerges is one in which *ad hoc* coalitions of particular individuals, aggrieved or disgruntled about particular matters, express their dissent in various ways. Nothing in the Conservative Party corresponds therefore to the structural divisions within the Labour Party.

This organisational manifestation of the 'Damn your principles, stick to your party' spirit is what in Berrington's view distinguishes the relative success of the Conservative Party from the difficulties that Labour experienced: 'the greater social homogeneity of the Conservatives, the more integrated character of the party, the extent to which opposition to the leadership on one issue cut across opposition on another, all helped to make them a more efficient electoral machine than Labour' (Berrington 1973: 225).

One of the ways in which this difference is shown is in the terms by which the organisation of the political parties is analysed. Whereas the Conservative Party can be regarded as a coherent and integrated organisation, the Labour Party has to be regarded as an amalgamation of rather disparate elements. In particular, it can be understood as an alliance of two distinct temporal strata of British politics: nineteenth-century radicals and twentieth-century collectivists (Berrington 1973: 213) and this in part helps us understand the 'tacit contract' between the working-class supporters of the Labour Party, interested in higher material standards of living, and its middle-class activists, interested in Third World development and humanitarian social reform. Moreover, different groups within the Labour Party pursued their different demands with different enthusiasm. Where it was possible to amalgamate their demands into a larger programme the Labour Party could be regarded as a 'system of institutionalized log-rolling' (Berrington 1973: 221). In this sense the Labour Party could be expected to find it much more difficult than the Conservatives to aggregate the demands of their supporters into a coherent programme.

What does this have to do with the critique of the traditional Westminster system of government? The answer, I suggest, is that political parties and political systems can both be regarded as institutions for aggregating diverse preferences where a collective or common choice has to be made. More particularly, within the traditional Westminister view political parties *are* the prime institution for accomplishing this amalgamation. Hence any pathologies of political parties will not only be analogous to pathologies of the political system at large, they will in fact be contributory, and probably prime, causes of it. The opposition to the system of checks and balances in *How Nations are Governed* rested upon a number of elements, but one that was central was the argument that divided government prevented the making of public policy in the light of a unifying programme (e.g. Berrington 1964: 72–3). But if political parties, like the Labour Party, are divided within themselves about their priorities and value preferences, then it will not be possible for the party system to provide the contest of unified programmes that is essential to democratic, accountable government. This problem, I suggest, is implicit in the concern about the functioning of national institutions and the decision-making capacity of political parties.

In the remainder of this essay I shall examine this problem in the light of contemporary social choice theory. Although an abstract account of political institutions, contemporary social choice theory provides the tools, I shall argue, for conceptualising the conditions under which preference aggregation is satisfactorily carried out, whether at the level of the nation state or at the level of political parties.

PREFERENCE AGGREGATION IN THE WESTMINSTER MODEL

In considering the relevance of the social choice results to the Westminster model of government and political parties, we need to note that the Westminster doctrine is in part a claim of principle and in part a claim of institutional design. The claim of principle is that democratic accountability is best served by the competition of competing alternative programmes of public policy, in which the electorate is given a clear choice between unified programmes. The proposition of institutional design is that this clear choice is best fostered by the competition of two parties for a winning share of the popular vote, with a voting system that delivers a clear majority in the House of Commons.

What conditions would need to be satisfied in order for the Westminster model to work in the way intended? One obvious condition is that it should be possible for political parties to present clear and unified alternatives to the electorate. But clear programmes have to embrace a number of different dimensions of public policy, ranging from economic policy, through questions of the welfare state and the limits of the criminal law to foreign policy and defence. So what are the constraints that will render commitments in these diverse areas consistent with one another? In essence, the constraints can come only from one of two sources: they must either be logical, that is, they must somehow be intrinsic to a given belief system, or they must be institutional, that is, they must represent a norm or practice among political actors to treat various commitments as a unity.

To see this, let us imagine a society in which the legislature has to debate only one set of issues, namely the domestic distribution of income and life chances generally. Under this heading there may be a series of policy measures (social security, health services, the trade-off between fiscal responsibility and public spending, etc.) but each of these individual measures can be evaluated by the members of the Parliament in terms of one set of underlying questions – say, the extent to which they promote or hinder a more equal distribution of life chances. Moreover, if the measures present themselves as a series of binary choices, such that one has to be either in favour of the measures or against them, then it is easy to see why, under the conditions of modern campaigning, there would be a tendency for two, and only two, parties to form. One is either for or against greater equality of life chances, and the organisational imperatives of structuring the political agenda, selecting candidates for office, and deciding on priorities within one's overall value commitments would supply sufficient pressure to create a two-party system. Moreover, such a system, once established, would create formidable barriers to entry for new parties seeking to compete for office.

Thus, aside from random fluctuations, we would expect the two parties to present a clear division of opinion between themselves over these issues but relative unity within themselves. Moreover, each party would have an incentive to elaborate a coherent doctrine to the electorate about why it took the position it did on any particular issue in the light of more general beliefs about how the social and economic world worked. Of course, a party that found itself permanently in a minority in terms of public opinion would either have to compromise its stand on the range of issues in question (the famous Downsian move towards the median voter) or introduce ambiguity into its position (another Downsian tactic) but there would be little reason for parties to be internally divided.

Suppose now that we introduce another set of issues, let us say those connected with the foreign policy agenda. Once we do this, we raise the question which, to the best of my knowledge, was first adumbrated by Sidgwick (1891: 563–77) in a delicious chapter of *The Elements of Politics* (a chapter which even anticipates the critique of adversary politics). Sidgwick in effect asks: why should we suppose, when we expand the political agenda into more than one dimension, that there should simply be two parties? As he points out with characteristic acuteness, there are good reasons why those in favour of some large public policy measure should compromise on their minor differences in order to determine jointly the line of action most favourable to their common end, but there is no logical reason to expect even large combinations of this sort to be all-inclusive. A libertarian party might oppose a socialistic party, but a third party might favour the cause of popular government, whereas a fourth might have an opposite aim. Similarly, a fifth party might want to promote a dovish foreign policy, whereas a sixth might collect together the hawks. In sum, he concludes:

> There seems to be no clear general reason why any one of these parties should coincide with any other; persons convinced of the expediency of extended popular control over government might easily differ on questions relating to the limits of governmental interference, or on the proper character of the foreign policy of the state.
>
> (Sidgwick 1891: 566).

Sidgwick believed that there was a tendency towards the creation of a two-party system in Britain and the United States but in his view this arose not from any reason connected with the tasks of legislation but from the organisational imperatives associated with appointing the chief or leading members of the executive. In the absence of this imperative, he argued (rightly, in my opinion) that the formation of parties in a modern state 'would probably be of a complicated and shifting kind' and even with the institutional imperative of choosing the members of the executive there is still a tendency towards plurality in the party system where 'each of the two opposing parties is often composed of parts which very imperfectly cohere . . .' (Sidgwick 1891: 567, 569).

If we follow Sidgwick's argument this far, as I think we should, then we have to look for institutional constraints to create the coherence that the members of a party lack in terms of the logic of their underlying ideology. Here modern social choice theory is helpful in identifying the institutional conditions under which stability and coherence can be given to a policy programme. In order to illustrate its lessons I shall work with a stylised example, which I shall adapt from *Backbench Opinion in the House of Commons*. The example is intended to be merely illustrative, and I am aware that it simplifies the interpretation of a complex data set. But, as so often with formal theory, simplified examples illustrate best the fundmental point of principle at issue.

Consider, then, the distribution of policy preferences in a world

Welfare state

		For	Against
	For	*w*	*y*
Alliance			
	Against	*x*	*z*

Figure 1

where there is more than one dimension of policy. I shall consider a world in which there are only two dimensions of policy, one concerned with the domestic distribution of life chances and the other with foreign policy. I shall also simplify by assuming that the issues have a binary character, so that in connection with domestic issues one can be either for or against a 'welfare state' and on foreign policy questions one can be either for or against a military 'alliance' like NATO. With two dimensions, and with two options of choice in each, we can represent the policy alternatives in terms of the two-by-two matrix of Figure 1. In this matrix *w* is the most preferred option of those who favour both the welfare state and the alliance; *x* is the most preferred option of those who favour the welfare state but not the alliance; *y* is the most preferred option of those who are opposed to the welfare state but in favour of the alliance; and *z* is the most preferred option of those who are opposed to both the welfare state and the alliance.

Incidentally, let me note that post-war British politics has contained groupings for whom counterparts of each of these options have been their most preferred choice. Thus *w* was the typically post-war Bevinite position supported by most of the Parliamentary Labour Party, whereas *x* was the position of the quarter or so of the 1945–50 Parliamentary Labour Party whom Berrington designated as the foreign policy left (1973: 62). The Conservative Party in the post-war period cannot easily be assigned to the *y* category, but it has moved between *w* and *y*, favouring *w* in the heyday of Butskellism and *y* in the heyday of Thatcherism. Finally, note that *z* is not empty: there is a tradition of market-oriented thinking, represented at various times by Enoch Powell, in which hostility to the Atlantic alliance has played a significant part.

It is important in this representation that each dimension of political opinion is logically distinct from the other. One of the ways of seeing this is to ask what the preference ordering might be over all the alternatives. Clearly, for most people the least preferred option is the one in the opposite diagonal of the matrix, but it is logically possible to order the preferences in any way, subject to that constraint. Thus the preference ordering of the Bevinite might be w, x, y, z or it might be w, y, x, z. Unless this were so, we would not be dealing with two dimensions of policy but one, for we should essentially be saying that a uniform ordering could be imposed upon preferences and partisan positions could be located along that single ordering. Thus the off-diagonal elements of the matrix are not simply intermediate stages between two extremes: they can be considered as reference points in their own right.

Since it is clear from Berrington's work that it was the Labour Party that contained the clearly distinct ideological factions, let us consider the pattern of intra-party bargaining and dissent that might be expected to arise from this pattern. Here a crucial institutional fact interposes itself. Within the conventions of the House of Commons, voting never takes place over all the dimensions of possible conflict simultaneously, except on the monarch's speech, where party discipline is very tight. Hence, whenever there is an occasion for voting or for a motion, it always represents a choice within these dimensions. It is as though members were voting on the welfare state questions, holding the debate about foreign policy in abeyance, and as though they were voting on foreign policy, holding the debate on the welfare state in abeyance. Given this institutional constraint on voting over issues in the two-dimensional issue space, the dilemma for the Labour left is now obvious. On any debate in which the welfare state is an issue they will always vote with the Bevinite majority of their party, since they always prefer w to y. On any debate in which foreign policy is an issue, they will always face the combined forces of the Bevinite wing of the Labour Party (for whom both x and z are always inferior to w) and the Conservatives (for whom x is always the worst option). The only place they could look for help would be to neutralist libertarians, for whom z is the most preferred option, and in the immediate post-war period there were not that many around (there are only a few now).

Thus it is not surprising that the left was so helpless in the 1945–50 period, with its only weapon the early day motion and occasional floor revolts but without the ability to shift the policy preferences of the Bevinite majority. The most obvious preference ordering to ascribe to the left would be x, w, z, y, in which case they got at least their second preference from the Attlee government, but it is possible that foreign policy issues were so important to them that their preference ordering might have been x, z, w, y. This latter ordering implies that foreign policy issues were so important that they would have been prepared to sacrifice working-class living standards at home to achieve their foreign policy goals. This is not an absurd interpretation. One could say that those who continued to resist the NATO alliance even after the announcement of the Marshall Plan were in effect choosing this course, even though they would probably have denied the trade-off implicit in their position had it been put to them. Had there been any 'third force' Conservatives there would have been the possibility of detaching the Labour left from the mainstream of the party in an attempt to push neutralist foreign policy priorities, but of course the distribution of opinion within the Conservative Party simply ruled this out.

If I have reconstructed the preference profile correctly, then it seems to me that the relation between the left and the Bevinite wing of the Labour Party was not so much a case of log-rolling as of fellow-travelling on the part of the left. Log-rolling requires the possiblity of vote-trading (compare Mueller 1989: 82–9), and in a sense the left had no votes to trade. They would not vote against the government on the welfare state issues, and they were always going to be outvoted on the foreign policy issues anyway. Vote-trading, like other forms of trade, works best when the parties have different endowments that they can bring to the trade, and this in turn usually arises when the parties are different in a number of key respects from one another. Hypothetically, therefore, the most likely log-roll would be between social democratic parties with a preference ordering of w, x, y, z and libertarian neutralist parties with a preference ordering z, x, y, w. Though both diverge in respect of their first preferences, they agree on their second preferences, leading to a situation in which the libertarians support the social democrats on the welfare state in exchange for the social democrats supporting the libertarians on a neutralist foreign policy. To my knowledge no such log-roll has ever emerged in West European liberal democracies. Of course, social democratic politicians of the post-war period, convinced of the need for a strong foreign policy towards the Soviet bloc, would have found it rational to lock themselves into international alliances to prevent their party falling prey in the future to the temptations of the neutralist log-roll, since an international alliance provides a strong institutional check upon such a strategy.

SOME NORMATIVE ISSUES

In this section I want to look in a little more detail at the normative properties of the sort of situation that I have so far discussed. In order to do this, I shall need to introduce two concepts. The first of these is that of the 'Condorcet winner'. The Condorcet winner in the context of majority voting is that alternative which can beat all the others in a pairwise contest, even though it may not be able to obtain a majority if it is put against all other alternatives simultaneously. To illustrate this concept consider Figure 2, which replicates the same sort of domestic/foreign policy alternatives that we have already considered in relation to the post-war House of Commons, but this time for a hypothetical chamber of 100 members. Below the matrix I have entered the preference ordering for the four imaginary parties (A, B, C and D) represented in the legislature along with the proportion of votes that each party controls.

It is easy to see that the overall policy programme of party A (pro-alliance/pro-welfare state) is not the first preference of an overall majority of the chamber, since party A controls only 40 per cent of the votes. Nonetheless, its policy programme is a Condorcet winner, since if it is pitched in a pairwise contest against each of the other programmatic alternatives it will beat each one of them under the rule

Welfare state

	For	Against
Alliance For	w	y
Alliance Against	x	z

Party A (40 per cent): $w\ x\ y\ z$

Party B (20 per cent): $x\ w\ z\ y$

Party C (20 per cent): $y\ w\ z\ x$

Party D (20 per cent): $z\ x\ y\ w$

Figure 2

of majority voting, provided parties are voting in accordance with their policy preferences. For example, w will defeat x because party C prefers w to x and will vote with A against the coalition of B and D, who both prefer x to w.

When there are more than two alternatives before a voting body, it is quite common to find that there is no outright majority winner. In these circumstances the notion of the Condorcet winner gives a second-best sense to the concept of majority preference, since although it is not an alternative that commands majority support when taken by itself, it has the property that no other alternative when pitched against it in a pairwise contest will be able to defeat it. This also means that the Condorcet winner forms the basis of a majority-rule equilibrium, in the sense that no coalition of voters, acting in accordance with their preferences, will be able to defeat it, to their own advantage, by uniting behind an alternative proposal. From the point of view of majoritarian values it seems an attractive property of any social choice procedure that it should pick the Condorcet winner if there is one.

The second concept to be introduced is that of the 'issue-by-issue median'. This is a weaker notion than that of the Condorcet winner. Figure 3 illustrates a variant on Figure 2, but this time in circumstances in which there is no Condorcet winner. Although alternative

Welfare state

		For	Against
	For	w	y
Alliance			
	Against	x	z

Party A (40 per cent): w x y z

Party B (20 per cent): x z w y

Party C (20 per cent): y z w x

Party D (20 per cent): z x y w

Figure 3

w beats *x* and *y* when pitched against them in pairwise voting, it does not defeat *z* but is instead defeated by it, since the majority coalition of B, C and D prefer *z* to *w*. But since *z* itself is not a Condorcet winner, being defeated by both *x* and *y*, there can be no Condorcet winner in this situation. In other words, if all programmes are pitched against all others, there is no alternative that can emerge as the victor under the rule of majority voting. Nevertheless, there is still an issue-by-issue median, namely that alternative which will emerge as the winner provided that the alternatives on which members vote can be constrained to each of the dimensions of choice one by one. In particular, if the preferences of members are separable, in the sense that their view on foreign policy questions is logically independent of their view on the welfare state and vice versa, then it will be possible to consider each dimension of policy separately. The issue-by-issue median will then be *w*, since it will be the culmination of a process in which the 60 per cent who favour the alliance will defeat the 40 per cent who do not, and the 60 per cent that favour the welfare state will defeat the 40 per cent that do not. The result of these two *separate* votes will lead to *w* as the issue-by-issue median.

An important property of the issue-by-issue median is that it is a *structure-induced equilibrium*, in the sense that, provided issue by issue voting is used, no majority coalition of voters will find it in their interest to defeat the issue-by-issue median. In this sense it is an analogue of the Condorcet winner, where no coalition, even with unconstrained voting procedures, would find it to its advantage to overturn the Condorcet winner. Moreover, an important property of majority rule is that if there is a Condorcet winner, then the issue-by-issue median under majority rule leads to that point. (For all these technical results see Ordeshook 1986: especially 245–51.)

In the light of Berrington's work on the post-war House of Commons, it looks as though the Bevinite position was a Condorcet winner between 1945 and 1955. On the welfare state both parties were Butskellite and on foreign policy the leaders of both parties were in agreement and could form a majority against their own dissidents on the back benches. It was this latter feature that lay behind Crossman's complaint about the L-shaped distribution of opinion in the House of Commons in the foreign policy debates of the early 1950s (Berrington 1973: 27).

In a period of consensus politics it was difficult to move from this position, either at the level of the legislature or at the level of the mass electorate. For most of the post-war period foreign policy questions were less salient to mass electorates than were welfare state issues, so that Conservative opponents of the welfare state, who knew that their position on defence and foreign affairs was favoured by the electorate, could not compete in that dimension but were forced instead to compete in the dimension in which the social democratic consensus was overwhelming.

In British politics the heyday of the social democratic consensus was also the heyday of two-party politics, so it is not surprising that the structure-induced equilibrium was also a Condorcet winner, since two-party majority contests will select the Condorcet winner, provided they are functioning with a reasonable approximation to standard assumptions about party competition (competitive agenda-setting, random abstention and the like).

I have described the Labour left as locked into the position of fellow-travellers of the Bevinite position essentially because there was no one else for them to team up with. But what happens if the proponents of x, the non-Bevinite form of social democracy, take control of the Labour Party so that the proponents of w, the traditional social democratic position, then have to decide whether they will be fellow-travellers with the left? In essence, the answer is that the happy coincidence of parliamentary majority and structure-induced equilibrium breaks down under some plausible assumptions. This was what happened in the 1980s under the impact of a variety of pressures, so that at the 1983 election the Labour Party presented the most non-Bevinite manifesto on which it had stood in the post-war period. The defections to the Social Democratic Party and the strength of the Liberals meant that the Conservatives were bound to be the largest party in the House of Commons. But since under Mrs Thatcher the Conservatives had abandoned their post-war commitment to the social democratic consensus, the majority position of the Conservatives meant that they had the ability to impose y rather than w as the overall programme.

What does this mean in terms of the normative criteria of social choice that we have discussed so far? It boils down to a number of specific questions. Was the Conservative Party or the Conservative programme of the 1980s either a Condorcet winner or an issue-by-issue median in the country at large or in the House?

In terms of the country at large it is difficult to decide whether the Conservatives were a Condorcet winner, but my conjecture is that they never were at any period in the 1980s. One way of imagining what this question involves is to ask what would have happened if a mysterious virus had led each of the three leading parties to withdraw their candidates from each constituency in which they were standing before the election. Which of the remaining two parties then would have received a majority of the votes cast? The most straightforward case is to suppose that the virus had struck all the Alliance candidates. Since we know that the Alliance drew its support more or less equally from the two major parties, the natural thought is that the second preference of Alliance voters would have gone equally to the other two parties, leaving the Conservatives with a majority over Labour. Labour could not therefore have been the Condorcet winner. This means that we have to ask what would have happened if the virus had struck all the Labour Party candidates. Would the Conservatives have had a majority over the Alliance or vice versa? In order to have had such a majority, they would have had to have picked up about a third of the Labour vote. Given that they picked up such a high proportion of the C2s anyway in their vote, who were those previous Labour voters who may be thought to have had the greatest interest in voting Conservative, it is seems doubtful whether the Conservatives ever were the Condorcet winner in the 1980s, although it is possible that they may have been in June 1983.

It is easier to answer the question of whether the winning Conservative programme of the 1980s represented an issue-by-issue median for the country at large. Here the relevant thought experiment is to ask how the vote would have gone in referenda on such issues as the welfare state and the Atlantic alliance, and the closest we can get to answering this question is to examine the opinion poll data. Examining these data, Ivor Crewe (1989) has shown that on welfare state issues the Thatcherite ethic of self-reliance was a 'crusade that failed'. Although in May 1979 public opinion was equally divided between those who wanted to cut taxation even at the cost of cutting services and those who wanted to improve services even at the price of increased taxation, by the mid-1980s there was an overwhelming two-to-one majority in favour of improving services, even at the cost of raising taxes. Issues connected with the Atlantic alliance are more difficult to plumb, but the Gallup data regularly report a majority or near majority of the electorate favouring the Conservative position on defence, and this looks like some measure of proxy support for the Atlantic alliance. There are no public data on the intersection of these sets of respondents, so it is difficult to know whether the results are consistent with the pro-welfare state/pro-alliance stance being a Condorcet winner, but it does look as though it was the issue-by-issue median. Hence it looks quite clear that the Conservative programme of the 1980s as implemented departed from the popular issue-by-issue median, which was still Bevinite.[1]

What happens when we turn to a consideration of the distribution of opinion in the House? Here we raise some intriguing questions that as yet cannot be answered. The standard social choice results on the structure-induced equilibrium presuppose 'sincere' voting, that is, that legislators vote in accordance with their underlying preferences. Since virtually all the work of the application of social choice theory to legislative voting has been done in the United States, where party discipline on floor votes is low, the principal reason, as conceptualised within the approach, for voting insincerely is strategic vote-trading. But in the House of Commons the 'insincerity' of voting has to be conceptualised more broadly, to encompass voting constrained by party discipline. In the 1980s party discipline meant that, by and large, the Conservatives could push through their party programme, although not without some setbacks, as on the issue of Sunday trading. But what would have been the distribution of opinion had all public policy issues in the fields of foreign policy and the welfare state been decided by a series of free votes?

Clearly, neither neutralist socialism nor neutralist libertarianism came near to large numbers in the House, so that a programme favouring an Atlantic alliance and market liberalism would have defeated either of those alternatives. The real question then concerns the choice between government intervention and the welfare state on the one hand versus market liberalism on the other. Here then the fundamental question is whether the 'wets', who for a variety of reasons, especially party discipline and the Conservative norm of loyalty, supported the Thatcherite programme, would have done so on free votes had the questions been taken issue by issue. Until the analysis of backbench opinion is conducted for the period 1979 to 1992, in the same way that Hugh Berrington has analysed the House of Commons in earlier years, we shall never know the answer to this question, but it would be fascinating to know whether the Conservative wets in the 1980s were in effect in the same position as the Labour left in the 1940s – unhappy with a central dimension of their party's policy but constrained to support the overall position *faute de mieux*.

What can be established, therefore, is that the programme of the Thatcher government was at odds with the issue-by-issue median preference of the population at large. In the absence of further empirical evidence it is impossible to know whether the divergence between the government's programme and popular preference can be attributed to the electoral system or the system of party discipline in the House of Commons, or some combination of both. Either way, key elements of the classic Westminster model doctrine come under strain once we recognise the dimensionality of the conflicts involved. Indeed, if the sincere issue-by-issue median in the House of Commons had diverged from the government's programme, the Westminster system would not only have failed to pick up the popular issue-by-issue median, which might not have worried its less populist proponents, but would also have failed to pick up the issue-by-issue median in the House, which ought to worry anybody.

SOCIAL CHOICE AND CONSTITUTIONAL REFORM

Issues of constitutional reform are unlikely to be settled by the niceties of social choice analysis, but such analyses can help clarify the questions at hand, and the seriousness of the matters involved. In particular, I have argued that when we apply social choice concepts to the workings of the Westminster system we begin to highlight the extent to which the defence of that system rests upon specific conditions and circumstances, many of which cannot be expected to hold in a general way. Following Hugh Berrington's lead in *How Nations are Governed*, we saw that a central element in the defence of the Westminster system was its ability to put forward and implement a public policy programme exhibiting coherence across the whole range of public policy. Yet this is possible in the Westminster system only under very specific conditions.

One such condition is that all issues can be reduced to a single dimension of difference between competing parties. If only two parties compete for a winning share of the popular vote, then under the normal circumstances of party competition they both have an incentive to gravitate towards the position of the median voter. Disproportionality between votes cast and seats obtained is not a problem in this situation, since the party programme advanced in the House of Commons will be that of the median voter, and it can be argued, along the traditional lines of defence of the Westminster model, that increasing the overall government majority in these circumstances, which is what the first-past-the-post system does, has certain practical advantages in terms of enabling the winning party to implement its programme.

Recognising that there is likely to be more than one dimension of political disagreement does not necessarily cast doubt upon the operation of the Westminster system in terms of its representativeness of public opinion. Thus the party rebels of the post-war Labour government were reflecting an underlying complexity in the dimensionality of political argument, but they found it impossible to shift the position of the government, simply because they lacked potential allies. Although the dimensionality of the conflict may be important, it does not have to be, and in the circumstance of the post-war Labour government it turned out not to be. The social democratic consensus around Bevinite values that was the majority preference in the country at large was also the majority position in the House of Commons.

What will destroy the ability of the House of Commons to represent the country is a combination of Labour factionalism, coherence on the right and three-party competition. In these circumstances the winning party may not hold to an overall policy position that corresponds to the issue-by-issue median in the country at large, and the ability to challenge that party on the most electorally salient issues may be undermined by the division of competing parties who cannot mobilise opposition effectively. Lack of electoral proportionality and strong party discipline do become barriers to the adequate representation of public opinion in the House of Commons in these circumstances.

The Westminster system was a tightly constructed set of institutions. Take away one of its elements and the whole edifice begins to collapse. By the time he came to write 'British government: the paradox of strength' Hugh Berrington had substantially altered his opinion about the merits of the Westminster system. The arguments from social choice theory that I have tried to develop suggest that the problem of preference aggregation over more than one dimension of public policy is a deep and serious one, and the ability of the Westminster system to solve it by providing the institutional means for producing coherent policy programmes is limited.

But perhaps the hardest question of principle for the proponent of the Westminster model is the one most familiar to the student of British government, namely the question of openness. For obvious reasons the Westminster system encourages that most English of practices, sweeping things under the carpet. The trouble is that after a while the accumulation of dirt becomes unbearable. Then a new constitutional broom is not only desirable: it is absolutely necessary.

NOTE

1 I should like to thank David Sanders for drawing my attention to the potential of the Gallup data to provide evidence on the question of popular opinion on these questions.

REFERENCES

Berrington, H. B. (1964) *How Nations are Governed*, London: Pitman.

Berrington, H. B. (1973) *Backbench Opinion in the House of Commons 1945–55*, Oxford: Pergamon.

Berrington, H. B. (1984) 'British government: the paradox of strength', in D. Kavanagh and G. Peele (eds) *Comparative Government and Politics: Essays in Honour of S. E. Finer*, London: Heinemann.

Brittan, S. (1975) 'The economic contradictions of democracy', *British Journal of Political Science* 5(2): 129–60.

Crewe, I. (1989) 'Values: the crusade that failed', in D. Kavanagh and A. Seldon (eds) *The Thatcher Effect*, Oxford: Oxford University Press.

Halévy, E. (1928) *The Growth of Philosophic Radicalism*, London: Faber, 1972 edn, ed. J. Plamenatz.

King, A. (ed.) (1976) *Why is Britain becoming Harder to Govern?*, London: BBC.

Lipset, S. M. (1963) *Political Man*, London: Mercury Books.

Mueller, D. C. (1989) *Public Choice II*, Cambridge: Cambridge University Press.

Ordeshook, P. C. (1986) *Game Theory and Political Theory*, Cambridge: Cambridge University Press.

Sidgwick, H. (1891) *The Elements of Politics*, London: Macmillan.

4 The awkward art of reconciliation

Sir Bernard Ingham

The date: 20 November 1990. The time: approximately 6.45 p.m. The city: Paris. The scene: the courtyard of the British ambassador's residence next to the Elysée Palace, where, like the rest of the world's political leaders gathered in the city to mark the end of the Cold War, President Mitterrand is bemused by the drama being played out in the Palace of Westminster across the Channel.

Suddenly there bursts upon the world's television screens a middle-aged and immaculately coiffeured woman of undoubted presence. The majestic doors of the embassy fly open. She marches resolutely down the steps, casting confusion into the ranks of the British Broadcasting Corporation as she more or less tramples on a live broadcast by their mellifluous political correspondent, John Sergeant.

She is pursued by what appears to be a raging and ageing prop forward who repeatedly asks, 'Where's the microphone?', a seemingly irrelevant question, bearing in mind the momentous history being made at this moment.

The woman is, of course, Margaret Thatcher announcing her long-rehearsed intention to fight on after failing to secure the necessary annihilating rather than simple majority over Michael Heseltine in her second defence of her leadership of the Conservative Party.

The puce prop is the writer, who was playing out to the bitter end the conflicts and tensions inherent in a civil servant who becomes Chief Press Secretary to the Prime Minister of the United Kingdom of Great Britain and Northern Ireland.

Mrs Thatcher, as she was then, was only doing what she, after consultation with her political advisers, had been programmed to do in the terminal events unfolding there. They had the previous week drawn up an elaborate coloured grid which dictated the sort of response she should make from Paris in any eventuality – in this case, to hold her support among MPs in Westminster. She made that response. She fought on to win.

That did not kid either me or Mrs Thatcher – or conceivably the media gathered in the embassy courtyard. She had confided as much even before we flew to France. If she did not win on the first ballot, she said, 'We,' – the ubiquitous 'We' in 'We are a grandmother' – 'are in trouble.'

I was most certainly in trouble. As a civil servant I had no role in the party political events being played out in Paris and London. The Government Information Service (GIS) represents only the policies and measures of government and the activities of Prime Ministers as distinct from party leaders.

Mrs Thatcher, in travail with her party, was no public concern of mine, whatever private views I may have had after eleven years with her. But the press, radio and television had no time for such constitutional niceties unless they provided them with a story. They lived only for the moment. They wanted Mrs Thatcher's announcement clear and quick, and no messing. And I had always conceived it to be part of my job to serve journalists – to build a bridge between the government and the media and to keep it serviceable at all times and in a good state of repair.

Had Mrs Thatcher had to cope only with the writing press – a luxury not enjoyed since the 1950s – she could have issued a quick message to the Press Association, Reuter's and AP and her position would have been safeguarded. But, on her behalf, I had also to think of a fiercely importunate radio and television who want – nay, demand – voice and pictures. That was why I arranged for a central microphone in the courtyard to ensure that not merely a privileged pool of some twelve writers and broadcasters, with the chance of questioning her, could hear what she had to say for herself at the foot of the steps but also so that the rest of the British journalists elsewhere in the courtyard could get a good quality sound 'feed' of her announcement directly. All of them were up against early evening deadlines.

This celebrated cameo of government–press relations has many lessons, not the least of which is the impossibility of satisfying British journalists. They subsequently charged me with anything from 'bullying' to 'activities unbecoming of a civil servant', even though I was serving their purposes.

It is, of course, true that I could legitimately have sat on my hands and my civil service neutrality and allowed Tory Party events to emerge as they developed and as they would. That would not have unduly discomfited Mrs Thatcher, who was as keenly aware as any other Minister I have served of the constitutional requirement to separate party from government. Indeed, as we once walked down a Westminster corridor to launch a book about her, published by a company headed by the Tory MP Sir Tom Arnold, she earnestly asked me whether it was proper for me to be present. I said it was: this was a Prime Ministerial/commercial event and not a party occasion. We all have to be on our guard, and there were many who argued that I overstepped the mark in Paris.

But imagine the consequences of my apparently abandoning the Prime Minister to a wholly unrestrained press pack at the moment when her hold on the leadership of her government as well as party hung in the balance. The interpretive headlines write themselves: 'Press Secretary admits Thatcher is a goner' . . . 'Rat deserts sinking Maggie.' My detachment could – and probably would – have created a political monster invested with its own significance for Mrs Thatcher's future. This is not to mention the odium that would have descended on the British ambassador – and his motives – for neglecting to cater for the needs of the media, who must be served, if not obeyed. 'FCO ditches PM,' the *Sun* might have screamed. Press secretaries have to be aware that doing nothing can have worse political implications than doing something.

I do not regret my instinctive choice. It was by far the line of least offence. I also know that I would have done the same for any other Prime Minister, whatever his or her political complexion. After all, I have served enough potential ones in my time – Barbara Castle, Tony Benn, Roy Hattersley and, not least, the late Labour leader, John Smith.

I mention this sketch from real life because, more than any other issue or event I encountered in my twenty-three and a half years in the civil service, it illuminates the conflicts inherent in the official life of a press secretary drawn from the ranks of an ethical civil service. Whether they serve a Prime Minister or a member of the Cabinet, a press secretary continuously practises the awkward art of reconciliation. And the conflicting interests to be reconciled are manifold.

These conflicts stem partly from the highly devolved nature of the British Cabinet system of government. While the Prime Minister is *primus inter pares*, he or she makes few policy pronouncements beyond those affecting constitutional issues, national security and appointments, including honours. Responsibility for devising policies and measures rests with individual Cabinet Ministers, according to their portfolio. Policies are hammered out within the department, where competing departmental interests have first to be reconciled. They then have to be refined to take account of other departmental concerns and the overriding Treasury interest in containing public expenditure. Having, fingers crossed, passed muster with other departments, the Minister tries to clear them through Cabinet. If successful, he announces them to Parliament and answers for their execution. The Prime Minister's role in all this is strategic: as the custodian of the government's overall philosophy, coherence, direction and thrust, he or she strives to keep the government train on the rails, driving forward and avoiding being shunted into embarrassing sidings or, worse still, suffering damaging reverses or crashes into buffers.

One of the departmental team of advisers who assists the Cabinet Minister in this process is his Chief Information Officer, or press secretary. His – or, almost as often these days, her – job has changed little fundamentally since I wrote my first job description on joining the Department of Employment in 1968, though it has become much more complicated with the growth of television and the speed of satellite communication. It is 'to promote an informed press and public about the government's policies and measures and to advise Ministers and officials on their presentation'. Operating within the constraints of a budget, he typically commands a division made up of three sections – a press office which is in the front line of relations with journalists; publications and briefing, producing written information; and publicity, handling such 'paid for' media as advertising, posters, films and videos and radio communication. At a price, he can call on the assistance of the Central Office of Information (COI), a common service government communications agency, to help with his department's publicity and its campaigns to promote, for example, road safety or energy saving.

The third leg of the government's communications apparatus is the No. 10 press office under a Chief Press Secretary whose first allegiance is to the Prime Minister, just as the departmental press secretary's first loyalty is to his Minister. But he has a wider responsibility for the government's overall presentation. He seeks to present the Prime Minister as leader of a government which is seen to be more rather than less coherent and to relate actions on one front with those on another, ideally to suggest a grand design. Thus he seeks to ensure that the government's communications orchestra is seen and heard to be playing from one score in tune and in time in the same way that the departmental press secretary conducts a more specialised chamber ensemble. It is a thankless task.

Because of the devolved nature of the British system of government, the Chief Press Secretary wields less authority in his role as a
co-ordinator than a departmental press secretary does on his own
patch. He cannot require action; he can only persuade. And departmental press secretaries, once persuaded by him of a particular course
of action, have in turn to convince their Ministers of its desirability.
Unfortunately, Chief Press Secretaries tend to be suspected of narrowly serving the Prime Minister's ends. Thus those MPs – Tory as
well as Labour – who invested me with great power by dubbing me
'the real deputy Prime Minister' served only to reveal their ignorance
as well as their mischief.

It follows that among the conflicts which a departmental press
secretary seeks to resolve in the course of a day's work is that
between the interests of the Cabinet Minister who heads his department and those of his Junior Ministers. They have their own ambitions and may have been placed in the department by the Prime
Minister to keep an eye on the Cabinet Minister – as first John
Smith and then Dickson Mabon watched over Tony Benn for Harold
Wilson and Jim Callaghan. He has also to reconcile these varied
interests with those of the accounting officer, the Permanent Secretary to the department, who answers for its expenditure of public
funds and is officially responsible for the activities of the press
secretary; the department's senior officials, who often have their
own agendas; the COI as a watchdog over the propriety of the
government's publicity output; the No. 10 Press Office in seeking
to present a coherent view of a government that is always a loose
coalition of attitudes and policies under constant refinement by
negotiation; the often bitterly conflicting requirements of the writing press, radio and television; a sceptical public whose credulity is
better not stretched; and MPs who are always the first to criticise
presentation when their party falls foul of public opinion.

The No. 10 Chief Press Secretary has to try to reconcile these
conflicting interests, plus one other: that of departmental press secretaries. It was not for nothing that I came during the 1980s to call my
information colleagues 'the robber barons'. They have, to repeat, to
be convinced of the wisdom of a proposed course of action. In my
experience, a Chief Press Secretary is likely to be the more persuasive
if he is an experienced professional who knows his job backwards,
takes personal responsibility for the co-ordination of government
presentation rather than devolving it on his deputy and manifestly
has the confidence of his Prime Minister. Politically motivated
journalists, whom the Labour Party has generally recruited to the

post, are probably less effective, partly because of their open political affiliation and partly because they lack knowledge of the government machine. What they gain in freedom from civil service constraints they probably lose in damaged credibility, though much depends upon the individual.

How these many conflicts are reconciled is the stuff of a British government at work. The drama is played out twenty-four hours a day and 365 days in a normal year. There is no respite for a press secretary, any more than there is for his Minister, at least on the big issues which arise, often without warning. The task of the No. 10 Chief Press Secretary is merely that of his departmental brother writ large, for the effect of ever more demanding media and international satellite television has been to focus attention on recognisable international symbols – the boss, not the responsible but obscure Cabinet Minister. Mr Major may be portrayed as a 'grey' man, but to the media he is a peacock compared, for example, with the Social Security Minister, Peter Lilley.

In examining how the awkward art of reconciliation in the information field works in practice, let us start with the most crucial relationship: that between Minister, Prime or otherwise, and his press secretary. Like every other civil servant, a press secretary has to take what he gets. He may loathe his Minister personally, though I came to enjoy all my Cabinet Ministers. He may think his attitudes and policies stink. But he cannot show any of this. If he cannot contain himself, he ought to resign or seek a transfer. His professional task is to help present the Minister's policies and measures to the public in the most effective way. His own inner thoughts are of no consequence whatsoever. Thus, the Minister's personality is neither here nor there in terms of the relationship, though it is germane to the conduct of the department's publicity operations, as I shall explain later.

It is also the case that Ministers have to be satisfied with their press secretaries. They want to feel they can trust them as individuals and professional advisers. There has to be a certain bond between Minister and press secretary. I was put to the test at least four times.

The first was with Robert Carr, the sincere, honest and, for politics, the altogether too decent Secretary of State for Employment who in 1970–2 sought, through the Industrial Relations Act, to bring the trade unions within a framework of law. At least for a time, he believed in the rationality of man.

From the outset he had a problem with me. I had been brought up in a Labour home. It was not a left-wing, revolutionary upbringing. Far from it. My parents, both cotton weavers, distrusted left-wingers and hated communists. They would have walked many miles to vote against either of them. They were solid, responsible, upright people who would have felt appallingly pretentious to be described as 'socialist'. They believed in order, discipline, paying their way and the Labour Party. They were the sort of people who, forty years later, would have found Mrs Thatcher quickening their blood, though probably not sufficiently, given their background, to vote for her.

I had written a blisteringly anti-Tory column for the Labour *Leeds Weekly Citizen* in the early 1960s under the pseudonym 'Albion', which confused no one in Leeds journalism. In 1965 I had unsuccessfully fought Moortown, arguably the most hopeless Labour ward in Leeds. I subsequently had offers, not all of them instantly to be rejected, to present myself as a prospective Labour candidate for half a dozen Yorkshire constituencies. I took none of them up because, either explicitly or implicitly, I was expected to secure trade union sponsorship. That stuck in my craw. I had an idealistic view of the sea-green incorruptible independence of Labour MPs. I had also been a Labour reporter for the *Guardian* at a time when all Labour correspondents tended to wear their hearts on their sleeves, though the imprint of my heart rapidly faded the more I had to do with the unions' headquarters. And I had been recruited by Barbara Castle, Mr Carr's Labour predecessor in the department, as her speechwriter and subsequently become the department's Chief Information Officer.

Ironically, I was 'investigated' by Paul (now Sir Paul) Bryan, Minister of State for Employment, who had thrice – and vainly – fought Sowerby, the constituency in which I was brought up and first voted. As a junior reporter, I had covered, entirely impartially, some of his election campaigns. As such – and no less as a civil servant in the Department of Employment – I had abandoned any party political activity or affiliation. Sir Paul must have 'cleared' me, for Robert Carr (now Lord Carr) told me within a few days: 'Your political past is no concern of mine. All I want is your professional service now and in the future.' That, I told him, was precisely what he had acquired.

Then came Tony Benn who cut a tragic figure in the Department of Energy in 1975. Prime Minister Harold Wilson had removed him from the Industry Department, the only department he confessed to coveting, in a straight swap with Eric Varley, with whom I had got on enormously well. For the first three months, Mr Benn saw as little of the Department of Energy as he could. He spent his time closeted with his political advisers, Frances Morrell and Francis Cripps. Eventually he conceived the idea of a Ministerial broadcast on North Sea oil, without giving the Opposition right of reply. I told him that it simply wasn't on. North Sea oil, in process of nationalisation, was, unlike energy conservation, highly controversial. I was nonetheless sent away to write the script of the proposed broadcast.

To cut a long story short, both No. 10 and the BBC rejected the text, as amended by Mr Benn, twenty-four hours ahead of the event. I made the mistake of telling Mr Benn I agreed with the BBC. His private secretary, Ronnie Custis, compounded the mistake by agreeing with my judgement. Mr Benn wrote us both out of his forthcoming trip to the USA which, in the event, did not take place. Mr Custis was given another post. As a specialist, I had a problem because, to repeat again, there is no future for a Chief Information Officer who cannot get on with his Minister. There are seldom alternative posts available. Only recently, I had been on 'gardening leave' when I was forced out of the Department of Employment on the appointment, to succeed Mr Macmillan, of Willie Whitelaw who returned with his head of information from Northern Ireland.

I consulted John Smith, the late leader of the Labour Party. He gave me the best personal advice I have ever had from any member of any government. It consisted of four words: 'Wedgie doesn't like rows'. So I contrived a private meeting with him which began with my saying: 'Can we start this meeting by my making the point that, of all the 1,300 civil servants in this Department, I have a vested interest in your success if only because the less successful you are the more problems I have to sort out?' Mr Benn did not, indeed, like rows. He and I never looked back, as his diaries reveal – until I joined Mrs Thatcher.

Which brings me to my third test in my role as Mrs Thatcher's Chief Press Secretary. It did not stem from the press comment about my political past when my appointment was announced. Instead, it arose from my dissatisfaction with the parliamentary lobby journalists – the 'Lobby' – as a means of communicating ideas in depth. Somewhat foolhardily, I therefore proposed that she should meet small groups of four or five political correspondents, each of which I had identified for myself, for a relaxed discussion. The horse fell at the first hurdle because the political correspondents of the *Financial Times*, *The Times*, the *Guardian* and the *Daily Telegraph*, the first beneficiaries of this intended series of briefings, came out with similar stories about the likely course of economic policy. This earned the Prime Minister much derision on the floor of the House.

The media wrongly alleged that she was reintroducing the 'White Commonwealth' – the name given to a group of journalists who had privileged access to Prime Minister Harold Wilson and whose existence caused him much difficulty. Mrs Thatcher was not best pleased at the time, though later she put it in context: 'If that's all you got wrong, it wasn't bad going.'

There was one other test: when Leon Brittan's press secretary at the DTI in 1986 asked me to leak the Solicitor General's comments on one of Michael Heseltine's frequent initiatives during the Westland affair. Had I not refused point blank to do so, saying that I had to keep the Prime Minister above that sort of thing, I have little doubt that the course of Britain's political history would have been changed. As a No. 10 private secretary put it to me at the time: 'I think you made your wisest decision.' In fact, I would no more have thought of leaking the contents of such a letter than I would have contemplated hara-kiri. So much for Westland conspiracy theory.

Each of these vignettes illustrates the forging of a relationship between a Minister and his or her press secretary. That relationship is subject to much stress and strain, trial and error and professional judgement and integrity. It can only survive if there is trust on both sides and a determination to make it work. That is the bedrock on which any Department's media relations are founded.

Without that bedrock there is a vacuum. And since nature – and politicians – abhor a vacuum, it will rapidly be filled either by a new Chief Information Officer or effectively by a Parliamentary Private Secretary (PPS) or a political adviser who would, in any case, be active in the Palace of Westminster on their Minister's behalf. That is why the head of information has to take account of their interests and activities, too. Imagine trying, as a written-off press secretary, to compete with a PPS or political adviser who has the Minister's confidence and his or her own ambitions to warm his activities. I have seen too many bear markets in heads of information who are being undermined and consequently carry little conviction. Yet a press secretary has but one stock in trade: his credibility as an informant. That is why I sought at all times to demonstrate that I was master in my own information house and to repel all boarders. At least those who might harbour ideas would know they had a fight on their hands.

Any new Chief Information Officer could be imported on the pretext, for example, of the Minister's alleged lack of personal chemistry with the existing incumbent or, better still presentationally, that the present information officer was required elsewhere, assuming a credible post could be found for him.

A Permanent Secretary, as the Departmental accounting officer and the top official answerable for the Chief Information Officer's behaviour, likes to have a Secretary of State and press secretary who are comfortable with each other. That is one fewer problem. They will, of course, worry if their relationship gets too close, as mine may have seemed to do with Maurice Macmillan, Secretary of State for Employment 1972–3. (Mr Macmillan was a former MP for Halifax, where I was born and for which he retained an abiding love. He even took as his title Viscount Macmillan of Ovenden – a district of Halifax. Halifax folk could do little wrong in his eyes.) This was not, however, why I caused the late Sir Denis Barnes, Mr Macmillan's Permanent Secretary, much distress when I failed to prevent the Secretary of State from flying to Geneva for an International Labour Organisation conference just as the Official Solicitor, a previously obscure law officer, was about to spring from prison a number of dockers detained for breaches of the requirements of the new Industrial Relations Act. Mr Macmillan had no more inclination than I had for him to be seen to be panicking by returning to his department from Heathrow

Similarly, Sir Jack Rampton, Permanent Secretary at the Department of Energy, found somewhat alarming my willingness to go along with Tony Benn's desire to place on record a detailed account of a Euro-agnostic's presidency of the European Community's Energy Council. He was not as alarmed as I was. Mr Benn had been smitten by my argument that he would do much to disarm his critics in Brussels and elsewhere if he took his presidential duties with manifest seriousness and reported assiduously to the various levels of the Euro-pyramid. There has never been a more conscientious President of the Energy Council. So, out of the clear blue sky of June 1976, he conceived the idea of a detailed public account of all his Community works over the previous six months. He was in no way deterred when I pointed out that this rested primarily on my ability to read all the shorthand notes which, much to his amusement, I had made of his European meetings. Sir Jack's relief was as nothing compared with mine when we got away with this interesting but little-noticed record.

If Permanent Secretaries prefer a quiet life, Deputy Secretaries and Under-Secretaries, the next two rungs down the civil service ladder, will settle for a more bruising existence with the press secretary. They – and the Minister's Principal Private Secretary, the man who runs his office – are closely involved in the formulation of policies. They are the chief custodians of the facts and therefore the range of possible options confronting a Minister. Naturally, they have their own ideas as to how things should be played and they do not take kindly to the media trampling all over them, with the active assistance, as they might see it, of press officers. They may therefore play things very close to their chests for all bureacracies tend to be secretive. Knowledge is power and information is not, therefore, lightly to be shared.

A Minister could command his machine to keep the press secretary informed of the formulation of policy but that could be counterproductive. He could be swamped with paper when what he needs, to supplement those policy meetings he attends – inevitably somewhat at random because his priorities lie with his Secretary of State and media relations – is a clear steer on the way policy is panning out, the problems along the way and the arguments for and against a particular course of action. He needs to be able intelligently to rehearse with journalists the options which confront government in developing policies. Thus a press secretary's relations with senior officials and the Minister's private secretaries are crucial.

The government machine is now much more positive in its approach to the media and public than it was when I first entered Whitehall in 1967. The prevailing view then seemed to be that the press secretary's job was to keep journalists quiet and at bay. He was not generally seen to be there, as I believe he is, to open up relationships but to hold Denis Thatcher's reptiles at arm's length. Again I was lucky in the Department of Employment, my first department proper, because its principal task in the 1960s and 1970s was the conciliation of national disputes which invariably ended up on the doorstep of No. 8 St James's Square, SW1. One of my principal tasks was to direct the industrial theatre increasingly played out before the television cameras in St James's. Even so, it never seemed to occur to some senior civil servants – or perhaps they did not care – that a press secretary was of limited utility if he was all smiles, words and bonhomie when the going was good and dumb, deaf and dead when all hell broke loose.

All my memorable rows in twenty-three years in the government's service were with obstructive senior officials. I was, of course, a joke among my fellow Chief Information Officers for a good ten years because of my chronic inability to recognise myself as a civil servant. I had good reason not to do so. All too often I felt myself to be an outsider looking in. I had had enough of that as a journalist. I spent seventeen years as a provincial reporter trying to drag informational blood out of a stone only to discover, when I came to London in 1965, that there the gen for journalists was provided on a plate and washed down with fine wine. I had no intention of returning to an informational desert, especially when I was supposed to be on the inside track.

Far from resolving the tensions which confront a press secretary in the execution of his duties, his positive approach to communication could then, and still might, increase them, though not usually with his Minister.

First, he might frighten the civil service horses. A Deputy Secretary in the Department of Energy once complained that I was altogether too certain of myself. I retorted that someone needed to be certain of something amid all the 'on the one hands' and 'on the other hands' I so frequently encountered.

Second, a positive press secretary's ambition will almost certainly outstrip his supply of information. As is abundantly clear from this account, I found throughout my career as an information specialist that my first requirement – reliable information – was hard to come by. For example, 'facts' on 'factsheets', prepared at the outset of an industrial dispute, would seldom survive until a settlement without amendment. And Lady Thatcher confirms the secretive nature of the system in the first volume of her memoirs, *The Downing Street Years*. Discussing the announcement of decisions on top salary increases in 1985 she writes: 'Fear of leaks meant those entrusted with explaining the rationale of our policy simply did not know about it in time. Even Bernard Ingham had been kept in the dark which, when he raised the matter with me afterwards, I conceded was absurd.'

This demonstrates what I found to be a continuing problem as a press secretary. He is at once an insider and an outsider. His Minister or Prime Minister may accept him as an insider, but this is no guarantee that other insiders will take the same view and furnish the information with which a fellow insider might reasonably be trusted. Why? The secretive nature of the British system of government is partly to blame. For me this reached utter absurdity when British information freely available under the more open Swedish or American systems was still held to be confidential in this country.

But there are other factors. Our system is highly geared to the protection of individual Ministers. This compounds its jealous guarding of information. Most officials, in my experience, prefer to keep the media at arm's length. They have a healthy distrust of all their works and, believing perhaps that press officers can survive only by casting their bread upon the waters of what used to be Fleet Street, extend it to them. In fact, press officers do not automatically communicate their every morsel to their best contacts in journalism. They are among the least leaky parts of Whitehall.

Exceptionally, some officials wish to do their own thing with the media. They can be very destructive of a press office's relations with the press. For example, I once thundered into the office of the Director of Establishments in the Department of Energy because the *Financial Times* was systematically so much better informed about certain issues than I was and could only have got its guidance from officials. It had to stop, I said. The Director took my point, though things did not improve much.

Inevitably, press secretaries create tensions and jealousies within a department because they have instant access to the Secretary of State and far more contact with him than the average higher-ranking divisional head or Deputy Secretary. Only a blundering press secretary fails to recognise this and to handle his position carefully in relation to those officials responsible for formulating policy. I would have been happier, however, if these officials had more readily granted me the right to have a policy, which I used to prepare for Ministers, setting out the principles governing presentation and providing a framework for its conduct over the next six to twelve months.

The concept of the supremacy of the administrator over mere mechanics such as press secretaries was at the root of my unresolved row with an Under Secretary in the Department of Employment in the 1960s. This began on the platform of London's Victoria Station and proceeded up Buckingham Palace Road, across the front of the Palace, through Green Park and the environs of Lancaster House and up Pall Mall right to the door of 8 St James's Square. I was seeking a professional partnership. The concept was also reflected in the complaint by some in the Department of Energy that I wanted to take it over completely. On the contrary, I retorted, I was concerned that no one – and most certainly not those blissfully ignorant of the communications business and negative about it to boot – took over my information division.

All this is paradoxical because government is not conducted in a vacuum. Ministers survive, in a democracy, by their ability to persuade, convince and win support – and votes. This entails presenting the facts and explaining them persuasively. Senior civil servants have to take account of presentation in their submissions to Ministers. A distinguished predecessor in No. 10 – the diplomat, Sir Donald Maitland, who was Chief Press Secretary to Edward Heath – even managed to require a paragraph on presentation in Cabinet submissions to No. 10. Yet, in my day, presentation usually – and curiously – still secured only cursory discussion once a policy had been settled.

I do not wish to exaggerate the present problem of which, after three years in 'retirement', I have only an impressionistic view. Progressively during the 1980s the government machine became more attuned to the practical implications of presentation for a variety of reasons. A proliferating media descended like locusts on that part of Whitehall currently in crisis. Sky TV especially covered government exhaustively. The televising of Parliament meant that senior officials would have to appear before Select Committees which might be bent not merely on bloodsport but televised blood-sport. That helped to concentrate the official mind wonderfully. A Treasury mandarin, Sir Peter Middleton, who had spent some time as Chancellor Denis Healey's press secretary, systematically used the Treasury's head of information post as a finishing school for his bright young men and women. Gus O'Donnell, who has just returned to the Treasury after three years as Prime Minister John Major's press secretary, is a notable graduate of that school.

There have been other small indications of a developing policy/ presentation partnership which I often sought in vain. The Foreign Office News Department, previously staffed solely by diplomats, now has expert GIS advice within its ranks, thanks to the late Brian Mower, one of my deputies at No. 10 who followed Douglas Hurd from the Home Office to the FCO. So, too, does the Treasury. Similarly, Gus O'Donnell persuaded his parent department that there was something to be said for the Treasury's information division having GIS expertise as well as, for example, an intimate knowledge of the exchange rate which caused me so much trouble.

But the fact is that I found myself constantly trying to strain the essence of communication – hard information – out of a tight-fisted system. It was never more difficult and frustrating than during the Falklands War when the Permanent Secretary to the Ministry of Defence, Sir Frank Cooper, actively sought to deny me information apparently to prevent my putting a political gloss on it. This greatly increased the tension at the heart of the government's presentational apparatus. It is one thing to interpret events when the nation is at peace; it is entirely another matter to do so when lives are at risk in war.

It follows from this that a press secretary lives dangerously. He would do so even if he had all the information he requires readily at his disposal. This is because if he is to do his job as an interpreter for the press he continually has to read the tea leaves, to sniff the wind, and to have a real sense of what will 'go' politically and what is simply not on. He derives much value from all his meetings with his

Minister, but he also needs hard briefing on paper to back up his assertions. He is only as good as his last reliable advice. And much of the advice he gives, in the hurly burly of the average day in Whitehall, can be validated only after the event. At best, I was able to clear directly with Margaret Thatcher only a fraction of the guidance I dispensed on her behalf. In other words, I was judged *post hoc*. This explains why Lord Whitelaw, consoling me when I was in another spot of bother, told me: 'You are the most exposed civil servant in Whitehall and have got to be protected.'

This brings me back to the personality of the Minister, which I have previously dismissed as a major influence on the overall presentational strategy. More than anything else, it is his policies – or lack of them – which govern a press secretary's activities. The better the Minister is at communicating policy and measures and the clearer and the better thought out those policies are the easier the task of securing an 'informed press and public.' It might be argued that this means that personality is crucial for, in this televisual age, the more appealing the Minister's personality the more effective he is likely to be in persuading the public of the sense of his approach. There is superficially something in this argument, but personality, as such, does not determine a press secretary's activity. It may simplify or complicate it, but it is not the decisive influence. That begins and ends with the Minister's policies.

In any case, under the rules and conventions of British government, the civil service is not in business to build up the image of a Minister or his department. It is there to help formulate and execute policies. Of course, the more tellingly a press secretary explains those policies the more credit may accrue to the Minister and his party. That has long been recognised and accepted as an incidental of office. But the point is that it is an incidental consequence of the presentation of policy and not its purpose. This doctrine was reaffirmed in the late 1980s after an internal civil service inquiry, in which I participated, had examined the possibility that modern communications and especially television advertising techniques might compromise the civil service tradition of playing no part in the cultivation of a ministerial image.

Nonetheless, a press secretary can no more ignore his Minister's personality than he can wisely discard any consideration of his political strength – whether he is on his way up or down the greasy pole – his reliability under fire and his skills as a communicator. I was blessed with powerful communicators in Barbara Castle, Robert Carr and not least Margaret Thatcher. Tony Benn would have been one, had a majority of the public been prepared to listen to him. Lord Carrington, whom I served for two months before the Tories' February 1974 election defeat, saw his task as a communicator more as a duty than a pleasure but was much better at it than he gave himself credit for. Eric Varley was no orator and a diffident communicator and Maurice Macmillan found the business of formal communication through the media, as distinct from relaxed informal conversation, a nightmare.

I could no more ignore these essential parts of a Minister's armoury than I could Barbara Castle's utter determination to present herself before the TV cameras looking – and feeling – a million dollars, however long it took. That meant that I had to carve great chunks out of a working day for briefing, hairdresser and make-up – and to build in a generous allowance on top to ensure that her toilet did not cause her to miss her deadlines for the 6 p.m. or 9 p.m. news. Robert Carr, as sure-footed as a mountain goat in front of a microphone, was never programmed to be early, though he always managed to catch his trains, even if they were about to move. I had to ensure that Maurice Macmillan always had in his hand a written set of, say, five points to get over to radio and television lest he panic and lose his way.

Eric Varley, as genuine an article as you could ever wish to meet, found the thespian aspect of politics not to his nature and consequently had to be persuaded to undertake some presentational programmes. Margaret Thatcher was altogether more complicated. Journalism is not her natural habitat. Unlike some politicians, she never longs for the company of journalists. So again she had to be persuaded to undertake some engagements just as she had to be dissuaded from other, more media-destructive operations when she got the bit between her teeth. With some Ministers, I knew I needed rockets to propel them into action. With others, lead weights were required. With Margaret Thatcher I required both, though not usually at the same time.

Of course, I dispensed advice to Ministers before major presentational events not merely on the nature and presentation of the message – wherever possible dreaming up some pithy summarising phrase such as 'Mr Gorbachev is a man I can do business with' – and the likely points of attack but also on the atmospherics of the occasion and the demeanour the Minister might usefully adopt. My aim, like that of the Minister's private office, was to ensure that he or she was prepared for every eventuality and did justice to himself and his message. This process was brought to its ultimate refinement in briefing Mrs Thatcher for Prime Minister's Question Time.

For half my career in the civil service I operated under Bismark's definition of politics: the art of the possible. The second half was a more rigorous experience. Mrs Thatcher thought Bismark was a wet. She adhered to an altogether more demanding concept of politics: the art of making possible that which is thought to be impossible. Of course, Barbara Castle and Robert Carr embraced this more rigorous philosophy in trying to reform the trade unions with respectively *In Place of Strife* and the Industrial Relations Act 1971. To the extent that politicians seek to introduce unpopular policies for the good of the nation, as they see it, so they break out, if only temporarily, from Bismark's confines. But they are generally governed by what they judge it is possible to get through the House of Commons. Ultimately, Mrs Thatcher had to take account of what was possible when in 1981 she avoided a clash with the miners because she knew the nation could not withstand a national stoppage. Similarly, she was eventually persuaded against her better judgement to join the ERM because she was running out of political options. But she never had to face the possibility of defeat in the Commons. That left her, leading from way out in front, freer than most to pursue demanding ideas. One of these was the poll tax.

I mention this because for me her valuable combination of personality and opportunity inevitably influenced my contacts with journalists. Whereas up to 1979 I had always had to leave a way out, I was afterwards able to brief with confidence, certainty and power. Mrs Thatcher did not change her mind. This made light of the continuing difficulty of securing enough solid information from the machine. It also reinforced the government's authority and Mrs Thatcher's command. But it was not a myth. Apart from the early tactical retreat over the miners, it was underpinned by the Prime Minister's performance during her first three years in No. 10 during which I played an enduring game of 'Spot the U-turn' with the lobby.

In this way, the Thatcher years underline the essentials of government presentation. The GIS cannot make a silk purse out of a sow's ear. Nor should it try to do so. But it may incidentally reinforce a public impression of power or palsy, depending on the circumstances. In short, Mrs Thatcher's reputation – and that of all the Ministers I have served – was not made out of the barrel of their press secretary's gun or the tube of a television set. Leave aside media hype; it was founded on the bedrock of her philosophy, ideas and very fibre.

So far I have concentrated on the press secretary's inner workings to reconcile conflicting interests within the machine to put his ministers and himself in a position to convey a positive message with conviction. This is entirely right. All the best presentational work is nine-tenths admininstration and preparation and one-tenth execution. And in the best conducted governments presentation flows from policy; only occasionally does it dictate it.

The internal tussle between conflicting interests within government is only half the picture. The press secretary is not merely a surrogate spokesman; he is also an adviser on how messages will be received and presented by the media and on their timing. If he is worth his salt, he is also the media's representative in government, arguing their case at least over the mechanics of presentation. During the 1980s I found that this concept of the press secretary's role usually left trainee journalists helpless with mirth, so indoctrinated were they with the conspiracy theory of government. (Personally, I go with the cock-up theory every time.) But who else do journalists think looks after their basic interests within government if is not the press secretary?

It is only when the media dimension is introduced to presentational discussions within government that the art of reconciliation comes to be practised in all its awkwardness. For it is only then that ministers have to confront and react to the gamut of current public scepticism, including the consequences of earlier briefing or leaking, devise the most persuasive line of presentational response, prepare defensive briefing, pore over the language to be used in any announcement, consider the parliamentary and any European or other international obligation, settle a timetable and agree a media programme designed to give the most comprehensive public exposition of their initiative.

This is only one aspect of the power of the media at work in a democracy. Its ability, working hand in glove with MPs, to inspire problematical or embarrassing questions on the floor of the Commons is another. But in those circumstances it is its own agent. When government presentation is being devised, it is no less powerful in absentia. Its brooding presence, waiting hawklike to pounce on every weakness, is palpable. It is a poor press secretary who does not use its capacity for criticism and ridicule to cut through the generalities of officialese, the pendanticisms of experts, notably lawyers, and the pedestrian language of those who do not have to capture public attention to refine and sharpen the 'product'. Passchendaeles continue to be fought over phrases in government announcements.

Yet at all times the press secretary must work within the other confines of his trade. He cannot indulge in polemic. He cannot deal in the language of party politics. He must find an inoffensive way of satisfying the reporter who does not distinguish between government and party interests. He must be factual. He must not mislead, though sensible journalists know he may be unable to tell the whole truth. He must uphold the spirit as well as the letter of the conventions which govern the conduct of civil servants. This means he must at all times ensure that the expenditure of public money on publicity programmes can be justified. He must not allow himself to be bullied or argued into spending taxpayers' money on advertising when other cheaper media should be used. While recognising that, to be effective, government publicity campaigns should be professional and arresting, he must not fall in with extravagance which could, for example, become the subject of such controversy as to cloud the intended message.

Yet if a press secretary is to reconcile conflicting interests he cannot just be negative. He has to devise and commend sensible, acceptable and effective ways of carrying the government's message to the people through the media.

After practising the art of reconcilation for nearly a quarter of a century, sometimes very awkwardly indeed, I parted from my departments with expressions of respect and regret and on excellent terms with the Cabinet Ministers I served. They, at least, did not wish to kill the messenger.

5 Loyalists and defectors
The SDP breakaway from the parliamentary Labour Party 1981–2*

Ivor Crewe and Anthony King

In March 1981 thirteen Labour MPs, including two Cabinet Ministers from the 1974–9 Labour Government, David Owen and Bill Rodgers, left their party to found the Social Democratic Party (SDP).[1] Twelve more Labour MPs joined them during the remainder of 1981, and another three came over in 1982. These twenty-eight defectors from the parliamentary Labour Party were joined by two more former Labour Ministers, Shirley Williams and Roy Jenkins, who had not been elected to the 1979 Parliament but who were returned as SDP MPs in by-elections in November 1981 and March 1982 respectively.[2] The full roll-call of these thirty ex-Labour SDP MPs is given in Table 1.

The resignation of twenty-eight Labour MPs to form the SDP was the largest breakaway from any party for nearly a century. Not since 1886, when seventy-eight MPs led by Joseph Chamberlain broke with the Liberals over Irish Home Rule, had any party suffered desertions in such numbers. The split appears even larger if account is taken of the eighteen Labour peers and thirty-one former Labour MPs – eight of them former Cabinet Ministers – who likewise joined the new party.[3] The SDP was the most substantial new political party to be launched in Britain since the formation of the Labour Representation Committee in 1900.

THE DEFECTOR–LOYALIST PUZZLE

Although the breakaway was historically large in absolute numbers, it constituted a small percentage of the parliamentary Labour Party (PLP). There were 269 Labour members of Parliament in 1981: the

* This essay is drawn from the authors' book, *SDP: The Birth, Life and Death of the British Social Democratic Party* (Oxford University Press, 1995).

Table 1 SDP MPs, 1981–3

Name	Constituency	Date of joining
Tom Bradley	Leicester East	March 1981
John Cartwright	Woolwich East	March 1981
Richard Crawshaw	Liverpool Toxteth	March 1981
Thomas Ellis	Wrexham	March 1981
John Horam	Gateshead West	March 1981
Edward Lyons	Bradford West	March 1981
Robert Maclennan	Caithness and Sutherland	March 1981
David Owen	Plymouth Devonport	March 1981
Bill Rodgers	Stockton	March 1981
John Roper	Farnworth	March 1981
Neville Sandelson	Hayes and Harlington	March 1981
Mike Thomas	Newcastle-upon-Tyne East	March 1981
Ian Wrigglesworth	Thornaby	March 1981
James Wellbeloved	Erith and Crayford	July 1981
Michael O'Halloran	Islington North	September 1981
Ronald Brown	Hackney South and Shoreditch	October 1981
James Dunn	Liverpool Kirkdale	October 1981
David Ginsburg	Dewsbury	October 1981
Dickson Mabon	Greenock and Port Glasgow	October 1981
Tom McNally	Stockport South	October 1981
Bob Mitchell	Southampton Itchen	October 1981
Eric Ogden	Liverpool West Derby	October 1981
John Grant	Islington Central	November 1981
Shirley Williams	Crosby	November 1981*
Jeffrey Thomas	Abertillery	December 1981
Ednyfed Hudson Davies	Caerphilly	December 1981
Bryan Magee	Leyton	March 1982
Roy Jenkins	Glasgow Hillhead	March 1982**
George Cunningham	Islington South & Finsbury	June 1982
Bruce Douglas-Mann	Mitcham and Morden	June 1982***

Note: In addition to the MPs listed above, Christopher Brockleback-Fowler (Norfolk North-West) defected from the Conservative Party in March 1981.
* elected at Crosby by-election, November 1981.
** elected at Glasgow Hillhead by-election, March 1982.
*** resigned to fight his seat in a by-election as an independent SDP candidate and was defeated.

twenty-eight defectors amounted to only about one in ten. More to the point, the defectors constituted only a small proportion even of Labour's right wing.

It is the limited size of the breakaway, not its magnitude, that forms the subject of this study. A large number of Labour MPs defected. But an even larger number did not. And many of those who remained loyal to the Labour Party held political views that were similar or even identical to the minority who switched. For every Bill Rodgers, there was a Roy Hattersley; for every David Owen, a Denis Healey or Eric Varley. There is, therefore, a considerable defector–loyalist puzzle. Two Members of Parliament hold similar or identical views. One defects to the SDP; the other does not. Why?

To answer this question one must compare the Labour defectors with those members of Labour's right wing who remained loyal. The term 'right wing' is used loosely in this essay to refer to all those Labour members and activists who did not think of themselves as left-wingers and did not belong to left-wing organisations like the Tribune Group or the Campaign for Labour Party Democracy. On this broad definition there were probably about 150 MPs on the Labour right in the House of Commons in 1981, comprising most of those who did not vote for Michael Foot on the first ballot in the 1980 party leadership contest. The twenty-eight Labour defectors to the SDP amounted to less than 20 per cent of this group. A somewhat narrower definition of 'right wing' might reduce the size of the Labour right in Parliament to about 120,[4] somewhere between the number who voted for Denis Healey on the first ballot in 1980 (112) and the number who voted for him on the second (129).[5] Even on this narrower definition, the proportion of Labour right-wingers who defected to the SDP still comes to well under a quarter. Either way, those who followed the 'Gang of Four' (Roy Jenkins, David Owen, Bill Rodgers and Shirley Williams) in quitting Labour's ranks were heavily outnumbered by those who might have done so but did not.

Moreover, the twenty-eight who did defect had never constituted even a loose grouping, let alone an organised faction, when they were in the PLP. Far from being a 'tightly knit group of politically motivated men' (to adopt Harold Wilson's description of the sea-men's leaders in 1966), the twenty-eight formed no more than a cluster of mini-groups, which only partly overlapped. One such group were the 'Jenkinsites', disaffected Labour backbenchers who kept in touch with Jenkins when he was king o'er the water in Brussels; and some defectors, including several of the Jenkinsites, had been officers in the Manifesto Group.[6] Similarly, some of them had been associated with Britain in Europe in 1975 (Tom Bradley, Dickson Mabon, Bill Rodgers, John Roper and Ian Wrigglesworth), and several more had been members of Labour's delegation to the European Parliament later in the same decade (Ron Brown, George Cunningham, Tom Ellis and Bob Mitchell). At least nine had personal ties to one or more of the Gang of Four, having been junior ministers under them or else their parliamentary private secretaries.[7] But there remained a number of defectors – Bruce Douglas-Mann, Ednyfed Hudson Davies, Edward Lyons, Bryan Magee, Tom McNally, Jeffrey Thomas – who stood outside even these mini-networks and whose switch cannot have been prompted by feelings of loyalty to any group or clique. What the Labour Party lost was not a group or even a splinter-group but a number of tiny fragments.

The defectors were not even united in their views. Obviously, none of them had been out-and-out left-wingers, but before defecting a considerable number would have described themselves as centrists. They certainly did not constitute an ideologically distinct group within the Labour right. On the issues that had divided the Labour right during the 1970s – notably Scottish and Welsh devolution and trade union reform – the twenty-eight were as divided as everyone else. Most of them were in favour of or indifferent to the Callaghan government's devolution proposals; but Richard Crawshaw, Eric Ogden and Bob Mitchell voted against them from time to time, and Cunningham and Douglas-Mann were leading figures (together with many left-wingers) in the main rebellions against the legislation. Cunningham indeed was largely responsible for the '40 per cent rule', which in the end killed the proposal for a Scottish Assembly (and also killed, indirectly, the Callaghan government).[8] The divisions on the issue of trade union reform were just as great, as SDP MPs' fragmented response to the Conservative government's trade union legislation was later to show.

THE EUROPEAN ISSUE

But the issue that most tellingly reveals the SDP's ideological disparateness is that of Europe. It is tempting now – and was tempting in 1981 – to regard commitment to the European Community as being at the very heart of the Social Democrats' beliefs. 'The 1971 split over Europe', wrote Peter Jenkins, the *Guardian*'s distinguished (and sympathetic) political columnist, 'prefigured the schism of 1981' (Jenkins 1987: 137). This assumption was also shared within the

Labour Party, as Tony Benn's postscript commentary on his diary entries for 1971–2 reveals:

> During the long and protracted argument about Europe which followed . . . it became clear that a group of pro-European Labour MPs would never accept an adverse Conference decision on this question, and had therefore decided that if their dream of an enlarged Common Market conflicted with their membership of the Labour Party, then the Party would have to be sacrificed. It was this commitment that ultimately led to the formation of the SDP in 1981.
>
> (Benn 1988: xiii)

But did it? It is true that the Gang of Four were united by their unswerving support for the Community. All four had voted to join Europe in the October 1971 debate; all four had resigned from Labour's front bench in 1972 on the issue; and it was on Europe that Owen, Rodgers and Williams had issued their first joint statement as the 'Gang of Three'. It is also true that constituency Labour Parties had increasingly come to regard opposition to the Common Market as a touchstone of doctrinal purity, with the result that several MPs who later joined the SDP were involved in rows on Europe with their local activists.[9]

But passionate commitment to Europe was not in fact what bound the SDP defectors together. Of the twenty-eight Labour MPs who defected, twenty-two had served in the 1970 Parliament and had therefore been in a position to vote in the House of Commons on 28 October 1971, when sixty-nine Labour MPs, organised by Rodgers, had supported the Heath government on the outcome of its negotiations with the EEC. If it were true that enthusiasm for Europe was an essential condition of subsequent SDP support, then the great majority of those twenty-two should have voted in 1971 in the pro-European lobby. In fact, however, only half of them, eleven, did so, with two others abstaining. The other nine voted with the Labour majority against joining the EEC on the Heath government's terms. Of these nine, some, like John Horam and John Grant, were indifferent rather than hostile to British EEC membership and were not positively anti-European; but at least two of them – George Cunningham and Michael O'Halloran – regularly defied the Labour whip in 1977 and 1978 and voted against direct elections to the European Parliament, as did one of the 1971 abstainers, Jim Wellbeloved.

Moreover, not only was devotion to the European cause not the ideological cement that bound the twenty-eight SDP defectors together; views on the issue hardly distinguished the Labour right-wingers who did defect to the SDP from those who did not. In 1981, thirty of the sixty-nine rebels in 1971 were still in the House of Commons. Eleven of the thirty, as we have just seen, defected to the SDP, but the other nineteen did not. In other words a majority of the 1971 'Euro-fanatics' remained loyal to the Labour Party.[10] There was thus no neat one-to-one relationship between being pro-European and defecting. On the contrary, most of Labour's Europeans did not join the SDP and some of the Labour MPs who did join were not notably pro-European.[11]

Policy differences within the Labour Party did, of course, play a part in the split: those who defected were united in their dislike of Labour's shift to the left. But even broad policy differences were certainly not a sufficient condition of a Labour MP's making the switch: only a small minority of those who disliked what was happening inside the party in fact defected. Indeed some SDP MPs (especially the later defectors such as Grant, McNally and Cunningham) were probably closer in their views to many of those they left behind than to their new SDP colleagues. Therefore we still need to ask: when two Labour MPs agreed on all major issues, what other factors persuaded one to stay but the other to leave? More precisely, when five were agreed on all the issues, what persuaded four to stay but the fifth to leave?

PERCEPTIONS OF LABOUR'S PROSPECTS

For some loyalists, their emotional attachments to the Labour Party were simply too strong for them to contemplate leaving. The loyalty of men like Roy Hattersley, Roy Mason, Merlyn Rees and Eric Varley can probably be explained in this way. They might or might not share the Social Democrats' diagnosis of the state of the party. But they were born in the party, they had spent their whole life in it, and they wanted to die in it.[12] Moreover, such an absolute commitment had the attraction of irrevocability; there was no need to agonise, no need to calculate or dissemble, no need to lose sleep. One simply made up one's mind to stay in the party and then carried on as normal.

A second, more cerebral factor was the differing assessments that MPs made of the Labour right's prospects. Labour MPs could share identical views on policy yet genuinely disagree about the right's chances of recovery. Optimism came more easily to some than to others, but everyone could, if they tried hard enough, find reasons for continuing to hope. The trade unions, for example, might switch their votes at the next party conference. Giles Radice, a leading Manifesto Group activist who remained loyal, instinctively took the long view: 'In politics patience is a virtue. Labour Party politics is a matter of time and tides.'[13] Another loyalist whom the SDP had hoped to recruit, Ken Weetch, made the same point: 'When I was his PPS, Bill Rodgers used to tell me to play Labour politics long; I followed his advice even if he didn't.'[14] Many of the loyalists believed – or persuaded themselves to believe (it was sometimes hard to tell which) – that, despite everything, the party could yet be saved.

A third factor in helping to make up people's minds was more strategic. Breakaways from a party always help the other side – whether outside one's old party or inside it. The departure of leading lights on the right would only serve further to strengthen the Labour left. Worse, to split the party might mean splitting the anti-Conservative vote and handing office to the Thatcherites, possibly for a generation. The historically aware referred back to the almost twenty-year Conservative hegemony that had followed the Liberal Unionist breakaway in 1886. The European-minded, like Denis Healey, remembered the role played by a divided socialist movement in the rise of German and Italian fascism and in the dominance of the right in post-war France and Italy (Healey 1989: 83). Loyalists like Giles Radice and Phillip Whitehead concluded on these kinds of grounds that it was better to quit politics altogether than set up in opposition to Labour. This was, in fact, a course taken quietly during this period by many disillusioned Labour activists and local councillors.

But, although assessments of the Labour Party's long-term prospects and a genuine fear of splitting the Opposition were undoubtedly crucial factors in many cases, they are not entirely satisfactory as an explanation of the overall pattern of loyalty and defection. On the one hand, many who remained loyal to Labour were not confident that the party could be saved.[15] On the other, most of the defectors were as well aware as the loyalists of the disadvantages of splitting Labour and setting up a rival party: the new party might fail, and under Britain's electoral system the Conservatives under Thatcher might indeed remain in power for an indefinite period on a minority vote. What distinguished defectors from loyalists cannot, therefore, have been only their differing judgements about Labour's future.

THE IMPACT OF DESELECTION

What role did deselection or the fear of it play? Labour loyalists and some Liberals claimed that many of the SDP MPs defected only because they were about to be deselected as parliamentary candidates by their local Labour Party: they jumped before they were pushed. There can never be certain answers to hypothetical questions; but the balance of evidence strongly suggests that deselection or the fear of it played only a marginal role in MPs' decisions to quit the party.

Altogether eleven SDP MPs had been seriously at odds with a substantial section of their local party, but of these no more than four would have remained in the Labour Party had they been reselected or expected to be reselected: Dunn possibly, Ogden and Ginsburg probably, O'Halloran certainly.

James Dunn's political views made him an unlikely Social Democrat, and his prospects of reselection by his Militant-dominated Labour Party in Liverpool's Kirkdale were slim; but poor health was forcing him towards retirement in any case and his constituency was due to disappear under impending boundary revisions. Dunn could have remained in the Labour Party and retired with dignity. Instead he joined the SDP. The other three cases are clearer cut. After being narrowly deselected by his Liverpool West Derby Constituency Labour Party (CLP) in June 1981, Ogden resisted the blandishments of SDP MPs to join them until he had learned that the local Liberals would allow him to stand as the Alliance's candidate for his seat.[16] Ginsburg had little chance of reselection in Dewsbury, having concentrated on his business affairs in recent years and chosen to live in Hampstead rather than the constituency. He joined the SDP a month before his local party was due to draw up its reselection short list, by which time he had received only one nomination from among the Dewsbury party's five branches. O'Halloran's defection was transparently opportunist. His ambivalence about the EEC and his taste for a Tammany Hall style of machine politics hardly made him a natural Social Democrat. At odds with the hard left in his Islington North constituency since his original selection in 1969, he was equally isolated from the right and would not necessarily have won their support in a reselection contest. After joining the SDP, he made little contact with its largely middle-class local membership and played no active part in the party nationally. In March 1983, after boundary changes had eliminated his prospects of securing the Alliance nomination for an Islington constituency, he resigned to become an Independent Labour candidate at the general election shortly afterwards.

Of the other seven MPs who had fallen out with sections of their constituency party, Cunningham deliberately waited until after he had succeeded in being reselected before defecting; and Crawshaw, Ellis, Lyons and Sandelson would have defected whatever the outcome: they were in the original tranche of SDP MPs and switched long before their reselection conferences took place. Their quarrels with their local party encompassed far more than their own position. Magee's late defection was not timed in relation to his reselection. An academic and writer with more interest in the arts than parliamentary politics, he was not unduly concerned at the prospect of being deselected and joined the SDP as a gesture of principled defiance, not of personal desperation.

McNally's case is the most marginal. His defection was unexpected, and it took place almost exactly a month before his constituency's selection conference. But his action was not that of someone calculating his prospects for survival: his chances of reselection were certainly good enough to make it worthwhile to stay on and fight; and, given the timing of his selection conference, if he had lost there still would have been time enough for him to switch to the SDP before the January 1982 deadline set by the SDP and Liberals for Labour MPs contemplating defection.[17]

Thus, only a handful of the SDP MPs, at most, joined because of actual or threatened deselection. In addition, fewer than half of those Labour MPs who actually were deselected as candidates seriously considered joining the SDP. Seven of the eight deselected Labour MPs were right-wingers but only one, Eric Ogden, defected.[18] A similar story can be told of those right-wing Labour MPs such as Stanley Clinton Davis (Hackney Central), Reg Freeson (Brent East) and William Hamilton (Fife Central) who either only just fended off left-wing challenges to their selection or, like Joel Barnett (Heywood and Royton) and Charles Morris (Manchester Openshaw) were squeezed out by left-wing MPs where boundary revisions obliged sitting members to compete for the same seat. Only one of them, Freeson, gave so much as a hint of wishing to join the SDP.[19]

RELATIONS WITH THE LOCAL PARTY

The deselected, the almost deselected, those who had been squeezed out for ideological reasons after the boundary revisions – all would seem to have had good reasons for joining the SDP. They had been rejected or nearly rejected on account of their political views, which were closer to the SDP's than to those of Michael Foot's Labour Party. Their struggle for political survival had often been unpleasant and exhausting and some had been very shabbily treated. Most would have been welcomed into the SDP and would then have had the support of a much more congenial and compliant local party membership. What stopped them from joining?

Some lacked the spirit and energy: switching to the SDP would have meant building up a local membership, attending countless fundraising functions and cultivating the local press, all the while knowing that the battle was going to be uphill. Potential aggravation from local Liberal activists was an added complication for some inner city MPs such as Arthur Lewis (Newham North-West) or Stanley Cohen (Leeds South-East). There seemed little point in wriggling free from the Labour left only to become entangled with an equally prickly collection of Liberals. Retirement, or a nominal campaign as an Independent, seemed easier options.

Some simply left it too late. Usually the possibility of deselection did not stare MPs in the face until sometime in 1982, and after the spring of 1982 joining the SDP was a less attractive option than it had been: SDP or Liberal candidates were largely in place, and by that time the SDP's ratings in the opinion polls had begun to slide.[20]

The SDP, therefore, was not, whatever people said at the time, mainly a refugee camp for casualties in Labour's civil war. But of course the ferocity of the fighting in someone's constituency often did have a bearing on whether that person switched or stayed. The SDP's three most unexpected recruits – Cunningham, Grant and McNally – escaped from especially bitter faction fights.[21] And some of the switchers who survived reselection – or expected to – emphasised that they were not so much afraid of death as unhappy at the idea of a guerrilla way of life:

> We always out-voted them [i.e. the local left] by out-organizing them, but there were increasing costs: endless phone calls, membership recruitment on Sunday mornings, and so on. I felt my independence was being gradually compromised. The temptation was not to do what I believed in because the moderates did not want trouble – and also had to have everything explained to them.[22]

Cunningham told the press how much he resented having to devote time to counter-intriguing:

If they get two votes here, can I get three votes there? If they control the Young Socialists, can I win the Women's Section? I cannot do my job properly and spend time on that kind of shenanigans as well.[23]

If some MPs defected because they were tired of in-fighting in their local party, the reverse is also true: some who might otherwise have defected remained loyal because their local party was moderate and supportive. Most CLPs had moved some distance to the left in the 1970s, but the advance of the hard left was extremely patchy, and many of Labour's traditional heartlands lay outside the party's main left–right battlezones and saw only sporadic fighting. One Labour member who almost defected said: 'But for the good relationship I had with my party I would have gone. But I had educated them about Militant.' Another waverer with a moderate CLP said: 'I simply couldn't go along to these people, with whom I'd been out in all weathers, and say I was leaving them. I simply couldn't.'[24] Political ties were reinforced by ties of friendship. As one of the Gang of Four put it:

In some places MPs had an uncharacteristically nice party and therefore either didn't see, or didn't feel in their guts, the pain of what it was like to be up against the other side of the party . . . They didn't really understand what we were going on about.[25]

Less impressionistic evidence confirms that MPs with moderate constituency parties were substantially less likely than those without them to be tempted into defecting. A CLP's vote in the 1981 deputy leadership contest provides a good indicator of whether or not it was moderate: a CLP that voted for Healey had obviously not been captured by the left. Table 2 divides CLPs according to whether they voted for Benn or for Healey in both rounds. (Those who voted for John Silkin, abstained or changed their vote between rounds are excluded.) In order to judge whether those Labour MPs who might have been expected to defect but did not were also among those who happened to have moderate CLPs, the table examines the CLPs not only of the twenty-eight actual defectors but of forty 'potential defectors'. These potential defectors comprise the October 1971 EEC rebels who were still MPs in 1981 and who stayed in the Labour Party – nineteen in all – plus twenty-one others who were mentioned in the press or in interviews as potential SDP recruits. Not all of them, it must be emphasised, ever talked or even thought of defecting; it is simply that others, such as journalists and SDP MPs,

Table 2 Whether Labour MPs switched to SDP or stayed Labour, by their CLP's vote for Deputy Leader*

| The potential defector: | Potential defector's CLP voted | |
	for Benn	for Healey
switched to SDP	22 (55%)	4 (20%)
stayed Labour	9 (23%)	14 (70%)
was de-selected or retired	9 (23%)	2 (10%)
Total	40 (100%)	20 (100%)

Note: * The table examines the 28 Labour MPs who defected plus the 40 'potential defectors' listed at the end of the chapter. It excludes the eight CLPs that voted for Silkin, changed votes between rounds, or abstained.
Sources: Labour Party, *Annual Report*, 1981, pp. 345–55; *The Times Guide to the House of Commons, June 1983* p. 287: Byron Criddle, 'Candidates', in David Butler and Dennis Kavanagh, *The British General Election of 1983* (London: Macmillan, 1984).

Table 3 The deputy leadership vote by CLPs of Labour MPs who were actual or 'potential' defectors to the SDP

| | CLPs of potential defectors who | | | |
| | joined SDP | did not join SDP | | All CLPs |
		EEC rebels	others	
Voted Benn	22 (85%)	11 (61%)	8 (47%)	443 (80%)
Voted Healey	4 (15%)	7 (39%)	9 (53%)	108 (20%)
Did not vote	2	1	4	49
Silkin/other*	–	–	–	23
Total	28	19	21	623

Note: * switched from Healey to Benn between first and second rounds.
Sources: see Table 2

thought of them in these terms. They are listed in the Appendix to this chapter.

Among the sixty-eight defectors and potential defectors the contrast between the decisions of those with Bennite CLPs and those with Healeyite CLPs could hardly be starker. Of those with Bennite local parties, a majority, twenty-two out of forty, actually did switch. Of those with Healeyite parties, only four out of twenty did so. Turning the same figures around emphasises the contrast (see Table 3). Of the 551 CLPs that recorded a double-vote for either Benn or Healey, no fewer than 80 per cent backed Benn. Among the actual defectors' CLPs, the proportion was even more overwhelming: 85 per cent.[26] By contrast, almost half of the loyalists' CLPs, 47 per cent, voted for Healey in both rounds. These constituency parties were thus not only more moderate than the defectors' CLPs, they were substantially more moderate than the total of constituency parties.[27]

THE PERSONAL FACTOR: FINANCIAL PROSPECTS

The character of a potential defector's constituency party was thus an important factor affecting whether or not he went over. Age also played a part – or rather old age did. As Table 4 shows, about half of the potential defectors in their thirties, forties and fifties did defect; the other half did not. But, of the sixteen in the group as a whole who were in their sixties in 1981, only three – Brown, Crawshaw and Ginsburg – made the move. Most of the other thirteen, the loyalists, were working-class stalwarts, men like Tom Urwin, Harry Gourlay and Alan Fitch, who were dubbed by one SDP MP 'the gold-watch brigade'. Saddened and disillusioned by what was happening in their party, they nevertheless could not bring themselves to make the break. There was anyway no need for them to do so: they would soon be retiring.

In 1981–2 the SDP's recruiting sergeants were convinced that one major determinant of a Labour MP's willingness to come over was his financial prospects. An MP who reckoned that if he lost his seat he could easily get another job without significant loss of income was much more likely to defect than one who risked a big drop in his income or even finding himself on the dole. One early defector reported a working-class Labour MP as confiding in him ruefully: 'It's all very well for you: if you lose your seat, you can easily get another job.'[28] This financial theory of defection is certainly plausible. It cannot, however, account for the loyalty of the thirteen potential defectors who were already in their sixties (several of whom had in any case planned to retire before the next election); nor is there

Table 4 Age, defection and loyalty

Age in 1981	Defected to SDP	Stayed Labour	% who stayed Labour
Under 40	2	2	50%
40–49	8	10	56%
50–59	15	15	50%
60 and over	3	13	81%
All	28	40	59%

Source: Who's Who, 1981

Table 5 Occupational class, financial prospects, defection and loyalty

		Defected to SDP	Stayed Labour	
Occupational class[1]	(N)			
Manual[2], clerical, technical	(25)	36%	64%	100%
Professional, business	(42)	45%	55%	100%
Financial prospects[3] Prospect of earning at least equal income shortly after losing seat:				
Probable	(32)	53%	47%	100%
Improbable	(23)	48%	52%	100%

Notes: 1 Based on occupation prior to entering Parliament. In one case the information was not obtainable.
2 Only six MPs were manual workers, two of whom defected.
3 This section of the table excludes the eleven potential defectors who retired in 1983, and two for whom the financial implications of electoral defeat were unclear.
Sources: *Dod's Parliamentary Companion*, 1980; *The Times Guide to the House of Commons, May 1979; Who's Who*, 1981

any real reason for thinking that money considerations weighed heavily among more than a handful of younger MPs.

One relevant bit of evidence lies in the occupational profiles of the actual defectors and the potential defectors or loyalists (see Table 5). The MPs with most to lose if they lost their seats were those who had had manual, technical or clerical jobs before entering Parliament and who, if defeated, might find it difficult to obtain a job straight away – and might find it impossible to match their current salary. At a time of high unemployment, this was especially true of those in their late forties and fifties. But in fact the defection rate among the small number of former manual, technical and clerical workers in the total group, 36 per cent, was only a little lower than among those who had held better-paid jobs, 45 per cent. The class profiles of the loyalists and defectors were actually remarkably similar. In both groups, as for Labour MPs in general, the majority had a background in the professions, research or business.

Of course not all MPs who had professional jobs before entering Parliament could count on picking up the threads immediately if they lost their seats (although David Owen declared that he would go straight back to medicine). But a tentative assessment based on the potential defectors' pre-parliamentary occupations and extra-parliamentary sources of income suggests that prospective financial loss was seldom a significant factor in a Labour MP's decision to stay or leave. We estimate that defection was almost as frequent among those who had good reasons to anticipate a drop in income (48 per cent) as among those who did not (53 per cent).[29]

THE PERSONAL FACTOR: ROOTS IN THE LABOUR MOVEMENT

Financial calculations thus counted for little. Far more important was the depth of an MP's roots in the labour movement. This was especially true of older members. The labour movement was the air they breathed. Their relationship with it was not unlike Ernest Bevin's explanation of Winston Churchill's loyalty to Lord Beaverbrook: ''E's like the man who's married a whore: 'e knows she's a whore but 'e luvs 'er just the same' (Bullock 1967: 178). Most older members represented solidly working-class areas in which they had lived for most of their lives. They were frightened of ending their public life under a cloud and retiring to a community where they would be vilified as traitors by former friends and colleagues.

The member for the Durham mining seat of Houghton, Tom Urwin, was typical. The son of a miner, married into a mining family, he had lived in Houghton all his life. A branch official of the Amalgamated Union of Building Trade Workers since 1933, its full-time organiser since 1954, a member of the Labour Party since 1940, the chairman of the local council's Planning Committee for fifteen years, he was elected as Houghton's MP in 1964. In one capacity or another – union organiser, local councillor, Member of Parliament – he had served the labour movement for almost fifty years. To divorce the Labour Party would be to divorce family and community, not just party. It was too much to expect.

Irrespective of age, the length and depth of an MP's involvement in the labour movement had a direct bearing on his or her decision about whether or not to defect. A person's connections with a trade union is a case in point. Members of unions were much less likely to leave (34 per cent) than were non-members (57 per cent). Union sponsorship was even more important: exactly half of the forty non-sponsored Labour MPs among the potential and actual defectors joined the SDP, whereas only 29 per cent of the twenty-eight who were union-sponsored did so. Active involvement in a union's internal affairs was even more important. Ten of the sixty-eight actual and potential defectors had held union office.[30] Of these, only one, Tom Bradley, the treasurer and then president of the Transport Salaried Staffs'

Table 6 Defection, loyalty and three aspects of roots in the Labour movement: trade union connections, local government service and residence in the constituency

		Defected to SDP	Stayed Labour	
Trade Union connections	(N)			
No trade union connections	(21)	57%	43%	100%
Trade union member	(47)	34%	66%	100%
Sponsored by a trade union[1]	(28)	29%	71%	100%
Held trade union office	(10)	10%	90%	100%
Local government service	(N)			
Had never been a councillor	(39)	51%	49%	100%
Served as a local councillor	(29)	28%	72%	100%
Residence in constituency[2]				
Lived away from constituency	(25)	56%	44%	100%
Lived in or close to constituency	(29)	28%	72%	100%

Notes: 1 Another seven MPs were sponsored by the Co-operative Movement, of whom four defected to the SDP.
2 This section of the table excludes fourteen MPs whose home address was not available.
Sources: as for Table 2

Association, switched to the SDP. The SDP recruits were almost entirely without union experience, certainly during their careers in parliament.[31]

Local government experience reveals a similar contrast between switchers and stayers. People who have served as local councillors, especially for a considerable length of time, are likely to be more firmly anchored in their local party. Their network of local contacts is more extensive; their obligation to local party workers is stronger; their acceptance of party discipline is of longer standing. The defection rate in 1981–2 of those with local government experience was just over one in four, 28 per cent, whereas the defection rate of those without such experience was nearly twice as high, 51 per cent (see Table 6). This contrast was similarly reflected in where the MPs in the two groups lived. Barely one-third of defectors, 36 per cent, lived in or near their constituency, whereas two-thirds, 66 per cent, of the loyalists did. The defection rate of 'local' MPs, 28 per cent, was likewise only half that of 'absentees', 56 per cent. In fact only five of the defectors – Bradley, Cartwright, Crawshaw, Mitchell and

Table 7 Defection, loyalty and roots in the labour movement

Roots in Labour Movement*	Defected to SDP	Stayed Labour
	(28)	(40)
Trade union *and* local government	1	5
Trade union only	–	3
Local government only	7	16
Neither trade union *nor* local government	20	16
of whom: live in/near constituency	4	6
live away from constituency	12	4
home address not known	4	6

Note: * Trade union involvement is defined as holding a local, regional or national office in a trade union. Local government involvement is defined as election as a local councillor
Sources: as for Table 2

Wellbeloved – can be said to have been heavily involved in the local politics of their area.[32]

If we combine all our indicators of Labour 'roots' – trade union and local government experience together with place of residence – the full contrast between defectors and loyalists is further underlined. Of the twenty-eight defectors, twenty had neither trade union nor local government experience; and of these twenty at least twelve (but probably more) were absentee MPs in the sense of living well outside their constituencies (see Table 7). Of the forty loyalists, only sixteen, 40 per cent, had neither trade union nor local government experience; and of these sixteen only four were absentees. There is therefore something in the accusation made by Labour loyalists at the time of the split that most of those who broke from Labour had not been all that tightly bound to it in the first place. Most of the defectors were MPs who happened to be Labour rather than pillars of the labour movement who happened also to be MPs.

CONCLUSIONS

Party rebellions and breakaways are traditionally depicted in terms of ideology and faction. Parties are regarded as more or less stable coalitions of overlapping groups united by a common adherence to one or more principle(s) of policy, constantly subject to internal strain. Only very occasionally does an issue of profound significance

– the corn laws, Ireland, the tariff, Europe – so divide a party that one or more of the groups leaves to join another party or establish its own.

The defection of Labour MPs to form the Social Democratic Party is commonly described in these terms. At the time of the breakaway it was seen as the inevitable surfacing of a structural fissure in the Labour movement between pro- and anti-Europeans, put under extra pressure by the party's internal constitutional reforms.

But a comparison of the backgrounds and motives of defectors as opposed to loyalists presents a very different picture. Had the breakaway represented the culmination of the Labour Party's deep-rooted divisions between left and right, and 'European' and 'anti-European', the size of the parliamentary SDP would have been much larger. In fact the twenty-eight defectors comprised only a small minority of the Labour right and less than half of the pro-European right. They did not constitute a faction or even part of one. They were not united by a common history of campaigning for 'Europe' or by a common position on any principle or policy.

To explain the size and composition of the SDP one must understand the motives of the individual MPs who belonged to it. To do that means turning one's attention from Westminster to the local constituency party and from the national policy positions of individual MPs to their political identities and relations. A pro-European outlook, or membership of a right-wing faction such as the Manifesto Group, were associated with defection but they were neither a necessary nor a sufficient cause: loyalty to local party workers often got in the way. Bad relations with the constituency party pushed some anti-Europeans and centrists into defection, but they were not sufficient or necessary either. The important factor was the depths of an MP's roots in the labour movement, the network of personal, local and organisational ties that bound him to the party irrespective of policy differences. The formation of the SDP is another reminder that the behaviour of MPs is often moved as much by the personal as the political.

APPENDIX: POTENTIAL RECRUITS TO SDP WHO REMAINED IN THE LABOUR PARTY

EEC rebels
Leo Abse (Pontypool)
Peter Archer (Rowley Regis and Tipton)
Joel Barnett (Heywood and Royton)
Tam Dalyell (West Lothian)

Ifor Davies (Gower)#
Dick Douglas (Dunfermline)*
Jack Dunnett (Nottingham E.)
Andrew Faulds (Warley E.)*
Ben Ford (Bradford N.)*
Roy Hattersley (Birmingham Sparkbrook)
Denis Howell (Birmingham Small Heath)
Alex Lyon (York)
Roy Mason (Barnsley)
Arthur Palmer (Bristol N.E.)*
Robert Sheldon (Ashton-u-Lyne)
Sam Silkin (Dulwich)
John Smith (Lanarkshire N.)
Phillip Whitehead (Derby N.)*
Fred Willey (Sunderland N.)

Mentioned as a potential recruit in the press or in interviews
Donald Anderson (Swansea East)
Betty Boothroyd (West Bromwich West)
Ian Campbell (Dunbartonshire West)
Stanley Cohen (Leeds South-East)
Donald Dewar (Glasgow Garscadden)
Alan Fitch (Wigan)
George Foulkes (Ayrshire South)
Harry Gourlay (Kirkcaldy)
Brynmor John (Pontypridd)
Jimmy Johnson (Hull West)
Walter Johnson (Derby South)
Harry Lamborn (Peckham)+
Giles Radice (Chester-le-Street)
Albert Roberts (Normanton)
George Robertson (Hamilton)
Shirley Summerskill (Halifax)
Tom Urwin (Houghton-le-Spring)
Ken Weetch (Ipswich)
James White (Glasgow Pollok)
William Whitlock (Nottingham North)
Alan Williams (Swansea West)

Davies died in June 1982
* Also mentioned as a potential recruit in the press or in our interviews.
Constituencies are those represented by the MP in 1981, which in a few cases differ
from those represented at the time of the EEC debate (October 1971).
+ Lamborn died in August 1982
Sources: On the October 1971 EEC vote: Norton 1975: 397–8. The other potential
recruits are names mentioned in our interviews; the twelve signatories of the state-
ment in *The Times* of 22 September 1980 calling for reforms in the party's structure;
and the MPs listed in Peter Rose, '12 Labour MPs set to join SDP', *Sun*, 27 July 1981.
These names largely overlapped.

NOTES

1 They were joined by a Conservative backbencher, Christopher Brockle-bank-Fowler, the only Conservative MP to defect.

2 In the 1979 election Shirley Williams was defeated in her Stevenage constituency and Roy Jenkins did not stand, having left Parliament in 1976 to take up the presidency of the European Commission.

3 The thirty-one ex-Labour MPs include six of the peers.

4 A quite different indicator produces a similar number. There remained in the 1979 Parliament 118 MPs who in July 1975 had signed a letter of support for Reg Prentice when he faced deselection by his local party in Newham North-East. See Chris Mullin, 'How the SDP tried to provide the Sunday Times with a new "hit list" ', *Tribune*, 11 December 1981.

5 Of course, not all Healey voters were committed right-wingers. But even the 'firm right' embraced many more loyalists than defectors. The Manifesto Group, which organised the right-wing slate in the annual shadow cabinet elections, could count on a core of eighty. In the 1976 leadership contest the combined first-round vote for the two indisputably right-wing candidates, Jenkins and Healey, was eighty-six, although this was in the previous Parliament when the PLP was larger and more right-wing in its make-up.

6 Dickson Mabon, Horam, Sandelson and Mike Thomas.

7 Bradley and Wrigglesworth had served as a PPS for Jenkins, and Ginsburg was an old friend from Oxford student days. Horam was a Junior Minister under Rodgers for whom both Ellis and Lyons had at some time been a PPS. Maclennan served under Shirley Williams as Under-Secretary for Prices and Consumer Protection from 1974 to 1979, for part of which time Mitchell and Cartwright each served as her PPS. Wellbeloved was Owen's PPS.

8 The rule required the government to repeal the Scotland Act if the Act failed to secure the support of '40 per cent of those entitled to vote' in the proposed referendum. Cunningham's amendment in fact superseded one calling for a one-third threshold, which was tabled by another defector, Bruce Douglas-Mann (Butler and Kavanagh 1980: 125–6; Dalyell 1977).

9 The most famous case was Dick Taverne in Lincoln. He forced a by-election on the issue in March 1973, at which he was easily re-elected as a 'Democratic Labour' candidate; he was narrowly defeated in the October 1974 election. He joined the SDP in 1981 and was a member of its National Committee. Others include Colin Phipps (Dudley West) and Neville Sandelson (Hayes and Harlington), both of whom joined the SDP in 1981.

10 The picture is the same if the fourteen abstainers are added to the thirty October 1971 pro-EEC rebels. Of the forty-four rebels and abstainers, thirteen defected to the SDP; thirty-one stayed in the Labour Party.

11 Of the six Labour defectors who entered Parliament after 1971, three (Magee, Mike Thomas and Wrigglesworth) were convinced Europeans – the same proportion as for those defectors who voted in the October 1971 debate.

12 'I accept that part of my inability to contemplate leaving the Labour Party is emotional rather than rational – the product of upbringing and

personal gratitude.' (Roy Hattersley, 'Why I will stay on and fight', *Observer*, 25 January 1981.) See also Hattersley's vivid description of the Labour Party's church-like qualities in his autobiographical *A Yorkshire Boyhood* (1983: 174).

13 Interview with authors. See also his explanation ('Labour is still the most effective vehicle for change') in *Guardian*, 14 December 1981, in which he argued that the SDP did not belong to the European social democratic tradition.

14 Interview with authors.

15 A number of the loyalists whom we interviewed thought that the right might well lose and that they would find themselves forced to leave the party within the forseeable future. One suggested to us that the 1981 split was going to be by no means the last.

16 After his deselection, which he had expected, he announced his intention of standing as a 'Labour candidate seeking re-election', but was then persuaded by Michael Foot to appeal to Labour's National Executive. Only after his appeal was rejected did he talk to local Liberals about the possibility of standing as the Alliance candidate in his seat. See Ian Aitken, 'Rejected MPs face new snub by Labour', *Guardian*, 9 June 1981.

17 The SDP and the Liberal Party agreed that Labour MPs who defected to the SDP would automatically be selected as the SDP candidate for their constituency so long as they joined the SDP before 31 January 1982.

18 Two others, Stanley Cohen (Leeds South-East) and Ray Fletcher (Ilkeston), announced at the time of their reselection difficulties that they were considering standing as Social Democrats but changed their minds. Arthur Lewis (Newham North-West) and Ben Ford (Bradford North) stood as Independent Labour candidates in the 1983 election; John Sever (Birmingham Ladywood) soldiered on as a Labour candidate in the safely Conservative seat of Meriden; and Fred Mulley (Sheffield Park) retired. Ben Ford later joined the SDP.

19 He faced an overwhelming challenge from Ken Livingstone, the left-wing leader of the GLC, but was saved by the early calling of the general election, which prompted Labour Party headquarters to intervene.

20 These considerations applied with particular force to those who lost out in the round of selections for the new merged constituencies – such as Clinton Davis in Hackney and Charlie Morris in Manchester – which was delayed until March/April 1983.

21 Grant and McNally were particularly anguished at leaving – Grant out of loyalty to his union, the ETU, McNally out of devotion to his Labour parents.

22 Interview with authors.

23 *The Times*, 1 December 1981.

24 Interviews with authors.

25 Interviews with authors.

26 The pull of moderate CLPs on potential defectors' loyalty was probably even stronger than the figures suggest. Eighteen of the potential recruits with Bennite CLPs did not switch. But as Table 2 shows, only nine of these 'loyalists' were reselected. Two were formally deselected (Ford and Cohen), one was squeezed out (Barnett), and six retired: Jack

Dunnett (Nottingham East), Jimmy Johnson (Derby South), Arthur Palmer (Bristol North East), Alfred Roberts (Normanton), Sam Silkin (Dulwich) and Fred Willey (Sunderland North). Of these six, Dunnett, Roberts and Silkin were widely tipped for deselection; rather than jumping before they were pushed, they stood aside. There was no parallel retirement pattern, however, among those MPs whose CLPs voted for Healey. If reselection rates are compared, therefore, the impact of having a right-wing rather than a left-wing party stands out: among potential defectors with Bennite CLPs, only 23 per cent stood as Labour candidates in June 1983; among those with Healeyite CLPs, the figure was 70 per cent.

27 The suggestion that right-wing Labour MPs were less likely to switch if they came from Labour's traditional strongholds because local parties in these areas tended to be more moderate was only partly borne out. It is true that only two of the eleven potential defectors from Scotland and three of the eleven from Wales actually joined the SDP; had the defection rates in Scotland and Wales matched those for England (51 per cent) the numbers would have been six from each. The SDP's recruitment of all but two of the eleven potential defectors from London reflects the much sourer atmosphere in the London Labour Party. However, four of the six potential defectors from the North East did join the SDP. Moreover, Scotland's CLPs were not moderate, judging by the 83 per cent that voted for Benn as deputy leader.

28 Interview with authors.

29 Another particle of evidence supports this view. Had fear of defeat and a subsequent loss of income been a crucial factor, one would have expected the defection rates to have been lower among sitting Labour MPs than among those Labour MPs who had retired or been defeated in 1979. This latter group, after all, had little to lose financially by joining the SDP, yet the defection rate among the 1981 PLP (10 per cent) was virtually identical to that among Labour MPs who had been defeated (11 per cent) or had retired (12 per cent) in 1979.

30 Tom Bradley (President of TSSA, 1964–7); Andrew Faulds (Council member, Equity); Alan Fitch (Secretary, Golborne Trades and Labour Council); Ben Ford (shop stewards convenor, AUEW); Denis Howell (President, APEX); Walter Johnson (Treasurer, TSSA and NFPW); Albert Roberts (Area Organiser, NUM); George Robertson (Scottish Organiser, GMWU, 1970–8); Tom Urwin (Organiser, Amalgamated Union of Building Trade Workers); William Whitlock (Area Organiser, USDAW; President, Leicester District Trades Council).

31 However, the SDP victor at the Portsmouth South by-election in 1984, Mike Hancock, was an AUEW convenor.

32 Bradley was a Northamptonshire county councillor and alderman for over twenty years; Cartwright led Greenwich Council in the early 1970s; Crawshaw was a local councillor in Liverpool and continued to immerse himself in local politics after being elected to parliament; Mitchell was deputy leader on Southampton council; and Wellbeloved was at one time leader of Bexley council. Another three – Ogden, O'Halloran and Sandelson – had served as local councillors but only for short periods.

REFERENCES

Benn, T. (1988) *Office Without Power: Diaries 1968–72*, London: Hutchinson.
Bullock, A. (1967) *The Life and Times of Ernest Bevin*, Vol. 2, *Minister of Labour*, 1940–45, London: Heinemann.
Butler, D and Kavanagh, D. (1980) *The British General Election of 1979*, London: Macmillan.
Butler, D and Kavanagh, D. (1984) *The British General Election of 1983*, London: Macmillan.
Dalyell, T. (1977) *Devolution: The End of Britain*, London: Cape.
Hattersley, R. (1983) *A Yorkshire Boyhood*, London: Chatto and Windus.
Healey, D. (1989) *The Time of My Life*, London: Michael Joseph.
Jenkins, P. (1987) *Mrs. Thatcher's Revolution: The Ending of the Socialist Era*, London: Jonathan Cape.
Kennet, W. (1982) *The Rebirth of Britain*, London: Weidenfeld and Nicolson.
Norton, P. (1975) *Dissension in the House of Commons, 1945–1974*, London: Macmillan.

6 'The Poison'd Chalice'
The European issue in British party politics

Philip Daniels and Ella Ritchie

INTRODUCTION

The process of European integration and Britain's role in it has been a recurrent theme in British political debate since the late 1950s. No other issue has produced such vacillations in the policies of the Conservative and Labour Parties and few other areas of policy have provoked such regular and frequent divisions within the two major parties. At times, intra-party divisions over Europe have been more pronounced than those between the two major parties. In contrast to other large member states such as Germany and Italy, in Britain no stable, long-term inter-party consensus has emerged on the 'European issue'. At the same time, the Conservative and Labour Parties have failed to develop consistent and distinctive European policies which would offer the electorate a clear set of choices.

The dynamics of party competition account in part for the major parties' frequent shifts in their European policies. The Labour Party in opposition, for example, has tended, at least until the late 1980s, to be more anti-European in order to attack Conservative government policy and to exploit the electorate's misgivings about Britain's role in Europe. The vacillations in party positions are also due to the dynamic nature of the integration process. It has been difficult for British parties to arrive at settled positions on the European issue since the process of European integration is inherently dynamic and each new stage in the development of the European Community (EC) has thrown up new challenges for British parties. Thus, the nature of the issue has constantly changed and evolved. From the late 1950s to the mid-1970s political divisions on the issue focused primarily on the question of whether Britain should participate in the integration process and on what terms. From the mid-1970s until the late 1980s the issue revolved primarily around the impact of EC policies on Britain and Britain's role in the EC. In recent years, a broad consensus has emerged across the party spectrum on the irreversibility of Britain's membership of the European Union (EU) but profound inter- and intra-party divisions remain over the scope and direction of the integration process. In this chapter, after giving a brief overview of the traditional positions of the Conservative and Labour Parties on the issue of European integration, we analyse the current sources of division over Europe in the two main parties.

TRADITIONAL PARTY POSITIONS

Both major parties showed little interest in the European Economic Community (EEC) during its early years. For the Conservative Party, in government at the time of the EEC's creation in 1957, opposition to British membership was based primarily on a perception of Britain's place in the world and fears about the surrender of national sovereignty to supranational European institutions. Britain had world-wide interests, embracing the defence and security links with the United States and an important trading relationship with the Commonwealth. While Europe was inevitably a sphere of British interest, the Conservative Party feared that Britain's membership of an integrated Europe would undermine the important political and economic links with the United States and the Commonwealth. In addition, the Conservatives were not interested in an integrated Europe based on supranational decision-making since this would challenge British national sovereignty. They preferred a looser, intergovernmental framework of co-operation with the emphasis on creating a barrier-free market rather than the longer-term political objectives implicit in the integration process.[1] A divergence of economic interests between Britain and the original six members of the EEC, particularly over the issues of agricultural policy and Commonwealth trade, also contributed to the Conservative Party's unwillingness for Britain to participate in the process of European integration.

By the early 1960s, however, the Conservative Party had changed its position on Europe and in 1961 Harold Macmillan, the Conservative Prime Minister, applied for British membership of the EEC. A number of factors accounted for this rapid shift in Conservative policy on Europe. The EEC was proving to be an economic success and the British government, and business interests, feared exclusion from a rich and dynamic market. At the same time, the economic and political links with the Commonwealth had declined and Britain's 'special relationship' with the United States had receded in importance. The Conservative government saw the EEC's potential to develop into a new political power and feared that continued non-membership would reduce Britain to a marginal status in Europe and damage its influence in international politics. The American government, keen that the EEC should develop as a bulwark against Soviet bloc communism, also encouraged Britain to seek entry. These developments led to a reassessment of Britain's foreign policy priorities and a reorientation towards Europe. In addition, Britain's earlier fears that the EEC would develop into a supranational organisation had not materialised.

The Labour Party shared many of the Conservative Party's misgivings about European integration in the late 1950s and it was not until the mid-1960s that the party showed much interest in British membership of the EEC. The Labour Party had initially dismissed the EEC as a club for the rich, an insular organisation which disregarded the problems of the Third World. In addition, Labour feared that British membership of the EEC, whose member-state governments were dominated by parties of the right, would frustrate attempts to carry through socialist policies in Britain (Berrington 1980). The Labour Party abstained in the Commons vote on the principle of British membership when Macmillan made Britain's first application in 1961. When Labour returned to office in 1964 the new government initially set a series of conditions for British entry which effectively ruled out the prospect of membership. However, the Wilson government rapidly converted to the idea of British membership and made Britain's second application for entry in 1967.[2]

The Labour Party's conversion to a pro-membership stance provoked considerable internal dissent and the issue continued to dog the party in government and in opposition until the mid-1980s. In October 1971 Labour voted in the House of Commons against entry into the EC but sixty-nine Labour MPs defied a three-line whip and supported the Conservative government's position on British accession. The party was deeply split on the issue of Britain's membership of the EC when it was returned to office in 1974. In an attempt to heal the party divisions, Harold Wilson's government renegotiated changes to Britain's terms of entry which were put to a national referendum in June 1975. While a majority of the Cabinet endorsed the new terms, they were rejected by a small majority in the parliamentary Labour Party, by the National Executive Committee, by the constituency Labour Parties and by the trade unions. Throughout this period, attitudes towards Europe within the Labour Party were bound up with intra-party conflict over the control and direction of the party and shifts in European policy reflected in part the changing balance of left and right forces.

The Conservative Party accepted membership more readily and, with only a small anti-Market element in the parliamentary party, it was able to present itself as the party of Europe from the early 1960s to the late 1980s. Neither party, however, positively embraced the ideal of a politically and economically integrated Europe: rather, membership of the EEC was grudgingly accepted as the only viable framework within which to promote Britain's long-term economic interests. There was certainly little enthusiasm in either party for supranational integration and moves towards a federal Europe.

PARTY DIVISIONS AND EUROPEAN INTEGRATION SINCE 1979

The Labour Party

The Labour Party's line on the European issue has shifted markedly since the early 1980s. Following Labour's defeat in the 1979 election the left gained ascendancy in the party. Strong anti-EC sentiments, always present in the party, resurfaced and the 1983 election manifesto committed a future Labour government to withdrawal from the Community. The anti-EC position, widely criticised as an irresponsible and unworkable policy, did not help the Labour Party's poor electoral image. Following its massive election defeat in 1983, the party, under the new leadership of Neil Kinnock, began the slow process of abandoning the withdrawal commitment.

By the late 1980s the Labour Party's stance had shifted once again and it was able to present itself as the more pro-European of the two major parties. The withdrawal commitment was dropped from the 1987 election manifesto and for the 1989 European Parliament elections the party adopted a positive attitude towards the EC, focusing in particular on the development of European social, regional, environmental and equal rights policies. A combination of domestic political calculations and developments at the EC level explain Labour's conversion to a more positive stance on the issue of Britain's role in the process of European integration.

The experience of the French Socialist government during the period 1981–4 had an impact on the thinking of left-wing parties across Europe. The Mitterrand government's attempts to reflate the French economy, at a time when its European partners were pursuing deflationary policies, ended in failure in 1983. The government was forced to make a policy 'U'-turn, introducing a package of austerity measures and dampening economic demand. The 'Mitterrand experiment' demonstrated that reflation in one country was no longer feasible. The growing interdependence of European economies and the mobility of capital rendered futile purely national reflationary strategies. The failure of the French Socialist strategy prompted a reassessment of national economic strategies by left-wing parties across Europe and reinforced the view that the growing interdependence of European economies required the coordination of economic strategies at the European level. For the Labour Party, the French Socialists' experience highlighted the inherent flaws in Labour's own Alternative Economic Strategy (AES) which proposed selective import controls and an expansionary economic policy. Elements of the Labour left, in particular, shifted focus from the purely national arena of policy-making to wider European strategies to achieve social and economic objectives.[3]

Electoral calculations were an important element in Labour's adoption of a pro-European position. The party's negative stance on Europe in the late 1970s and early 1980s contributed to the split in the party in 1981 and the formation of the Social Democratic Party (SDP). Labour's commitment to withdraw from the EC, contained in its 1983 election manifesto, was widely viewed as unrealistic and damaged its credibility as a party of government. The more positive approach to Europe was part of the Labour leadership's attempts after 1983 to make the party electable and to win back voters lost to the breakaway SDP. The 1989 Policy Review confirmed the party's pro-European stance, focusing on the EC as an appropriate arena for the co-ordination of industrial, employment, environmental and regional policies (Labour Party 1989).

The changing attitude of trade union leaders towards Europe also contributed to the Labour Party's move to a more pro-European line. In the second half of the 1980s the trade unions, traditionally quite hostile to the European Community, adopted a more positive approach towards Europe. A number of factors account for the change in union attitudes. The long-term experience of working with other trade unionists within trans-European organisations such as the Economic and Social Committee (ECOSOC) and the European Trade Union Confederation (ETUC) is likely to have had an impact on the attitudes of British trade unionists. At the same time, the trade unions' exclusion from national policy-making processes following the election of a Conservative government in 1979 encouraged them to look towards the EC as an alternative arena for influence over policy. The trade unions' more positive approach to Europe was reinforced by the address given by Jacques Delors, President of the European Commission, to the Trades Union Congress in Bournemouth in 1988. Delors sought to win the support of European trade unions for the Community's single market programme and in his speech outlined proposals for the development of a 'social Europe' in which social rights would be guaranteed and workers and their representatives would have rights to representation on company boards.[4] These EC policy initiatives were attractive to British trade unions which had experienced a marked erosion of their rights and a diminution of their political role during a decade of Conservative government. Given the trade unions' institutional links with the Labour Party and their influence at every level of policy-making in the party, a shift in the unions' stance on Europe inevitably had an impact on Labour's approach to the issue.

The Delors' proposals for a 'social dimension' to the single market programme became an issue of domestic political division and helped to galvanise Labour's pro-European policy. Margaret Thatcher, the Conservative Prime Minister, favoured a free, deregulated European market, a position consistent with her domestic policy of limited government intervention in the economy. She confirmed this view in her address to the College of Europe at Bruges in September 1988 when she attacked the proposals for a social charter:

> we certainly do not need new regulations which raise the cost of employment and make Europe's labour market less flexible and less competitive with overseas suppliers. . . . And certainly we in Britain would fight attempts to introduce collectivism and corporatism at the European level.[5]

The EC's new dynamism from the mid-1980s onwards posed a number of difficulties for the Conservative government which opposed proposals for the social dimension, plans for economic and monetary union (EMU) and reform of the EC's institutional structure. Thatcher's increasing hostility towards the EC and her difficulties in reconciling the divergent views on Europe inside the parliamentary Conservative Party encouraged Labour's more positive approach to the EC. European issues became enmeshed in domestic political debate as Labour portrayed Thatcher as increasingly isolated in the EC and condemned her approach as inimicable to Britain's interests. The adversarial style of British politics encouraged Labour to develop a European policy distinct from that pursued by the Conservative government. In order to capitalise fully on the Conservatives' difficulties with Britain's European partners and internal divisions over European policy, Labour had to develop a coherent set of policies on the key issues on the European agenda. Labour endorsed the social dimension, gave qualified acceptance to EMU and supported reform of the EC's institutions and was thus in a position to present itself as more pro-European than the Conservatives. In addition, Labour's support for sterling's membership of the Exchange Rate Mechanism (ERM) and its qualified support for moves towards a single currency were motivated by the party's desire to present an image of itself as a responsible and credible party of government. According to opinion surveys, Labour consistently trailed the Conservatives in the public's perceptions of each major party's competence to manage the economy. The obligations of ERM membership, and the policy constraints which it imposed, were seen as a way of insulating a future Labour government against the pressures for increases in public expenditure and at the same time reassuring key business and financial interests of the party's 'responsible' approach to economic management.

Labour's pro-European policy since the late 1980s has largely concealed the divisions which remain within the party over the issue of Europe. As a party in opposition, Labour has not had to take key decisions on European issues such as political union and EMU and therefore its internal splits have not been as evident as those in the governing Conservative Party. In addition, internal criticism of the Labour leadership's European policy has been muted in the interests of party unity and in order to make political capital out of the public rifts in the Conservative Party. Nevertheless, divisions over Europe have not disappeared and a future Labour government is likely to face difficulties uniting the party behind its European policy. The moves towards EMU pose a particular difficulty for the Labour Party. Monetary and fiscal policies will increasingly become responsibilities of the European Union and thus limit national governments' room for manoeuvre in economic policy. Labour critics of EMU argue that the EU's emphasis on budgetary discipline and on achieving sound money will lock Britain into a framework of deflationary policies which will cost jobs, reduce growth and threaten welfare spending. The Labour Party's support for European integration, and in particular that of the trade union movement, may also wane if the competitive pressures of the single market force down labour and social costs.

The Conservative Party

The European issue has caused frequent difficulties for the Conservative Party during its long period in office. Following the Conservative Party's election victory in 1979, Mrs Thatcher, the new Prime Minister, made the issue of Britain's contributions to the Community budget the centrepiece of her European policy. Britain demanded cuts in its net contribution to the EC budget and at the same time pushed for budgetary discipline to rein in Community spending. The dispute over the budget soured relations between Britain and its European partners and dominated the EC agenda until an agreement on annual refunds for Britain was negotiated at the Fontainebleau summit in June 1984.

The resolution of the British budgetary problem allowed the Community to focus on new issues and from the mid-1980s the integration process gathered a new momentum. Thatcher's combative approach to EC politics did not abate, however, and the Conservative government resisted the growing pressures for fundamental reform of the Community's institutional structure and further political integration. In an attempt to influence agenda-setting and to convey a more positive approach to the EC, in 1985 the Conservative government clarified its European policy in a paper entitled 'Europe: The Future' (HM Government 1984). The paper reaffirmed the government's view that the EC should remain as an association of sovereign states based on an intergovernmental mode of decision-making. The government's positive initiatives proposed the creation of a liberalised and deregulated internal market and an enhanced role for the EC in foreign policy through the intergovernmental system of European political co-operation (EPC).

The EC's new dynamism from the mid-1980s posed significant difficulties for the Conservative government. Mrs Thatcher rejected a number of EC policy developments which conflicted with her domestic economic strategy. The proposals for a social dimension to the single market, for example, were opposed on the grounds that they would limit labour market flexibility, increase costs to industry and thereby undermine European competitiveness. Thatcher also resisted moves towards economic and monetary union because of her unwillingness to cede national economic sovereignty and her preference for a system of free-floating exchange rates. Throughout the 1980s Thatcher resisted calls for sterling to enter the ERM, arguing that it would join 'when the time is right'. The government's decision to enter in October 1990 was clearly the result of the Prime

Minister bowing to internal party pressures.[6] Political developments in the EC also provoked rifts between the Conservative government and most of Britain's European partners. The proposals for a 'double acceleration' of the EC, with economic integration matched by political and institutional reforms, were consistently opposed by the Conservative government. Fearing moves towards a federal Europe, and the erosion of national sovereignty, Britain consistently opposed a strengthening of the supranational powers of EC institutions and attempted to preserve the intergovernmental basis of EC decision-making.

Thatcher's reaction to developments in the EC was forcefully expressed in her speech to the College of Europe at Bruges in September 1988. The speech, allegedly toned down by the Foreign Office, acknowledged that Britain's future was irrevocably bound up with the European Community: 'Britain does not dream of some cosy, isolated existence on the fringes of the European Community. Our destiny is in Europe, as part of the Community.' The speech, however, conveyed a negative message in distancing Britain from mainstream European opinion on a number of developments in the EC. The Prime Minister reiterated Britain's commitment to intergovernmentalism, arguing that 'willing and active co-operation between independent sovereign states is the best way to build a successful European Community'. She warned of the dangers of centralisation: 'We have not successfully rolled back the frontiers of the state in Britain, only to see them re-imposed at a European level, with a European super-state exercising a new dominance from Brussels.' She dismissed proposals for institutional reform arguing that the Community was not 'an institutional device to be constantly modified according to the dictates of some abstract intellectual concept'. And the proposals for a 'social Europe' were firmly rejected.[7] The essentially negative assessment of developments in the EC continued in the Conservative Party's campaign for the elections to the European Parliament in June 1989.

The Conservative government's problems over Europe during the period 1988–90 stemmed from its inability to control the EC policy agenda. The new dynamism in the integration process and the pressures for political and institutional reform could not be dampened by British opposition. Most member states and EC institutions saw the single market as an initial step in an ambitious project of economic and political integration. Thatcher's growing hostility towards the EC, and the essentially reactive nature of her European policy, left Britain increasingly isolated among the twelve member states. At the same time, the government's difficulties over European policy posed problems for party management: there was frequent criticism of the government's stance from within the parliamentary party and the divisions in the Cabinet over Europe were well publicised. Over the course of Thatcher's premiership four Cabinet Ministers resigned over issues related to Europe (Michael Heseltine in 1986, Nigel Lawson in 1989, Nicholas Ridley in 1990 and Sir Geoffrey Howe in 1990) and Mrs Thatcher's own downfall owed much to her handling of European policy.

Mrs Thatcher's successor, John Major, declared his intention to locate Britain 'at the heart of Europe' and attempted to convey a more positive tone in the government's relations with the EC. In spite of the change in style, the European issue has continued to bedevil the Conservative government and highlighted the divisions over Europe running through the party at every level. Major has inherited the troublesome European issues which had so afflicted the Thatcher government in the late 1980s and for much of his premiership has had to confront the difficult issues of EMU and political union. In an attempt to placate the Euro-sceptics in the parliamentary party, Major negotiated British opt-outs from the social chapter and the single currency provisions contained in the Maastricht Treaty. These concessions did not, however, mollify opposition among 'Euro-sceptic' Conservative MPs who viewed the Maastricht Treaty as a significant advance in the integration process and a further surrender of national sovereignty. An organised group of Conservative MPs persistently flouted the official party line and ensured that the Maastricht Bill had a tortuous passage through Parliament with a series of government defeats and climbdowns.[8]

The deep divisions over Europe within the Conservative Party did not abate, as the government had hoped, following the passage of the Maastricht Bill. They quickly resurfaced with disagreements about the content of the Conservative manifesto for the 1994 European Parliament elections and over the issue of reform of qualified majority voting in an enlarged European Union. The latter issue saw the British government oppose proposals to increase the number of votes required, following enlargement, to block legislation in the Council of Ministers.

These episodes once again demonstrated that the government could control neither the timing nor the content of the issues on the European agenda. Developments at the European level have frequently disrupted a fragile party unity and caused Major persistent problems in party management. His efforts to pacify the Euro-sceptics while simultaneously retaining the support of the pro-European majority in the parliamentary party has proved an increasingly difficult balancing act and cast doubts on his leadership. At the same time, Major's concessions to the Euro-sceptics over issues such as the reform of qualified majority voting strained Britain's relations with its European partners.

The contemporary divisions within the Conservative Party over Europe are complex and cut across the traditional left–right cleavages which characterise divisions on issues of domestic policy. While the anti-marketeers are located almost exclusively on the right of the parliamentary party and federalists predominantly on the left, attitudes towards Europe do not coincide neatly with a left–right cleavage in the party. A large majority in the parliamentary Conservative Party, spanning left and right, support membership of the EU. Nevertheless, within this broad consensus there are clear divisions over the nature and scope of European integration. Ashford has identified six tendencies among Conservative MPs: the 'Tory Gaullists', the 'Tory modernizers', the free-market neo-liberals, the federalists, the anti-marketeers and the passive supporters of Europe (Ashford 1992: 139–41). The 'Tory Gaullists' or confederalists wish to see Europe limited to an association of sovereign states which co-operate only in those policy areas where they can achieve more by working together. The 'Tory modernizers', predominantly from the 'wet' wing of the party, share a confederalist view of European co-operation but believe that 'British interests are best protected by Britain playing a more active leading role within the EC, which may sometimes involve the sacrifice of short-term interests for wider goals' (Ashford 1992: 139). The free-market neo-liberals support a Europe based on a wide barrier-free internal market and readily accept the loss of British national sovereignty which this entails. The federalists see a substantial surrender of national sovereignty to EU institutions as necessary if Britain is to realise the full benefits of membership. The anti-marketeers opposed Britain's entry into the EC and now attempt to limit further integration. The 'passive supporters of Europe' acknowledge the benefits of membership and accept that there is no realistic alternative for Britain outside the EU; nevertheless, they do not 'share either the enthusiasms or the hostilities of the various groups' (Ashford 1992: 141) in the Conservative Party.

A recent analysis of this broad spectrum of Conservative opinion on European integration suggests that there are two cross-cutting cleavages within the party which explain Tory divisions on Europe (Baker, Gamble and Ludlam 1993: 420–34). On the 'sovereignty/

interdependence' continuum, opinion is divided over Britain's place in the world and the nature and extent of European integration. The 'extended government/limited government' continuum describes the range of opinion from those who favour interventionist government to those who support a deregulated, free market economy with minimal state intervention. These two axes crosscut and Conservative opinion on Europe is distributed across each of the four quadrants. For example, those located in the quadrant 'national sovereignty/limited government' oppose moves towards a federal Europe and favour minimal state intervention in the economy. Conservative opinion in the quadrant 'interdependence/limited government' also favours minimal state intervention but acknowledges that Britain's economic interests are inextricably bound up with Europe. Both these groups are 'Thatcherite' in terms of domestic economic policy and the role of government but are split over the issue of Europe. Lord Tebbit, for example, would be located in the national 'sovereignty/limited government' quadrant while Lord Howe would belong to the 'interdependence/limited government' quadrant. The Conservative 'wets' are located in the remaining two quadrants and while they agree on 'extended government' in domestic policy they are divided over Europe.

The divisions over Europe within the parliamentary Conservative Party are not based on stable, organised factions; rather, they are tendencies or issue groups which share a common attitude towards European integration but on issues of domestic policy, such as economic management, revert to traditional left–right divisions. This distinction between domestic and European policy is becoming increasingly blurred, however, and helps to explain why the European issue has provoked such bitter disputes in the Conservative Party and has become embroiled in intra-party ideological conflicts. European policy is not simply a part of external relations: a number of policy areas, once the sole preserve of the member state, now fall increasingly within the policy competence of the EU. As a result, European issues become entangled in domestic politics: for example, European proposals for a 'social Europe' have clashed with the Conservative government's policy of deregulation. Similarly, the processes of European economic and monetary integration mean that a government's room for manoeuvre in domestic economic management will be increasingly curtailed.

CONCLUSION

The European issue has posed persistent problems for both major parties over the course of the last thirty years. In the 1960s and the 1970s the Labour Party was more internally divided over the issue and the Conservative Party, with only a small element opposed to membership, was able to present itself as the party of Europe. By the second half of the 1980s the positions were reversed. The European issue became a persistent source of division within the ruling Conservative Party and contributed, directly or indirectly, to the resignation of four Cabinet Ministers and Prime Minister Thatcher. The Labour Party became progressively more pro-European from the mid-1980s onwards and projected itself as the party of Europe. As a party in opposition, Labour has been able to present a united policy and exploit the Conservative government's frequent difficulties over Europe.

Two dynamics have determined party attitudes to Europe: on the one hand, the dynamics of inter- and intra-party competition and, on the other, the dynamics of the process of European integration. In contrast to most other member states, in Britain the European issue has become entangled with interparty competition and intra-party factional conflict. While a broad parliamentary consensus has emerged on Britain's membership of the European Union, deep divisions remain within and between the parties over the scope and direction of European integration. With public opinion consistently unenthusiastic about the integration process, neither major party has perceived significant electoral benefits in a strong pro-Europe policy. At the same time, the adversarial style of party competition has encouraged both the Conservative and Labour Parties to emphasise policy differences over Europe rather than a consensual approach.

Both the Conservative and Labour Parties have faced difficulties in adapting to the developing European framework of British policy-making and the dynamism in the process of European integration is likely to continue to cause problems for the parties. For the Conservatives, for example, the traditional conception of the nation state and national sovereignty has been undermined by Britain's participation in the integration process. For the Labour Party, the idea of 'a national road to socialism' has been challenged by the growing interdependence and interpenetration of Europe's economies and the mobility of international capital: elements of the party's left, traditionally anti-European, now endorse 'a European road' and the 1989 Policy Review made much of the European dimension of party policy. The impact of Europe on party competition and party ideology is likely to become more pronounced as the European Union encroaches upon policy areas (such as economic management, defence and foreign and security policy) which are traditionally at the heart of domestic political concerns.

The European issue will continue to be a 'poison'd chalice' for British governments. Prime Ministers will have the difficult task of maintaining internal party cohesion over Europe while at the same time satisfying the demands of Britain's European partners. The latter, with their own domestic audiences to address, are unlikely to make repeated concessions to ease the political difficulties of a British Prime Minister. There is no sign of the European issue being 'settled' or receding in importance in British politics; rather, the dynamics of the integration process may provoke deeper divisions within and between the parties and reopen the debate about Britain's continued membership of the European Union. There is little enthusiasm for a federal Europe within the pro-European majority in the House of Commons and significant moves in a federalist direction may encourage opposition from party elements which have traditionally supported pro-European positions.

NOTES

1 The European Free Trade Association, set up in 1960, was organised on an intergovernmental basis and posed no threat to national sovereignty. The original members were Britain, Sweden, Switzerland, Austria, Norway, Denmark and Portugal.
2 On the reasons for the Wilson government's conversion to the idea of membership, see Ashford (1992: 126) and Pimlott (1992: 432–42).
3 On this theme, see Tindale (1992).
4 On Labour's reaction to 'social Europe', see Tindale (1992).
5 Speech given by the Prime Minister on Europe in Bruges, 20 September 1988. Office for the Minister of the Civil Service and the Central Office of Information, December 1989.
6 For the Prime Minister's own account of sterling's entry into the ERM, see Thatcher (1993: 690–726). See also Lawson (1992).
7 Speech given by the Prime Minister on Europe in Bruges, 20 September 1988, op. cit.
8 On the Maastricht vote, see Baker, Gamble and Ludlam (1993b; 1994).

REFERENCES

Ashford, N. (1992) 'The political parties', in S. George (ed.) *Britain and the European Community: The Politics of Semi-Detachment*, Oxford: Clarendon.

Baker, D., Gamble A. and Ludlam, S. (1993a) '1846 . . . 1906 . . . 1996? Conservative splits and European integration', *Political Quarterly* 64: 420–34.

Baker, D., Gamble, A. and Ludlam, S. (1993b) 'Whips or scorpions? The Maastricht vote and the Conservative Party', *Parliamentary Affairs* 46: 151–66.

Baker, D., Gamble, A. and Ludlam, S. (1994) 'The parliamentary siege of Maastricht 1993: Conservative divisions and British ratification', *Parliamentary Affairs* 47: 37–60.

Berrington, H. (1980) 'The Common Market and the British Parliamentary Parties, 1971: tendencies, issue groups . . . . and factionalism', unpublished paper presented at the European Consortium for Political Research workshop on Factionalism, Florence, March.

HM Government (1984) 'Europe – the future', *Journal of Common Market Studies* 23: 74–81.

Labour Party (1989) *Meet the Challenge, Make the Change: Labour's Policy Review for the 1990s*, London.

Lawson, N. (1992) *The View From No. 11: Memoirs of a Tory Radical*, London: Bantam.

Pimlott, B. (1992) *Harold Wilson*, London: HarperCollins.

Thatcher, M. (1993) *The Downing Street Years*, London: HarperCollins.

Tindale, S. (1992) 'Learning to love the market: Labour and the European Community', *Political Quarterly* 63: 276–300.

7 The industrial privatisation programmes of Britain and France

The impact of political and institutional factors

Vincent Wright

Privatisation has become a policy fashion throughout the world. In 1992 alone nearly fifty countries sold public-sector firms worth $69 billion to private investors, bringing the running total since 1985 to $328 billion (*Economist*, 21 August 1993). Sales proposed in Western Europe could raise $150 billion by 1998 (Debbasch 1989; Vickers and Wright, 1989; Wright 1993).

Nowhere in Western Europe has privatisation been more active than in France and the United Kingdom. By whatever criteria employed their programmes must be classified as radical.[1] The privatisation programmes of Britain and France provide a particularly rich field of investigation – both empirically and theoretically – for political scientists. They may be analysed as an exercise in rational choice (Dunleavy 1986; Pint 1990) – as a method of distributing costs and benefits amongst groups – as illustrations of the impact of technology on public decision-making, or they may be studied from the angle of their electoral impact. (McAllister and Studlar 1989) Equally, they can be viewed as examples of the changing nature of the state (in a more indirect and regulatory direction) or of the adjustment which is taking place in state–market relationships. For students of public policy the two programmes are rich in lessons concerning, for example, policy diffusion, policy emulation, policy paradox, policy fashion, policy paradigms, policy slippage. Finally, they enable the political institutionalist – that most modest member of the political science profession – to evaluate the effect of institutional arrangements on the shaping of public policy. (Zaharidis 1991) It is this final political science dimension of the two programmes which serves as the focus for this essay. More specifically, after briefly describing the convergent pressures which led to the programmes, the programmes themselves and the differences between the two, the essay addresses two central questions: how have institutional arrangements facilitated the pursuit of the two radical privatisation programmes? How do such arrangements explain the differences between them? The study concentrates on the definition and implementation of the programmes, and does not raise the complex and problem-ridden issues of the *impact* of the programmes where the evidence seems to point to a differentiated balance sheet according to the criterion evaluated.

The argument of the essay is threefold in nature and may be stated quite simply. First, two ideologically committed governments were able to exploit the policy opportunities provided by powerful and convergent exogenous pressures. Second, they were able to do so also because the policy environment – in some respects restructured by those pressures as well as by state action – was especially conducive in the two countries to radical policy-making. Finally, a close look at the two programmes reveals not only striking similarities but also significant differences, and these differences are due not only to somewhat distinctive ambitions but more particularly to differing patterns of political, constitutional and institutional constraints. France – traditionally depicted, however misleadingly, as the archetypal strong state – emerges as more inhibited than Britain, frequently alleged to be a weak state.

CONVERGENT PRESSURES

The first pro-privatisation pressure has been the general paradigm shift rooted in disenchantment with Keynesianism, industrial policy and *dirigisme*. Scepticism about the efficacy of state intervention, which permeated Conservative Party circles after the failure of the Heath government, crossed the Channel in the 1980s. Even France's socialist government, after the early heady days, was quickly to lurch into many of the policies which it had previously denounced in opposition: 'Thatcherism with a human face' was the cruel jibe employed by left-wing critics.

On both sides of the Channel reactions against high taxation, worrying levels of inflation and ballooning public deficits and public indebtedness have forced governments to call into question the bases of many of their economic policies and to dismantle some of the collusive relationships which they enjoyed with budget-expanding 'distributional coalitions'. Nowhere were those coalitions more powerful than in the public industrial sector. The financial squeeze on governments has meant that they no longer have the resources to feed an ailing public sector with a panoply of state aids. And although these remain a familiar feature of the West European industrial landscape they are everywhere in decline. Increasingly, governments are demanding that nationalised industries cut losses by acting more like private industries. The French socialist government poured FF 136 billion into the public industrial sector between 1981 and 1983, but recognised that such profligacy was not sustainable, and by mid-1984 it was granting public-sector bosses greater autonomy to pursue strategies based on the exigencies of the market.

The second major pressure has been the changing nature of public-sector industries. (Heath 1990) Part of the argument for nationalisation had always resided in the need for the state to control natural monopolies in strategic areas – railways, gas, electricity, telecommunications – or, to aid high-risk industries demanding heavy investment and promising low returns. Yet new technology is dramatically weakening the extent of natural monopoly in several industries (notably telecommunications and electricity distribution) and transforming single-product monoliths into complex multi-product enterprises. There are many reasons why the publicly owned monopolies Deutsche-Telekom and France Télécom are pressing for privatisation. One of the most important is that British Telecom, US Sprint and several others can now transmit data across frontiers and offer attractive deals to major French and German enterprises. Arguments about the need to control 'the commanding heights' of the economy to justify nationalisation now appear weak, given the shape of those industries: shipbuilding, steel, coal are everywhere in decline and in financial crisis. The new strategic industries in high tech are much less susceptible to state control because they are more fragmented, function in mercilessly competitive markets and are subject to rapid product innovation. Furthermore, since they require massive capital injections which states can ill afford to supply they are increasingly obliged to go to the international financial markets. The massive capital needs of major companies constitute one of the major pressures for escaping the shackles of state control. And this leads us to the third major pressure on the traditional public sector: the liberalisation and globalisation of both product markets and financial circuits – twin processes linked to and facilitated by technological change.

Many industries have become much more complex and necessitate international cooperation because of problems of comparability. Economies of scale are no longer national in character. Take-overs, mergers, joint research agreements, joint ventures, equity swaps are increasingly common at the international and European levels. These processes of internationalisation are blurring the identities of many major enterprises – private and public – and render them problematic as 'national champions'. Nevertheless, throughout Western Europe governments are tolerating or even encouraging such processes. However, privatising governments or governments with extensive private sectors are demanding reciprocity. Thus, the United Kingdom has taken a less than friendly view of foreign public-sector firms buying British equity or subsidiaries – 'nationalisation by the back door', particularly as the same firms are not vulnerable to the same treatment. Finally, it is alleged that, in an internationalised and liberalised environment, flexibility and speed in decision-making are at a premium. The luxury of an industrial decision-making process shaped by cumbersome politico-bureaucratic compromises can no longer be afforded.

The challenges of the European Union and, more particularly, of an increasingly integrated market, present the fourth major pressure. In principle, the existence of national public sectors is perfectly compatible with the stipulations of the Treaty of Rome. However, there are aspects of economic integration – monetary convergence, competition policy, public procurement policy – which clearly inhibit *dirigiste* governments from fully exploiting their public enterprises as instruments of industrial policy. Moreover, the increasingly tight control exercised by Brussels over state-controlled firms has infuriated governments and irritated managers. State aid to Renault, Air France, Bull (the computer group), Usinor (steel), and Thomson (defence and electronics) has been stopped or frozen in widely publicised rows between the Commission and the French government. This control of the Commission – which has not always been consistent or coherent – is one of the reasons often cited by public-sector managers who advocate privatisation.

A final significant pressure for privatisation has been the emergence and diffusion of a pro-privatisation model based on the experience of the United Kingdom. The apparent success of the British programme fed the ideological aspirations of the neo-liberals of other European countries, including France, pushed sceptics on to the defensive, provided ammunition to pro-privatisers in public-sector management, and whetted the financial appetites of revenue-starved governments of all political hues. It clearly influenced the Chirac government in its privatisation strategy (Balladur 1987: 93).

There have been, therefore, several broadly convergent pressures at work in Western Europe which have combined seriously to call into question the bases of the traditional public sector. However, it should be emphasised that each of these pressures was felt with varying degrees of intensity and at different times. And sometimes for very obvious reasons. Thus, governments with little to privatise felt the pressures less acutely. It should also be noted that whilst privatisation was placed on the political agenda everywhere, it was not always the most pressing policy priority. Not all governments in Western Europe felt the same need or desire or enjoyed the same ability to take the radical privatisation path of Britain and France.

THE PROGRAMMATIC RESPONSE

The British privatisation programme is too well known to warrant a detailed account. Suffice to say that from the sale of the first tranche of British Petroleum in November 1979 to the sale of the third tranche of British Telecom in July 1993, British government transferred into private hands almost the whole of the industrial public sector. Only a dwindling number of coal mines, parts of the railway system, of the electricity generating industry and most of the Post Office remain under state control. And all are scheduled – whatever the political and technical problems – for privatisation. The firms involved include major public utilities – gas, water, electricity, telecommunications, those considered as 'strategic' (BP, British Aerospace, Britoil), a number with a high national profile (Jaguar, Rolls-Royce) and even British Airways, the national flag carrier. According to the proud claim of the 1993 Conservative Party election manifesto, 46 major enterprises employing 900,000 people have been sold to the private sector. No industrial sector has been spared: energy, steel, automobile, air and road transport, shipbuilding, ports, airports, water, gas, electricity, telecommunications. Small wonder that the privatisation programme should become the model for zealous neo-liberals throughout Europe, and especially since the programme has been so immensely lucrative, raising nearly £70 billion. Some flotations have been amongst the biggest financial market operations in post-war European history: several (BP in October 1987, BT in December 1986, the water industry in December 1989 and electricity distribution in December 1990) topped £5 billion. The programme also rapidly and dramatically expanded the number of industrial shareholders to over 11 million.

The French privatisation programme has been less drastic, but its true significance lies in the fact that it has occurred in a country frequently characterised as a quintessentially *dirigiste* state. It has had two distinct phases: that of the Chirac government which was defined in the Privatisation Acts of 2 and 6 August 1986, and that of the Balladur government enacted by the Law of 19 July 1993. Unlike the British, the French provided a list of the enterprises to be privatised within the duration of a five-year legislature. The 1986 list contained twelve major groups, comprising sixty-five major companies with a total of 1,454 subsidiaries, employing some 755,000 employees. It included nineteen insurance companies (with over 200,000 employees) and almost 350 companies in the industrial sector (with some 350,000 employees). The list included some of the flagships of French industry such as Bull, the ailing computer group, and Elf-Acquitaine, France's biggest group, employing 88,000 workers and long-considered as one of the linchpins of the country's *dirigisme*.

By the time of the presidential elections of May 1988 which saw the re-election of François Mitterrand and the end of the right's privatisation drive, twelve major flotations had taken place (Saint-Gobain, Paribas, Sogénal, Banque du Bâtiment et des Travaux Publics, Banque Industrielle et Mobilière Privée, Crédit Commercial de France, Compagnie Générale d'Electricité, Havas, Société Générale, Suez, Matra, and TFI). To these must be added the off-market privatisations of CGCT and the Mutuelle Générale Française. Almost half the 1986 privatisation programme was implemented in about eighteen months. A total of thirty (of the sixty-five envisaged) and 138 subsidiaries were transferred to the private sector, and the capital raised amounted to FF 71 billion (more than twice the amount projected for the entire programme). This figure may be compared with the FF 22 billion which had been raised by private corporations on the Bourse between 1983 and 1985: the short privatisation burst of 1986–8 comfortably exceeded the total that had been raised on the French equity market in the previous three years. Nearly 300,000 employees were moved from the public industrial groups to the private sector, and in the banking sector over 100,000 were transferred. The popularity of the programme was clear. Most of the sales were vastly oversubscribed, and the number of shareholders rocketed: 1.5 million for Saint-Gobain, 3.8 million for Paribas, 1.6 million for Crédit Commercial de France, 2.25 million for the Compagnie Générale d'Electricité. By May 1988 the number of individual shareholders had risen from the 1985 figure of two million to eight million. The impact on the Paris Bourse was real, since it increased market capitalisation by an estimated 10 per cent and sharply increased trading on the secondary market.

The stock market crisis of October 1987 brought the first privatisation programme to a crashing halt even before its official

Table 1: French privatisation programme, 1986–93

1986 List implemented	1986 List not implemented – on 1993 list	1993 List additions
Saint-Gobain	AGF	Aérospatiale
Paribas	GAN	Air France
CGCT	UAP	Caisse Centrale de Réassurance
Banque BTP	Bull	Caisse Nationale de Prévoyance
BIMPT	Thomson	Compagnie Générale Maritime
Havas	Banque Hervet	Renault
CGE	Crédit Lyonnais	SEITA
Mutuelle Générale	BNP	SNECMA
CIC	Péchiney	Usinor-Sacilor
Suez	Rhône-Poulenc	
Matra	Elf-Acquitaine	
	Société Marseillaise de Crédit	

abandonment in May 1988 after the Mitterrand victory. But it was judged a success, and whetted the appetite of the right, which advocated, in its 1993 electoral programme, the progressive privatisation of the equity of the public sector transport, energy and telecommunications monopolies. The second programme reflected, at least in part, this increased appetite. The 19 July 1993 Law extended the 1986 list by adding nine new groups to the fifteen (reduced to twelve by mergers) which had not been sold.

There are some notable differences between the 1986 programme and that of 1993: these include a more market-oriented approach to pricing, a change of the rules concerning the state's golden share, a decision to sell some groups by *tranches* and not in their entirety as in 1986, and a strengthening of the role of the Independent Privatisation Commission (see below). But the biggest difference lies in the scope and scale of the new programme. The new programme includes defence-related industries such as Aérospatiale, the politically sensitive Renault car company (taken over by the state at the time of the Liberation to punish the company's owners for their collaboration with the Germans), and even the national flag carrier Air France. The radical nature of the programme may be judged not only by the scale and scope of the programme or the inclusion of certain sacred cows of French industry, but also by the speed of implementation.

Within six months of the promulgation of the 1993 Law four major privatisations had taken place: the reduction of the state's direct and indirect stake in Crédit Local de France from 50.5 per cent to 20 per cent; the highly successful flotation of the BNP which raised FF28 billion and attracted 2.8 million shareholders (a figure beaten only by the Paribas privatisation of 1986); the no less successful sale of the state's 43 per cent stake in Rhône-Poulenc which raised FF13 billion; the flotation of most of the 54 per cent of the state's equity holding in Elf-Acquitaine for FF33 billion in February 1994 – France's biggest ever financial market operation. All the signs are that the Balladur government will maintain the hectic pace of most of its programme.

THE CONDITIONS FOR RADICAL POLICY-MAKING

Radical policy-making may be motivated by acute needs or desires, but its implementation requires a capacity to establish the appropriate instruments and to avoid possible constraints. This point is made very clear by a study of the British and French privatisation programmes.

At a number of levels, the privatisation drives of Britain and France might be seen, somewhat paradoxically, as evidence of state-led 'heroic' decision-making. The extent and wider ambitions of the programmes as well as the persistent intervention of the state in ensuring their success lend credence to this view. Certainly, the British and French experiences contrast sharply with the half-hearted privatisations of many other West European countries.

The speed and extent of the programmes highlight the conditions which are propitious for radical policy-making. They are worth outlining, since they underline certain distinctive features of British and French policy making.

- The policy-makers were able to form small, ideologically like-minded, politically cohesive and relatively closed policy units which were not bogged down in 'the quagmire of corporatism' (the case in several other West European countries), were served by an efficient administrative apparatus, were unhindered by the querulous reluctance of sponsoring ministries or state holding companies (an all too evident phenomenon in other West European states), and were able, when necessary, to restructure the traditional – and potentially disruptive – policy communities, either through judicious appointments or through a process of marginalisation or exclusion (Richardson, Maloney and Rüdig 1992). Thus, in France, the first privatisation programme was spearheaded by a small group of friends and political associates of Finance Minister Edouard Balladur who, with the public support of Prime Minister Chirac, retained a tight grip on the entire programme (Denis 1987).

- They were able to rely on the backing of a strong and united government. Indeed, in Britain privatisation appeared to be one of the few policies which united the Cabinet. The Chirac government provoked the irritation of several of its members – but over the means by which Chirac pushed through the programme, rather than over its substance: right-wing ministers were divided over the privatisation of part of the television network but were in agreement over industrial privatisation. This broad agreement was also clearly in evidence in the Balladur government. It is worth emphasising that in both Britain and France the inner core of the executive was able to exploit the traditional segmentation of Cabinet decision-making: privatisation was a 'policy-turf' or '*chasse-gardée*' not to be violated by ministers not specifically involved.

- The decision-makers could count on the blessing of their respective party or party coalition in power (once again a situation which rarely prevails elsewhere in Western Europe). Certain right-wingers in Britain expressed unease at the privatisation of public-sector enterprises with their monopolistic positions intact, but were easily ignored. Harold Macmillan's caustic remarks on the sale of the family silver were received favourably only by those who had none. Party opposition to rail privatisation came from unexpected quarters – from Nicolas Ridley, a champion of the Thatcherite cause – but had little real impact. On the whole, the Conservative Party overwhelmingly approved the programme. Only postal privatisation, clumsily handled, was to run into effective party opposition. In France, some centrists (including ex-Prime Minister Raymond Barre) criticised certain aspects of the 1986 programme, notably the use of the proceeds of the privatisation sales and the politically inspired choice of the hard-core groups (see below). But the principles of the programme were fully approved. Moreover, by 1993, the right-wing coalition electoral platform gave privatisation prominent place, and even promised the liberalisation and privatisation of the state monopolies.

- They enjoyed the necessary support and constitutional mechanisms to push their programmes through Parliament. In Britain the opposition to clauses of certain privatisations was able to exact concessions in the form of amendments (notably in the water and railway privatisation bills), but in no case did Parliament question the basic elements of a privatisation programme. The sole exception was the privatisation of the Post Office in 1994. In France, the first privatisation programme was subject to sustained guerilla tactics (over 400 amendments were proposed), and the Chirac government amended the 1986 bill in a number of ways (see below) although there was never any doubt that the substance of the programmes would be respected. The 1993 programme ran into a barrage of parliamentary opposition from socialist and communist Deputies and Senators who proposed over 3,500 amendments. Indeed, an extraordinary session of Parliament was required to push through the legislation. Once again, however, in spite of a number of concessions, the main lines of the government's proposals were never in any danger.

- The privatisers were able to mobilise some powerful group support. Private-sector financial and industrial interests which gained most from the programme were at the forefront of the privatisation drive in both countries. Perhaps more significantly, the privatisers were able to enlist the backing of important elements *within* the public sector – most notably the chairmen (who were often selected to prepare their company for privatisation or to privatise the culture of their company). Such appointments included Sir Robert Reid at British Rail, Sir George Jefferson at British Telecom, and, of course, Lord MacGregor – Mac the Knife – of British Steel and British Coal. Lord Kearton, Chairman of BNOC, who was one of the very few public-sector bosses to oppose the privatisation of his enterprise, was swiftly replaced by Philip Shelbourne, an ardent privatiser (Pitt, 1990). Public-sector managers, even those appointed by the French Socialists, generally yearned for greater autonomy to pursue market-oriented international strategies or to raise capital on the private financial markets – without political interference or bureaucratic delay. Furthermore, in both countries opposition from employees was frequently stilled by the offers to buy the shares of the company at below market price. Thus, no fewer than 95 per cent of the employees of Saint Gobain bought shares in their company at discounted prices.

- The privatisers were confronting an opposition which was weak, demoralised or divided – the case of the Labour Party throughout the 1980s, as well as the French left, especially after the electoral *débâcle* of spring 1993. Furthermore, there has been a clear dilution of the ideological commitment of the European left for nationalisation. Even the British Labour Party, disenchanted with Morrisonian concepts of the public sector, aware of the abuses of the 1970s and conscious of the financial and political cost of reprivatisation has quite clearly rethought its position on the virtues of nationalisation. It is also revealing that several left-wing governments in Europe have advocated or tolerated partial privatisation of public enterprises. Indeed, French Socialist governments after 1984 accepted the sale of public enterprise subsidiaries (the controversial policy of *respiration*), and had encouraged the recapitalisation of the public sector through private (often foreign) finance (Wright 1990). Trade union reactions in Britain have been muted or ineffective or divided (Bulford 1983; Thomas 1986). Indeed, future historians of the 1980s may wonder why the biggest transfer of wealth since the dissolution of the monasteries raised so little effective organised opposition. In France, as will be noted below, the first privatisation package provoked little trade union opposition. However, the post-1993 programme may not be received with the same indifference.

- The privatisers were confronted with a public which was profoundly ambivalent. General support for privatisation slackened during the 1980s, and opposition to certain privatisations was overwhelming (the case of the public utilities). But such opposition was generalised and diffuse, and it did not prevent the public (especially the middle-class public) from purchasing shares at the time of privatisation. This was scarcely surprising, since the price of the stock was politically fixed in both countries to ensure such a response. Premiums to investors at the end of the first day of trading could be substantial (36 per cent for British Gas, 73 per cent for Rolls-Royce, 70 per cent for British Airways, 19 per cent for Saint-Gobain, 24 per cent for Paribas and 80 per cent for Sogénal). Criticisms of underpricing were not restricted to the political opposition. The House of Commons Public Accounts Committee as well as the independent National Audit Office were amongst the sternest critics.
- The privatisers were able to construct a legitimising discourse for the programme – a discourse which combined a virulent anti-state and anti-public sector rhetoric with arguments in favour of industrial efficiency and innovation, competitiveness, entrepreneurship, private initiative, freedom and a property-owning democracy (Henig, Hamnet and Feigenbaum 1988). Privatisation held out promise as a means of cutting taxes or reducing public debt. It is true that the privatisers often garbed their pragmatic needs

(money) with a legitimising rhetoric: privatisation often gave the impression of being a programme in search of a rationale, to borrow John Kay's pithy phrase. But it corresponded to the ideological requirements of sections of the right, and it touched a responsive chord in a public which often perceived the performance of public enterprises as inadequate or even disastrous.

- Finally, it is worth emphasising the importance of prolonged and sustained political will in pushing through the programmes. Although the British Conservatives have been in office since 1979, it was not until the second Thatcher administration that the programme took on a decisive direction; hitherto, it had stumbled rather clumsily into the programme. Since then, it has had adequate time to push through its programme. Furthermore, the government has shown sustained commitment to privatisation – a fact recognised by most actors. Electoral defeat brought the first privatisation drive in France to a halt – a situation similar to that in Norway and Greece – but the programme was immediately resumed (and extended) when the right returned to office in 1993.

If the political and institutional situation was highly propitious for the pursuit of a radical privatisation programme, so, too, were certain industrial and financial conditions in both countries. The major public firms to be privatised have all been eminently privatisable – they were profitable (a testimony, incidentally, to the efficacy of public-sector management when given autonomy and the right incentives), were already imbued with 'an enterprise culture' thanks to the import of private-sector managers, and held solid or strategic (often monopolistic) market positions. It is revealing that the two industrial sectors on the bottom of the British privatisation list – coal mining and railways – were either technically difficult to privatise (witness the desperate muddle surrounding rail privatisation) or financially unattractive – or both. Technical and political problems together forced the government to withdraw nuclear power from the electricity flotation.

On the financial front, the privatisers have benefited from a generally bullish investment environment. The stock market crash of October 1987 brought both programmes to a resounding halt, but the halt proved temporary. They have also been privatising in financial markets which have been liberalised and increasingly internationalised (by British Conservatives and French Socialists) and have expanded (ironically, in the case of France with state aid). French fears that the Bourse would be too small to absorb British-style massive privatisation issues have so far proved unfounded and there is no evidence that these fears determined the list of firms to be privatised. The French and British governments have not, therefore, been hampered by financial market considerations – the case in many other West European countries where privatisation of major enterprises evokes fears of foreign takeovers.

In short, compared with many other West European countries, Britain and France have enjoyed a political and economic environment which is highly conducive to radical policy-making, and their privatisation programmes perfectly illustrate the capacity of determined governments to exploit those environments. The preconditions, the resources and the will have all been present – a rare combination by West European standards. However, placing the Franco-British experience in a wider European context masks the differences between the two countries which we will now examine.

THE DIFFERENCES

The French and British programmes have striking similarities. But these similarities mask some very significant differences. Differences between the two programmes may be seen in the procedures governing privatisation (the French specification of the entire list of groups to be privatised compared with the piecemeal and disjointed British approach) and in the use of the proceeds (which, in France, have sometimes been earmarked for specific purposes). However, the major differences between the two programmes lie in three directions. In the first place, there is a major difference in the scope of the two programmes. In spite of its radicalisation, the French programme does not envisage the denationalisation of the major public monopolies – gas, electricity, railways, telecommunications, and postal services. The British government has seriously contemplated the transfer to the private sector of the postal services and is pressing ahead with the progressive privatisation of the railway system. The latter has been seriously questioned by most transport specialists, many Conservative backbenchers and even ardent Thatcherites such as Nicolas Ridley and Lord Young. It may not be 'the poll-tax on wheels' but it may eventually be a source of considerable political embarrassment for the government.

The second major difference relates to the precautions taken by the state to protect certain privatised industries against unwelcome – and often specifically foreign – actions. Both governments have placed a cap on permissible foreign holdings in certain privatised enterprises:

the size of the stake permitted and the period of the applicability of the rule varies considerably from company to company in Britain and, in practice, the rule has been frequently violated (as the experiences of the Rover car group and of Rolls-Royce clearly demonstrate); whereas, in France, a uniform ceiling has been fixed by law: in the 1993 Law this was fixed at 20 per cent, but for any enterprise involved in health, public order or defence the figure drops to 5 per cent. Both governments, too, have created a golden share or *action specifique* in certain companies. This golden share arms the state with veto powers to protect the privatised company against unfriendly predatory activity. For instance, the French government may veto any purchase of 10 per cent or more of Havas, Elf-Acquitaine or Bull. In Britain, the duration of the golden share is fixed by the specific privatisation legislation. In France, in 1986, a general rule of five years was enacted. But, in 1993, it was decided to place no limit on the time the *action specifique* could apply. It is worth noting that the rights conferred by the golden share have not been activated in Britain (even in the highly controversial BP takeover of Britoil), and have been used only once in France (to foil a complicated operation involving Havas, the privatised communications group). Both governments, finally, have placed state representatives on the boards of some privatised companies – although, again, their powers are not always very clear. However, the French, unlike the British, in their attempt to shield their privatised industries against hostile action have decided to retain on a permanent basis a minority shareholding in some companies (Elf-Acquitaine, Framatome, for example) and have created a system unknown in Britain – that of the *noyaux durs*. The system inspired by a mistaken perception of the role of the 'house banks' in the German system, involves the creation of a core of stable shareholders which are given privileged rights to acquire stock in exchange for the obligation to remain faithful. Initially reserved for French companies (sometimes with close links to the Gaullist Party), the Balladur government in 1993 extended the range of *noyaux* to encompass major foreign enterprises. Thus, when 43 per cent of the equity of Rhône Poulenc was sold in 1993, 6 per cent was reserved for core shareholders (bringing the total to 24 per cent), which included Fiat and Crédit Suisse. The privatised Banque Nationale de Paris now has sixteen friendly institutional shareholders which control 30 per cent of the capital and which include the bank's German partner, the Dresdner Bank, Britain's BAT, General Electric from the USA, Hoffmann-La Roche, the Swiss group, and two Kuwaiti government-controlled investment agencies.

The third major difference between the two programmes lies in the policy environment in which industrial privatisation has been embedded. In the first place, privatisation in Britain has already been linked with a major drive to deregulate, to liberalise and to reshape the very nature of the state apparatus (through, for instance, marketisation, and the introduction of private sector managers, management and criteria of evaluation as well as the creation of agencies through the Next Steps Initiative).

Second, the British industrial privatisation drive has been part of a much wider programme of privatisation which has included:

● The sale of public housing stock at discount prices.

● A vast contracting-out programme, often of a compulsory nature, not only at local (where it may also be seen in France) but also at national level. This programme has touched sensitive areas such as the escorting of prisoners, the prison education service, the servicing of the Immigration Centre near Heathrow airport. By the end of 1993, the United Kingdom government was exploring the means of handing over the tax codes and assessments of 34 million individuals to a private company.

● The curtailing of public services or the funding of public services in the hope that the private sector would compensate.

● The transfer to the private sector or to quangos of previously public regulatory or promotional responsibilities (certain training policy programmes; care for the mentally handicapped and the aged).

● The encouragement given to private entrepreneurs to share in the funding of public works – the so-called Private Finance Initiative, launched in 1992, and which included seventy-eight major projects in 1993 (*Economist*, 30 October 1993) (seen, for example, in the high-speed rail link from the Channel Tunnel to London).

● The introduction into the public sector of the ethos and managerial techniques of the private sector.

In France, many of these other dimensions of privatisation are not even seriously considered.

EXPLAINING THE DIFFERENCES

Any explanation of the above differences between the two programmes must disentangle those which spring from the nature and salience of the pressures, those which arise from ambitions or motives, and those which are rooted in the pattern of constraints in both countries. Each difference has a specific mix of reasons.

The pressures, as noted above, have been largely convergent, although it might be argued that the financial squeeze was more keenly and more quickly felt in Britain. Ambitions and motives have also been strikingly similar in many respects. Yet, there are differences. For instance, the French have made clear that one of the reasons for their programme is to boost a weak and vulnerable domestic financial market. More importantly, the British have remained committed to an anti-state ideologically inspired programme. This was the case in 1986 in France. By 1993, however, the privatisation programme was *dépassionné*: 'le débat idéologique est clos', declared the Economics Minister to a bored Senate during the June 1993 debate on the Privatisation Act. It is worth noting that whilst the relationship between the state and its public sector had always been problematic (under both right- and left-wing governments), the image of the public enterprise was not universally bad. Indeed, successive governments, especially Gaullist, had used the public sector as a major and dynamic instrument of industrial policy. And although the balance sheet was mixed, defenders of the public enterprise could point proudly to the achievements of France Télécom, the TGV and to Airbus. Furthermore, a close look at the rationalisation for privatisation, at least in some right-wing circles, suggests that the programme was advocated in order to *strengthen* an overloaded state. In other words, privatisation has come to be seen in largely disaggregated and functional or instrumental terms. This pragmatism has unquestionably been reinforced by the perception of the constraints which have been more apparent in France.

In terms of these constraints, there have been similarities. Hence, legal problems hindered the swift privatisation of British Airways and have contributed to the slowing down of the privatisation of Renault, whilst technical unfeasibility helps to explain the protracted nature of the British Rail privatisation programme and of the prudence in programming the privatisation of Framatome in France. However, in some respects, the pattern of constraints differs sharply. Thus, the absence of a financial market of the size of London, of pension funds and of massive institutional investors, has worried the French about the capacity of the Bourse to absorb a massive privatisation programme and about the danger of crowding out investment for non-privatised firms (Jenkinson and Mayer 1988). The capitalisation of the Bourse represents only 10 per cent of GDP, compared with nearly 60 per cent in the United Kingdom, over 50 per cent in Japan and

Switzerland, and over 40 per cent in the USA and Canada. The privatisation of France Télécom, with a value of some FF 200 billion, would clearly present a problem for a Bourse which accounted for 'only' FF 150 billion worth of transactions in 1992. The sale of the state's 51 per cent stake in Elf-Acquitaine, France's biggest company, with a market capitalisation of over $18 billion in August 1993, could only be implemented in stages (*Economist*, 7 August 1993). So, sensitivity about the capacity of the Paris financial market may not have determined the list of *privatisables*, but it certainly shaped the pace and method of privatisation.

At a more general – and more significant – level, the privatisation programme of France is much more powerfully hindered by constitutional, legal, political and cultural constraints, each acting upon and reinforcing the other.

Constitutional constraints

Unlike Britain, France has a written constitution and it has acquired a tradition of judicial review. There is no doubt that the Chirac and Balladur governments would have encountered severe constitutional obstacles had they attempted to dismantle and privatise the great public utilities of gas, electricity, core telecommunications, and railways. Such an attempt would have constituted a breach of the Constitution – a point readily conceded by Balladur during a National Assembly debate on 22 April 1986. The 1986 Bill was referred to the Constitutional Council and, as a result, was significantly amended. The Council insisted, for instance, that a panel of independent experts carry out an assessment of the value of the company to be privatised and that this panel – the *Commission de la Privatisation* – should fix a minimum price for the shares at the point of flotation. Overall, the reaction – real or anticipated – of the Council led the Chirac government to amend five of the eight articles of the initial text – even though the underlying principles and major thrust of the programme were left intact. It may even be the case that the Council provided some legitimacy for the programme by meeting some of the objections of the political opposition. The *Commission de la Privatisation*, disbanded in 1988, has been recreated and strengthened by the 1993 Act.

Any attempt radically to widen the scope of the privatisation programme to embrace the police, prisons, key welfare services, immigration services and tax collection would also be effectively prevented by the Constitutional Council, jealous guardian of the inalienable prerogatives of the regalian state.

Legal constraints

These have not only slowed down the pace of some privatisations because of the complex and time-consuming requirements to change the legal status of certain firms to be privatised. More importantly, in some industries such as telecommunications and postal services some workers enjoy the same status as civil servants and are protected by a *statut du personnel* – a *statut* which is protected by the Council of State, France's highest administrative appeal court. Any change in the *statut* would require difficult and protracted negotiations with very reluctant trade unions.

Political constraints

The first, and obvious constraint is that of time. Whereas the Conservative government has had many years of uninterrupted office, the same cannot be said of the French right. The 1986 programme was brought to a resounding halt with the victory of the left two years later. However, even in office, the French government has faced greater political impediments. Effective political opposition did not emanate from the Presidency, even though François Mitterrand has always voiced his hostility to elements of the privatisation programme. In 1986, he refused to sign the *ordonnance* authorising the programme, thus forcing the Chirac government to seek parliamentary authorisation by way of a law. This had the minor effect of postponing the promulgation of the programme by one month. In 1993, the President again couched his hostility in terms of the threat posed to national independence of the privatisation of strategic and defence-related enterprises. At the Council of Ministers on 26 May and on television on 14 July he specifically mentioned Elf-Acquitaine, Air France, Aérospatial and SNECMA. However, the President may advise and warn but not obstruct. As in the United Kingdom, Parliament in France has not forced the government to abandon the major objectives of its privatisation programmes. But in 1986 and in 1993 it forced out of the government important concessions relating to the golden share, the ceiling on foreign stakes, and the role of the Privatisation Commission. It also successfully insisted that the government present an annual report to Parliament on the implementation of the programme.

The final source of opposition which has been more effective in France than in the United Kingdom is that of the trade unions. They have been ineffective – as in Britain – in the internationalised and competitive sectors. But in Renault and in the postal services they have proved difficult partners in renegotiating the terms of the *statut du personnel*. In Elf-Acquitaine they have organised strikes to protest against privatisation, and in Air France they belatedly but successfully organised opposition to a moderate restructuring plan which was deemed necessary for a successful flotation of the firm. A nine-day strike in October 1993 brought air traffic to a standstill, forcing the government into humiliating retreat and leading to the resignation of the chairman of the company.

Cultural constraints

The constitutional, legal and political constraints which have moderated and shaped the French programme are embedded in a wider tissue of cultural constraints. Indeed, they are often the articulation or formalisation of those cultural constraints. The parameters of public policy-making are forged by a set of intertwined preoccupations rooted in a dramatic and divided history: national independence; the republican ideal; the conception of the state, with its limits, rights and obligations; the notion of the public good and of the public service. They sit in uneasy equilibrium, and each is inconsistently applied and protected. But they are given constitutional and legal expression, and, collectively, they generally constitute a significant inhibiting barrier to those whose ambitions appear seriously to call into question their legitimacy. Many aspects of radical privatisation *à l'anglaise* would represent a questioning of each of the preoccupations mentioned above. For that reason it is unlikely to be pursued. Indeed, each of the more muted aspects of the French programme could be explained by reference to one or other of the preoccupations.

SOME GENERAL CONCLUSIONS

The first major conclusion to emerge from this brief study is that powerful, interrelated, international, European Union and technological pressures may force change, but they do not dictate the scale, the timing, the pace and the means of programming such change. Clearly, political ambition, will, durability and skill are important. But national political and institutional environments also matter: domestic opportunity structures shape policy responses. These opportunity structures must be widely interpreted, since they encompass constitutional, legal, political and cultural factors at the general level, and factors which are specific to the sector under pressure.

Second, in terms of pushing through a radical programme such as industrial privatisation, the British and French governments have proved very effective – certainly much more so than their European partners. Their experience tends to suggest that at the initiation, agenda-setting and formalisation stages of public policy, the British and French governments have a capacity for 'heroic' decision making. Through the judicious use of incentives, manipulation and exclusion they are able to restructure policy networks and communities in a way favourable to their ambitions.

Finally, the autonomy of a determined British government, although not unlimited, appears to be greater in this sector than that of the French government with its more limited programme. The doubtful assertions of the traditional weak state/strong state literature appear even more dubious in the light of the privatisation experience of the two countries.

An analysis of the implementation phase of the programmes and of their effective impact might well lead to a more nuanced set of conclusions. But such an analysis would require another chapter.

NOTE

1   On the United Kingdom the literature is vast. See, notably, Vickers and Yarrow (1988); Kay *et al.* (1986); Beesley and Littlechild (1983); Brittan (1984); Curwen (1986: 157–285); Dunleavy (1986); Graham and Presser (1991); Heald (1983; 1984; 1985); Hastings and Levie (1983); Jackson (1985); Kay and Silberston (1984); Shackleton (1984); Steel and Heald (1984); Whitfield (1983); Young (1986). The best single account of the privatisation programme in France is Balladur (1987). See also Banc and Monnier (1985); Corntreau (1986); Rapp (1986); Bizaguet (1988).

REFERENCES

Balladur, E. (1987) *Je crois en l'homme plus qu'en l'Etat*, Paris.

Banc, P. and Monnier, L. (1985) 'The privatization of public enterprises in France' *Annales du CIRIEC*, 45–67.

Beesley, M. and Littlechild, S. (1983) 'Privatization: principles, problems and priorities', *Lloyd's Bank Review* 149: 1–20.

Bizaguet, A. (1988) 'The French public sector and the 1986–1988 privatizers', *International Review of Administrative Sciences* 54: 553–70.

Brittan, S. (1984) 'The politics and economics of privatization', *Political Quarterly* 55(2): 109–28.

Bulford, C. (1983) 'British Telecom' in S. Hastings and H. Levie (eds) *Privatization?*, Nottingham: Spokesman.

Corntreau E. (ed.) (1986) *Privatisation: l'Art et la Manière*, Paris: l'Harmothen.

Curwen, P. (1986) *Public Enterprise: A Modern Approach*, Brighton: Harvester Press, 157–285.

Debbasch, C. (ed.) (1989) *Les privatisations en Europe*, Paris, CNRS.

Denis, S. (1987) *Le Roman de l'argent*, Paris: Albin-Michel.

Dunleavy, P. (1986) 'Explaining the privatization boom: public choice versus radical approaches', *Public Administration* 64(1): 13–34.

Graham, C. and Presser, T. (1991) *Privatizing Public Enterprises*, Oxford: Clarendon.

Hastings, S. and Levie H. (1983) *Privatization?* Nottingham: Spokesman.

Heald, D. (1983) *Public Expenditure: Its Defence and Reform*, Oxford: Robertson.

—— (1984) 'Privatization: analysing its appeal and limitations', *Fiscal Studies* 5(1): 34–46.

—— (1985) 'Will the privatization of public enterprises solve the problem of control?', *Public Administration* 63: 7–22.

Heath, J. (1990) *Public Enterprise at the Crossroads*, London: Routledge.

Henig, J. R., Hamnet C. and Feigenbaum, H. B. (1988) 'The politics of privatization: a comparative perspective', *Governance* 1(4): 451.

Jackson, P. (1985) *Implementing Government Policy Initiatives: the Thatcher Administration 1979–1983*, London: Royal Institute of Public Administration.

Jenkinson, T. and Mayer, C., (1988) 'The privatization process in France and the United Kingdom', *European Economic Review* 32: 482–90.

Kay, J., Mayer, C. and Thompson, D. (eds) (1986) *Privatization and Regulation: The U.K. Experience*, Oxford: Clarendon Press.

Kay, J. A. and Silberston, Z. A. (1984) 'The new industrial policy – privatization and competition', *Midland Bank Review* Spring: 8–16.

McAllister I. and Studlar, D. T., (1989) 'Popular versus elite views of privatization: the case of Britain', *Journal of Public Policy* 9(2): 157–78.

Pint, E. M. (1990) 'Nationalization and privatization: a rational choice perspective on efficiency', *Journal of Public Policy* 10(3): 267–98.

Pitt, D. (1990) 'An essentially contestable organization: British Telecom and the privatization debate', in J. J. Richardson (ed.) *Privatization and Deregulation in Canada and Britain*, Aldershot: Dartmouth.

Rapp, L. (1986) *Technique de privatisation des entreprises publiques*, Paris: Librairie Technique.

Richardson, J., Maloney W. A. and Rüdig, W. (1992) 'The dynamics of policy change: lobbying and privatization', *Public Administration* 70: 157–75.

Shackleton, J. R. (1984) 'Privatization: the case examined', *National Westminster Bank Quarterly Review* May: 59–73.

Steel, D. and Heald, D. (eds) (1984) *Privatizing Public Enterprises: Options and Dilemmas*, London: Royal Institute of Public Administration.

Thomas, S. (1986) 'The union response to denationalisation', in J. Kay *et al.*, *Privatization and Regulation: The U.K. Experience*, Oxford: Clarendon.

Vickers, J. and Wright, V. (eds) (1989) *The Politics of Privatization in Western Europe*, London: Frank Cass.

Vickers, J. and Yarrow, G. (1988) *Privatization: An Economic Analysis*, London: MIT Press.

Whitfield, D. (1983) *Making it Public*, London: Pluto.

Wright, V. (1990) 'The nationalisation and privatization of French public enterprises 1981–1988: radical ambitions, diluted programmes and limited impact', *Staatswissenschaften und Staatspraxis* 2: 176–98.

Wright, V. (ed.) (1993) *Les privatisations en Europe: Programmes et problèmes*, Paris: Actes Sud.

Young, S., (1986) 'The nature of privatization in Britain 1979–1985', *West European Politics* 9: 235–52.

Zaharidis N. (1991) 'Explaining privatization in Britain and France: a new institutionalist perspective', unpublished paper presented to the APSA Meeting, Washington.

8 Backbench opinion revisited

Iain McLean

INTRODUCTION

> Their help has been quite invaluable. The same is true of the help given us by Miss Pat Heneage, B.A., who has acted as computer.
>
> (Finer, Berrington and Bartholomew 1961: ix)

> Let me add that a computer (expensive or otherwise) has been used only for one stage of this study, namely the carrying out of chi-squared tests.
>
> (Berrington 1973: x).

In 1961 a computer was still a person; in 1973 it was a statistical calculator; now it is a prop, a panacea, a panjandrum. This chapter re-evaluates Hugh Berrington's research programme, enquires why it has been so little followed up in the UK on the House of Commons, and suggests some lines to follow now that computers can do more things than used to be dreamt of in your philosophy.

Hugh Berrington has produced three major research works on rollcall voting in the House of Commons. Listed in the order that the major work was done, they are 'Partisanship and dissidence in the nineteenth-century House of Commons' (Berrington 1968), *Backbench Opinion in the House of Commons 1955–59* (Finer, Berrington and Bartholomew 1961; cited below as *BBO*); and *Backbench Opinion in the House of Commons 1945–1955* (Berrington 1973; cited below as *BB45*). The Backbench Opinion project continued on a reduced scale, hampered by the ever-pressing demands of running an understaffed (overstudented) department and by the premature death of Berrington's main statistical collaborator. Publications arising from the later work are Leece and Berrington (1977) and Berrington (1982). These works do nothing like full justice to the vast quantities of data about legislators and their votes which Hugh

Berrington has accumulated over the years; it is very much to be hoped that more will be published.

IN QUEEN VICTORIA'S GLORIOUS DAYS

Berrington's 1968 paper starts with Lowell's (1919) lists of divisions in the House of Commons in seven selected years in the nineteenth century. Berrington re-analysed Lowell's lists in greater detail, adding data for three further years. Lowell used these lists to show how party discipline gradually eliminated independent voting. As a prominent American scholar of Congress (not to mention a president of Harvard), Lowell was interested in why the British and US legislatures had evolved so differently after 1800. Even granted that the constitutional framework is quite different, British MPs and US Congressmen were much more like one another in 1832 than they were in 1886 (or are today). In 1832 MPs were not bound by a strong party whip, had real opportunities to initiate legislation, had constituency patronage to offer when their party was in office, and saw themselves as representatives of their district (sometimes of its patron), not of their party. By 1886 all of these had been reversed. In 1832 the House of Commons was somewhat like Congress; in 1886 it was more like the Electoral College. How and why, during the ninteenth century, did the Mother of Parliaments turn itself into an appendage of the executive?

Lowell counted rollcalls in 1836, 1850, 1860, 1871, 1881, 1894, and 1899. He deliberately selected uneventful years, as did Berrington (1968) when he came to expand Lowell's study. Lowell's data (Table 1) measure the decline of the cross-party division, in other words the increasing importance of party discipline.

The classical interpretation of the rise of party discipline is due to Ostrogorski (1902). According to Ostrogorski, the Second Reform Act of 1867 introduced the politics of electoral pressure via the party caucus. Constituencies became too big to be managed on behalf of patrons; voters responded more to candidates' party labels and less to their willingness to distribute favours than before; MPs' voting behaviour came under stronger party discipline, so that the 'independent MP' was virtually extinct by 1886. Ostrogorski catalogued and deplored the domination of the caucus over the independent MP, and Ostrogorski's normative judgements continue to hover over most writing on the subject.

Lowell's data lend support to Ostrogorski, but it is not unqualified support. The first column of Table 1 shows that whipped divisions

Table 1 Whipping and cohesion, House of Commons, selected years 1836–99

Year	% of divns whipped by Govt	Unwhipped divns, indices of cohesion: Cons.	Lib.
1836	48.6	0.687	0.582
1850	67.9	0.531	0.617
1860	67.3	0.557	0.617
1871	81.6	0.738	0.614
1881	92.2	0.236	0.678
1894	90.2	0.591	0.602
1899	88.5	0.673	0.982

Source: Derived by Cox (1987: 24) from figures originally reported by Lowell (1919).

Note: Cox's Index of Cohesion may be expressed as

$$C_j = \frac{\sum_{i=1}^{n} 2\ [(V_j^{maj}/V_j) - 0.5]}{n}$$

where there are n divisions in a session, the parties are labelled $1, \ldots i, j, \ldots m$; C_j is the jth party's index of cohesion, and V_j^{maj}/V_j is the ratio of votes cast by the majority of that party's MPs who voted in a division to all votes cast by MPs of that party in that division. The range of V_j^{maj}/V_j is between 0.5 and 1, and the scale is therefore normalised to the range 0–1. The overall cohesion indices are the means for the session. Note that this measure cannot capture the rare but significant cases where the leadership of a party was in a minority of its own supporters.

climbed to around 90 per cent of all divisions by 1881 and stayed there, thus tending to confirm that MPs' independence declined after (but not immediately after) the Reform Act 1867. An increase in the indices of cohesion for unwhipped divisions implies an increase in internal harmony: the trend for Liberals is in this direction, but there is no trend for Conservatives. Lowell's data therefore tend to smooth away the abruptness of the 1867 shift postulated by Ostrogorski.

Berrington (1968) took the process further. He pointed out a defect in the measure of cohesion used by Lowell, which we have summarised as the 'index of cohesion' in the legend to Table 1. Lowell had judged where majority opinion in each party lay from the majority of its votes cast in any division. But late Victorian Liberalism was too factious to be captured by this measure. Not infrequently, the Liberal front bench did not vote in the same way as the majority of Liberals who voted. Typically when the Conservatives were in office, a small number of radicals forced a division in which their own front bench did not vote. And when the Liberals were in office, they often relied on Conservative support against their own backbench rebels. As Berrington notes:

> *In 1883, the leadership of the two parties were on the same side in 46% of the 'Whip' divisions.* It was not the independents, but the official Liberals, who supplied the moderating element in the Parliament of 1880–1885. Government in the early eighties was almost as much 'government by the centre' as it was 'party government'. . . . [It] bears some resemblance to the situation twenty years before when the Palmerston government, dependent on Whig and *radical* support for office, relied on Whig and *Conservative* support for the passage (or to prevent the passage) of legislation.
>
> (Berrington 1968, pp. 361–2, stress in original)

Ostrogorski had painted a powerful picture of moderate Independents cowed by an extremist caucus; Berrington showed for the first time how often the opposite was the case. He also revealed his love–hate fascination with irregulars of the left that was to reappear in *BBO* and *BB45*. Henry Labouchère is the Sydney Silverman of 1883 and Emrys Hughes is the Charles Bradlaugh of 1955.

The demolition of Ostrogorski was completed with beautiful economy by Gary Cox (1987). Cox undermines Ostrogorski's anecdotal evidence of the power of the caucus to suborn MPs. In the first place, Ostrogorski's evidence of the malign power of the caucus, although purportedly applicable to both parties, derives only from the Liberals. Conservative mass organisations were non-ideological. Furthermore, a survey of Conservative associations in 1874 ranked them as 'strong' or 'weak'; but there is no association between the strength of an MP's constituency party and his loyalty to his front bench (Cox 1987, pp. 37–44). Cox records how MPs voluntarily deprived themselves of backbench power over a long period of years. In particular, between 1832 and 1855 they allowed government business to take up a far higher proportion of parliamentary time than ever before; and they excluded themselves from the barrel of pork labelled Private Bill procedure. In the 1870s and 1880s they consented to still further extensions of the power of the executive over the legislature, by consenting to the guillotine and closure procedures which were brought in to counter Irish obstruction and filibustering. If one of the main British parties had supported the filibuster, it would have survived. It was a party which neither had nor sought a role in governing the UK which perfected the classically negative instruments of obstruction and timewasting: the two parties which had and sought power therefore united against the Irish (but curtailed their own powers) in approving the guillotine and other closure procedures (Cox 1987; McLean 1992; McLean and Foster 1992). All these changes in parliamentary procedure were freely voted through by MPs themselves; they cannot be put down to the power of a determined executive. The procedural changes conferred that power; they cannot have sprung from it. In this story, the Reform Bill of 1867 plays almost no part. The monolithic uniformity of the parties belongs to a later era. It was canonically described by W.S. Gilbert in *Iolanthe* (1882), although every boy and every gal who had been born a little Liberal very soon had to make a painful choice between Gladstone and Chamberlain in the Home Rule split of 1886.

It is notable that Berrington is the only Briton among the three scholars who have done most work on the Ostrogorski hypothesis. As we shall see below, American political scientists have consistently shown more sophisticated interest in the nineteenth-century House of Commons than their British counterparts. We must return to this curious state of affairs.

BACKBENCH AND SON OF BACKBENCH

What could Berrington and his colleagues do for the study of the twentieth-century House of Commons, given that the whips had by now reduced division lists to meaninglessness? *BBO* and *BB45* explore the alternative of early day motions with great ingenuity.

The bizarre title Early Day Motion may have attracted Hugh Berrington the psycho-political scientist. However, there is nothing anal in its meaning. *BBO* explains it thus:

> Any MP has the right to table a Motion, but in the last forty years it has become increasingly common for those who agree with its sentiments to add their names in support. (Today, some such Motions attract as many as two or three hundred supporters.) They are put down on the Order Paper without any specific day having been fixed for their discussion and so appear under the heading: 'For an Early Day': hence their technical name, Early Day Motions (henceforth abbreviated to EDMs). Thus the fiction is maintained that they are subjects for serious debate . . . [b]ut few if any are debated, and it is doubtful whether any but a small fraction are put down in the serious hope that they would be debated.
>
> (Berrington 1973: 7)

Table 2 Labour backbench MPs 1955–9, post-1945 entrants by occupation

	Workers		Miscellaneous occupations		Business		Professions		
	No.	%	No.	%	No.	%	No.	%	Total
Consistent rebels	4	17	8	32	3	60	2	9	17
Non-consistent rebels	3	13	5	20	–	–	5	22	13
Loyalists	16	70	12	48	2	40	16	70	46
Total	23	100	25	100	5	100	23	100	76

Data grouped. Miscellaneous occupations plus Business vs. All others. Consistent Rebels against Loyalists. χ^2 = 5.86. Significant at 2.5%.

Two Members who came on to the backbenches in 1954 and rebelled once in that year but did not rebel again have been excluded.

Source: Berrington 1973: 207, Table 54

Thus EDMs are, in sociologese, expressive gestures, and in economese, cheap talk. How could anybody draw worthwhile conclusions from such dubious data?

The primary data for *BBO* were all EDMs tabled between 1955 and 1958, and for *BB45* all EDMs tabled between 1945 and 1955. For both periods, some data on floor revolts and unwhipped divisions were also available. Signatures on EDMs were taken as the dependent variable; facts about MPs' backgrounds, such as their class background, schooling, occupation, military service and membership of other political bodies, were taken as the predictors. The statistical techniques used were cross-tabulations and Guttman scaling. Tables 2 and 3 show three characteristic cross-tabulations.

Table 2 is one of a number that show consistent differences among Labour MPs by occupation. All Berrington's occupational categories are self-explanatory except the 'Miscellaneous Occupations'. He waxes lyrical about these. Miscellaneous occupations were white-collar jobs that did not require a professional qualification. Of those, Berrington concentrates on the journalists and authors. Drawing on Kornhauser (1960), he argues that

Freelance intellectuals, in short, are not likely to enjoy such stable rewards (whether these be psychic or material) as intellectuals in corporate bodies, and are not integrated into old and stable organizations. As a result, they are likely to contain in their ranks a disproportionate number of the socially alienated and discontented.

(Berrington 1973: 206)

Table 3: Conservative backbenchers: votes on two divisions on corporal punishment

The Conservative Party and penal reform: by universities

Bullus Bill, 1953

	Humane No.	%	Severe No.	%	Total No.	%
Oxford	19	56	15	44	34	100
Cambridge	10	48	11	52	21	100
Others	4	36	7	64	11	100
Sandhurst	2	40	3	60	5	100
None	3	10	28	90	31	100
Total	38	37	64	63	102*	100

Graduates vs. Non-graduates: χ^2 = 12.84. Significant at 0.1%

Arbuthnot Amendment

	Humane No.	%	Severe No.	%	Total No.	%
Oxford	18	67	9	33	27	100
Cambridge	7	39	11	61	18	100
Others	2	18	9	82	11	100
Sandhurst	–	–	2	100	2	100
None	2	7	27	93	29	100
Total	29	33	58	67	87	100

Oxford vs. Cambridge vs. Others; χ^2 = 8.26. Significant at 2.5%
Graduates vs. Non-graduates: χ^2 = 11.97. Significant at 0.1%
*It was not possible to trace the age or education of one Member who voted for the Bill.

Source: Finer, Berrington and Bartholomew 1961: 203, Table 47

Berrington thus portrays his miscellaneous occupations as so many Jude the Obscures, embittered, and turned to leftism, by their repulse from Christminster.

The leftism of the literary petty-bourgeoisie has been, appropriately and self-referentially, a long-standing theme of literature from Hardy to Forster to Orwell. Berrington *et al.*'s findings about Conservatives, corporal punishment and universities (Table 3) contain a more surprising element. The Bullus Bill was a proposal to reintroduce corporal punishment for crimes of violence. The Arbuthnot Amendment, in 1956, would have permitted convicted murderers to be flogged as well as imprisoned for life. Conservative graduates were overwhelmingly more hostile to corporal punishment than Conservative non-graduates. But note also that in 1956 Conservative Oxford graduates were more hostile to corporal punishment than Conservative Cambridge graduates. This was only one of several points on which the Oxford Conservatives differed from their Cambridge counterparts. Oxonians tended to be pro-European; Cantabrigians tended to be imperialist. Oxonians were (in modern parlance) dry on economic issues, Cantabrigians wet (Finer, Berrington and Bartholomew 1961: 90, 100; Berrington 1973:169).

In both books, Berrington and his collaborators constructed scales for various attitudes, particularly 'leftness' in the Labour Party. In the earlier book, this led to a controversial table of the fifty most 'left' Labour MPs, constructed on the simple basis that an MP was more left, the more left-wing EDMs s/he signed. The later book occasionally supplemented the numerical and *ad hoc* scales used in both by Guttman scales, as did Leece and Berrington (1977). As Berrington explains,

> The aim of Guttman scaling is to discover a single dimension running through the answers to a series of separate questions, or, in legislative terms, running through the responses of Members to a series of separate issues posed in legislative votes or resolutions.
> (Berrington 1973: 226)

The benefit of such techniques is to show consistency where none was suspected; the risk is that they may purport to show consistency where none exists. Underlying this is a deeper question: should we investigate primarily questions that conform to a scale, or questions that do not? As posed, this is a silly question: some analysts are interested in the one, some in the other. Berrington, like the Iowa School whose work we consider in the next section, has been primarily interested in underlying consistency. I happen to be more interested in underlying inconsistency. This is partly a matter of taste, and partly because social choice has shown that multidimensional politics is the most interesting and disturbing politics.

To put flesh on these abstractions, consider the row that broke out in the Labour Party about German rearmament in 1954. The *Economist* described the Labour opponents of German rearmament as

> an oddly assorted collection of Labour groups – the lunatic left, the ordinary Bevanites, the bloc of Jewish MPs, ex-servicemen of both wars, some MPs who are unexpectedly emotional on this subject without being emotional on anything else, and many of the party's old women of the male sex.
>
> (27.2.1954, quoted by Berrington 1973: 105)

The penultimate category, and perhaps the last, were clearly jibes at Hugh Dalton, who never forgave the Germans for starting the war that killed his beloved, and perhaps lover, Rupert Brooke. German rearmament, in other words, was *not* just another left-wing cause, but one that brought the Jews, the ex-servicemen, and some of the homosexuals into the rebel camp. It added at least one other dimension to the Labour Party's internal warfare. In principle, whenever there are two or more political dimensions, the possibility exists that there is a majority-rule cycle. In other words, there is no unique winning proposition; each of the propositions in the cycle would lose by a simple majority to another. (For readers unfamiliar with cycling and manipulation, there are introductions in Riker 1982 and McLean 1989.)

No cycle was revealed in the 1954 debates about German rearmament. In the event, it sparked off only a private war, one of many, within the Labour Party. But it is perfectly possible that there existed a House of Commons majority against the motion approved by the House. The Conservative ranks contained no leftists and no Jews (Berrington 1973: 209), but many ex-servicemen and possibly men who had lost their lovers in war. If such a majority existed, it was frustrated by the institutions of the House – especially the party whips. Following Ostrogorski, it is customary to deplore whipping, especially when it leads MPs to vote against their preferences. But if preferences are cyclical, then there must be institutions to secure some outcome that is regarded as legitimate. The whips may turn out to be a disagreeable necessity after all. We return to the issue of cycling in the Conclusion.

Unfortunately, no deep issues were raised by the public reception of *BBO* and *BB45*. A review in *Parliamentary Affairs* (Fellowes

1962) was one of several which queried whether signatures on EDMs were a valid measure of anything. The most pungent review was by Richard Crossman. For some years, Hugh Berrington would bring it out at methodology lectures and sundry other suitable places and read it out as a talisman:

> I cannot resist a brief comment on the most statistical book about politics that I have ever read – 'Backbench Opinion in the House of Commons 1955–59'. . . . Once [the authors'] results had been dealt with by an expensive computer at Stoke University, they provided . . . 'an X-ray of the two major parliamentary parties'. Any lobby correspondent could have told poor Professor Finer that the reasons why members add their names to motions are many and mysterious and that it would be unwise to assume that you can estimate the intensity of MPs' convictions by adding up the number of motions they sign. I will leave the Tories to speak for themselves, but there is something wrong when an X-ray which reveals Mr Robert Mellish and Mr Roy Mason among 'the fifty most Left members' of the Parliamentary Labour party excludes Mrs Barbara Castle. It passes my comprehension how three portentously serious students of political institutions could have failed to question their own basic premises when they found themselves led to such a plainly nonsensical conclusion. Remote and ineffectual don. . . . I have no choice but to award the Hilaire Belloc Memorial Prize for Pretentious Pedantry to Professor Finer and to recommend that his two lieutenants should share the G.K. Chesterton Bronze Medal for Statistical Gamesmanship.
>
> (Crossman 1961)

In response to such criticisms, the first twenty pages of *BB45* are a sustained defence of the methods used, interspersed with digs at Crossman and other critics which can be appreciated once their attacks are in focus, but are easily overlooked otherwise. In the academy, though not perhaps elsewhere, the battles of statistical method fought so valiantly by Hugh Berrington in the 1960s and 1970s are now won. Though the motives for signing any one EDM may indeed be frivolous, the systematic associations revealed by Berrington's data cannot be. Indeed, opportunities exist now to do far more with his data than was easily possible in the 1960s and 1970s. The two Berrington books used only bivariate analysis. That is, each vote was compared with only one social characteristic at a time. Thus we know that Conservative MPs who went to Oxford were ideologically distinct from those who went to Cambridge but we do not know whether that is a mere artefact of, say, different age or class profiles. Multivariate analysis can, and should, be used to settle such questions. It would be nice to be able to show that something about the curriculum in Oxford and Cambridge affected the ideology of future Conservative MPs. On the face of it, it appears that Oxford men (they were nearly all men) followed J. S. Mill and Cambridge men followed Alfred Milner. But without multivariate analysis such a conclusion would be premature. It is to be hoped that the Berrington data will be examined by logistic regression methods, now that easy methods for doing so have been added to the main statistical packages used for social science data analysis.

OTHER ROLLCALL VOTING STUDIES IN BRITAIN

Professor W. O. Aydelotte of Iowa has been the other main analyst of rollcalls in Britain. Over many years he compiled a massive database on the Parliament of 1841–7, and his graduate students did the same for 1852–7 and 1874–80 (Aydelotte 1966, 1967, 1970, 1972, 1977; Bylsma 1977; Hamilton 1968; other work inspired by the Iowa programme includes Heyck and Klecka 1973; Cromwell 1980, 1982). For each of these Parliaments, the Aydelotte databases collected a record of the votes of each MP on a large number of divisions (186 for 1841–7). As much information about the MP's background, class, personal relationships, occupation and ideology as could be obtained was also gathered. The result, for 1841–7, was a database comprising over 800 cases (MPs) with up to 368 pieces of information on each MP (his vote on as many of the 186 divisions as he took part in, plus up to 182 pieces of background information about him). This is the richest, and most underused, database on individual legislators that I have encountered.

The Parliament of 1841–7 has a claim to be the most interesting of the century. The General Election of 1841 introduced a Tory administration under Sir Robert Peel with a secure majority. There is considerable evidence that it was a 'modern' election in the sense that the voters understood what the parties stood for and voted along party lines in accordance with their interests or ideology. Much of the domestic agenda of that parliament has a curiously modern ring. Parliament debated free trade and tariffs, factory legislation, sanitary reform, public order in Britain and Ireland, and the regulation of natural monopoly. Peel's administration ended with the most damaging split the Tories have ever suffered. In 1846 Peel, who had been gradually converted to free trade during his administration, proposed to repeal the Corn Laws which excluded grain from the UK when the domestic price was below a threshold. He carried Repeal with the support of a majority of the Liberals, but only a third of his own party. The protectionist rump of the Conservatives was rallied and led with great skill and verve by the young Benjamin Disraeli, but the Conservatives were out of power, apart from two brief minority administrations, until 1874.

Why did a Tory administration repeal the Corn Laws? This is again a question to which Americans have recently made more contributions than Britons (see McLean 1992: 503–8 and the sources cited there). Earlier explanations related to the intellectual hegemony of arguments for free trade failed to explain the actual mechanics of passage by a Parliament in which the party of agriculture, the interest group which on the face of it had most to lose from Repeal, held a commanding majority. A full explanation must rely heavily on the dominant personality and strategy of Peel, who coupled the dimension of free trade with the dimension of social order (he believed that both the famine in Ireland and industrial unrest in Britain must be placated by free trade in grain, and that Tories should concede their short-term interests in favour of their long-term interest in social order). But it must also study the correlates of those who voted on each side in the crucial debates. With the Aydelotte database to hand, this could be one of the most promising areas for the development of legislative studies in the UK.

PROSPECTS AND CONCLUSION

The rollcall studies reviewed in this chapter are extremely valuable. But the data they report undoubtedly have more secrets to yield. As we have already stressed, both Berrington and Aydelotte looked mostly for consistency. Looked at with an eye for inconsistency, the data might show great potential for the analysis of cycling and of majorities achieved artificially through institutional constraints. In an earlier paper (McLean and Foster 1992), I have analysed a division in Aydelotte's Parliament, on the Regulation of Railways Bill 1844, which escaped from all his Guttman scales and yet showed that there were significant divisions among MPs, according to their social and economic backgrounds, on the issue of regulation of natural monopoly.

The point may be generalised. In principle, there are as many producer interests as producer groups, and many of them are represented in Parliament. Each producer group typically seeks legal protection for the commodity it produces. Each of these issues forms a dimension of its own. On each of them, the minority interest of producers clashes with the majority interest of consumers. None the less, producer-group protection is often put into law through the lobbying and log-rolling processes which are amply documented in some legislatures. Berrington (1968: 357–8) records 'an interesting bi-partisan revolt' on the Sale of Food and Drugs Bill 1899, in which '21 Liberals voted with 28 Unionists in support of a new clause designed to forbid the sale of margarine coloured like butter'. Unfortunately, he does not pause to investigate this bizarre vote.

On contemporary American evidence, it was not so bizarre. Miller (1989) gives a full and entertaining account of the stratagems used by the dairy industry to prevent or discourage people from eating margarine. In 1885, the Pennsylvania legislature enacted that 'no person . . . shall manufacture out of any oleaginous substance . . . any article designed to take the place of butter . . . , nor shall sell or offer for sale, or have in his . . . possession with intent to sell the same as an article of food.' In New York, 'an office of dairy commissioner specifically charged with uncovering and prosecuting violators of the margarine law' presumably raided homes and shops in search of bootleg margarine (Miller 1989 pp. 113–14). Anti-margarine legislation was pure producer-group protectionism smuggled in under a bogus claim to consumer protection. It would be fascinating to find out how many of the twenty-one Liberals and twenty-eight Conservatives who wanted to outlaw yellow margarine represented dairy-farming constituencies.

The politics of interest-group log-rolling has been much less studied in Britain than elsewhere, although there are some pioneering studies of the 'railway interest' (especially Williams 1952 and Alderman 1973). The Berrington and Aydelotte datasets remain the starting point for any serious research.

It is only too easy for the armchair reviewer to say 'there ought to be a multidimensional spatial analysis of British legislators' ideologies'. There certainly ought to be, but even a general review like this essay must discuss some of the technical problems, in fairness to all those who have tried to do it. There are two basic stratagems: either to let one's statistical technique define the dimensions, or to define the dimensions from inspection of the issues and general knowledge of the context. Both have their characteristic pitfalls.

Letting the data, the statistics, and the computer define the dimensions was the strategy of Aydelotte (1966, 1967, 1972, 1977), of Heyck and Klecka (1973) and of Cromwell (1982). The advantage of this approach is that it does without the researcher's possibly erroneous preconceptions – links the researcher believes in may not exist, while links the researcher does not suspect may truly exist. The main drawback of the method is that the data it generates can be very hard to interpret. Aydelotte found no fewer than twenty-four Guttman scales linking subsets of the 186 divisions in 1841–7, and was able to classify many MPs by their positions on many of the scales. But it was hard in many cases to see what the scales meant. Many of them seemed to reflect very similar clusters of ideology and it is unlikely that they all represent different ideological dimensions. One of the Guttman scales, the 'Miles's motion scale', also reveals another problem. Philip Miles was a protectionist who proposed strategically to reduce the duty on corn: not because he wanted to reduce the duty on corn, but in the hope of confusing the free-traders in both parties. Whichever side an MP took on Miles' motion, he may have taken it for either sincere or strategic reasons; each side would therefore contain some free-traders and some protectionists. It is therefore not surprising that the Miles's motion scale differs from the other scales. But it is hard to believe that it shows anything significant.

The attempts by Heyck and Klecka and by Cromwell to deal in two dimensions were not totally successful. Heyck and Klecka wish to find out from the division lists who should really count as a 'radical' between 1874 and 1895, having found out that MPs' self-descriptions were unreliable and incomplete. However, in my view they take an interesting problem and turn it into an uninteresting one by collapsing the many dimensions of voting among Liberal MPs into a unidimensional index of radicalism. Cromwell preserves two dimensions in her analysis of the MPs of 1861, and shows that there are three clusters of MPs (Liberals, members of the administration and Conservatives) with different degrees of internal cohesion. But the dimensions themselves are not labelled and she cannot (or at any rate does not) say what issue positions they represent.

The alternative approach is that mainly[1] adopted by the Berrington team and by many less rigorous observers. The researcher studies the issues voted on and categorises them into dimensions before seeing how far MPs' votes on one dimension correlate with their votes on another. This method inevitably relies on the researcher's subjective judgements. '[T]he authors and the authors alone are responsible for "identifying" these viewpoints and arranging them in a scale. This is a subjective exercise' (Finer, Berrington and Bartholomew 1961: 142). The better the judgements, the better the researcher – but there is no external check on the process. Most of Berrington's judgements, both of nineteenth- and of twentieth-century MPs, seem good to me, but inevitably some seem dubious. Consider again the various issues used to compile scales for the leftness of Labour MPs between 1945 and 1959. As already indicated, German rearmament in 1954 divided the Labour Party in ways that cannot be called left–right. The problem of policy towards Germany re-emerged in 1958: '[Labour] Members have been divided into Left-, Centre-, and Right-wing factions on the issue of European disengagement and the future of Germany' (Finer, Berrington and Bartholomew 1961, p. 168).

How then can Berrington be certain that MPs' location on the scale constructed out of EDMs in 1958–9 did not reflect the mixed and cross-cutting pressures of 1954? He might well retort that it was obvious by inspection and by the company they kept that the EDMs represented various factions of the left and the non-left – but then his argument comes close to being circular. In *BB45*, in response to the widespread criticism of the list of the fifty leftist Labour MPs, Berrington stressed that there were many different kinds of left – 'pacificism, neutralism in foreign policy, anti-colonialism, libertarianism, humanitarianism, and zeal for social welfare' (Berrington 1973: 17). But this is to go too far down the road of collapsing dimensions. If John Bright had miraculously found himself in the Parliament of 1955, he would have scored highly on all except the last of these, whereas Harry Pollitt would have scored only on anti-colonialism (anti-British-colonialism, at any rate) and zeal for social welfare. Should John Bright be regarded as more left-wing than Harry Pollitt?

Berrington and his colleagues were wisely much more reluctant to classify Conservatives as 'right' or 'left', 'centrist' or 'extremist'. Three successive Annexes to *BBO* discuss three dimensions of disagreement among Conservatives: 'foreign affairs and Commonwealth policy', penal reform and social policy. All three dimensions are very old and very new. The division on foreign affairs, with imperialists and autarkic thinkers on one side and anti-imperialists and internationalists on the other, is as old as 1846 and as new as 1993. From the Repeal of the Corn Laws to the votes on the Maastricht Treaty it has seemed to be the deepest and most divisive cleavage among Conservatives (for an insightful commentary see Baker, Gamble and Ludlam 1993). In the 1950s it was represented by the division between MPs who clung to the Commonwealth and MPs who were interested in the European Community (Finer, Berrington and Bartholomew 1961: 87–94, 185–94)

The division between the 'Humane' and the 'Severe' (Finer, Berrington and Bartholomew's terms – 1961: 195–206 and see Table 3) is also old. A Conservative election leaflet of 1904 proclaimed:

"LET 'EM ALL COME!" is the Radical cry.

The Radicals, by their obstruction to the Aliens Bill, are evidently glad to see all foreigners who are criminals; who suffer from loathsome diseases; who are turned out in disgrace by their fellow countrymen; who are paupers; who fill our streets with profligacy and disorder. *The Radical Welcomes Them All.* The Unionist Government wants to keep these creatures out of Great Britain. They don't want to see the honest Britisher turned out by these scourings of European slums. They brought in a Bill to check this evil flow of aliens. But Radicals said, No! we don't want to stop the foreign criminal and diseased outcast from coming into this country.

(National Union of Conservative and Unionist Associations leaflet No. 325, quoted by McKenzie and Silver 1968: 60)

This is a far cry from Lord Hugh Cecil's assertion that

Moreover, the defence of individuals against injustice involves also the preservation of at least the most essential parts of personal liberty. At the present time Liberalism is much more likely to be tempted to transgress the principles of liberty than Conservatism.

(Cecil 1912: 247)

Conservative divisions on social policy (Finer, Berrington and Bartholomew 1961: 207–13) are now assimilated to the labels 'wet' and 'dry', but they surely go back at least to Lord Shaftesbury. The patron of the Ten Hours' Bill of 1847 ought to be hailed as the father of the Wets. Most of his contemporaries who were the intellectual ancestors of the Dries (Edwin Chadwick, Nassau Senior) were Whig, Liberal, or Radical by party affiliation, but those whose ideology was moulded by classical economics mostly came over to the Conservatives between 1886 and 1918.

I believe that this shows that it is more fruitful to find political dimensions, or candidates for political dimensions, from some external source and investigate whether legislators' ideologies fit these dimensions, than to attempt to derive dimensions from legislators' votes themselves. But where should the researcher go for these dimensions? Two possible sources are political philosophy and public opinion.

If ever a warning has been absorbed by political scientists, it is Converse's (1964) classic demonstration that popular ideologies do not fall neatly into categories derivable from political philosophy. This is equally true of the ideologies of political elites. In the period covered by the two *Backbench* studies, the dominant ideology of the Labour Party mixed some socialism with some welfarism – articulated by the collectivist Liberal William Beveridge – and some classical liberalism especially in foreign affairs. The dominant ideology of the Conservative Party had an element of classical liberalism among those who would now be called Dries (a much smaller proportion of the parliamentary party then than now), an element of imperialism and an element of traditionalism. The most coherent of these philosophies are socialism and classical liberalism. But socialism was never more than a component of Labour elites' ideology, and it has now vanished except among constituency activists, Dennis Skinner and Tony Benn. Classical liberalism was sundered in two around the time of the First World War. Social liberalism, including pacifism and the belief that what one does with one's body and one's relationships is the business of nobody but those involved, is regarded as a doctrine of the left. Economic liberalism is regarded as a doctrine of the right. A consistent libertarian in Britain must look in vain for a party manifesto she can support. So political philosophy is no help in providing a structure for possible issue dimensions.

But Converse went too far in decrying the structure, and the stability, of mass beliefs (on this see, e.g., McLean 1982: 65–7; Heath *et al.* 1991: 41–5). There is growing evidence

> both in Britain and elsewhere, that the attitudes of the mass public towards social and political issues tend to group together in broadly predictable ways. Analyses of British Election Study data have consistently found that attitudes towards economic issues such as nationalisation, income redistribution and government intervention go together and are largely unrelated to attitudes towards moral issues.
>
> (Heath, Evans and Martin 1994: 115)

Heath, Evans and Martin were able to construct two stable and reliable scales of popular attitudes: a 'socialist/*laissez-faire*' scale and an 'authoritarian/libertarian' scale. People's positions on one scale are not strongly associated with their positions on the other, nor with the traditional 'left' (socialist and libertarian) or 'right' (*laissez-faire* and authoritarian) bundles.

This approach does not help in constructing an issue dimension relating to foreign affairs. There is overwhelming evidence that, in a country which is not a superpower, mass attitudes to foreign questions are less salient and less stable than mass attitudes to domestic policy questions. However, 150 years of British political history suggests that there is a strong foreign policy dimension that cross-cuts traditional party alignments. Baker, Gamble and Ludlam (1993: 476) label it 'interdependence' v. 'sovereignty'. Though they apply it only to Conservatives, I see no reason not also to apply it to twentieth-century socialists and nineteenth-century Liberals. Imperialists, protectionists, supporters of *Realpolitik* and (Scottish and/or Irish) Unionists are towards the sovereignty end; anti-colonialists, free-traders and believers in international agreements are towards the interdependence end.

Finally, the politics of interest-group lobbying should be brought into a multidimensional model. On one view, as suggested above, there are as many political dimensions as interests. This should mean that politics is chronically chaotic – in the social choice theorist's sense that all possible platforms are in a global cycle. Observed interest-group politics, however, tend to display remarkable stability, through log-rolling or institutional sclerosis. Therefore, perhaps the dimension that should be tested is 'producer v. consumer'. Some politicians may systematically tend to favour producer interests, others consumer interests.

Two of the main thrusts of empirical politics research over the last thirty years have been:

● that political actors make rational choices on the basis of stable beliefs; and
● that politics is multidimensional.

Hugh Berrington's research programme on the British Parliament has gone far towards establishing both of these facts. The time is ripe, and the techniques and hardware are available, to build on the foundations he has laid.

NOTE

1 But in Berrington (1982) he analysed Labour MPs' ideologies by factor analysis of EDMs for seven sessions between 1960 and 1973, finding that 'for six of the seven sessions a factor emerged as the main factor . . .

which seemed from its content to approximate to the traditional left–right scale', and that it seemed stable from session to session. Two other factors were identified but not labelled (Berrington 1982: 72, 92).

REFERENCES

Alderman, G. (1973) *The Railway Interest*, Leicester: Leicester University Press.

Aydelotte, W. O. (1966) 'Parties and issues in early Victorian England', *Journal of British Studies* 5: 95–114.

—— (1967), 'The country gentleman and the repeal of the Corn Laws', *English Historical Review* 82: 47–60.

—— (1970) *Study 521 (Codebook) ' British House of Commons 1841–1847'*, Iowa City: Regional Social Science Data Archive of Iowa.

—— (1972) 'The disintegration of the Conservative Party in the 1840s: a study of political attitudes', in W. O. Aydelotte *et al.* (eds) *The Dimensions of Quantitative Research in History*, Princeton, NJ: Princeton University Press.

—— (1977) 'Constituency influence in the British House of Commons, 1841–1847', in W. O. Aydelotte (ed.) *The History of Parliamentary Behavior*, Princeton, NJ: Princeton University Press.

Baker, D., Gamble, A. and Ludlam, S. (1993) '1846 . . . 1906 . . . 1996: Conservative splits and European integration', *Political Quarterly* 64: 420–34.

Berrington, H. B. (1968) 'Partisanship and dissidence in the nineteenth-century House of Commons', *Parliamentary Affairs* 21: 338–74.

—— (1973) *Backbench Opinion in the House of Commons 1945–55*, Oxford: Pergamon.

—— (1978) 'Backbench attitudes in the House of Commons, 1959–1976', dataset and codebook deposited at ESRC Data Archive, University of Essex.

—— (1982) 'The Labour left in Parliament: maintenance, erosion, and renewal', in D. Kavanagh (ed.) *The Politics of the Labour Party*, London: Allen and Unwin

Bylsma, J. R. (1977) 'Party structure in the 1852–1857 House of Commons: a scalogram analysis', *Journal of Interdisciplinary History* 7: 617–35.

Cecil, Lord Hugh (1912) *Conservatism*, London: Williams and Norgate.

Converse, P. (1964) 'The nature of belief systems in mass publics', in D. Apter (ed.) *Ideology and Discontent*, New York: The Free Press.

Cromwell, V. (1980) 'Computer analysis by multidimensional scaling of House of Commons division Lists, 1861', dataset and codebook deposited at ESRC Data Archive, University of Essex.

—— (1982) 'Mapping the political world of 1861: a multidimensional analysis of House of Commons division lists', *Legislative Studies Quarterly* 7 (2): 281–97.

Cox, G. (1987) *The Efficient Secret: The Cabinet and the Development of Political Parties in Victorian England*, Cambridge: Cambridge University Press.

Crossman, R. H. S. (1961) 'How poor are the poor? ', *Manchester Guardian* 15 December.

Fellowes, Sir E. (1962) 'Back-bench Opinion in the House of Commons, 1955–59', *Parliamentary Affairs* 15: 244–5.

Finer, S. E., Berrington, H. B. and Bartholomew, D. J. (1961) *Backbench Opinion in the House of Commons 1955–59*, Oxford: Pergamon.

Hamilton, J. C. (1968) 'Parties and Voting Patterns in the Parliament of 1874–80', unpublished dissertation, University of Iowa.

Heath, A., Curtice, J., Jowell, R., Evans, G., Field, J. and Witherspoon, S. (1991) *Understanding Political Change: the British Voter 1964–87*, Oxford: Pergamon.

Heath, A., Evans, G. and Martin, J. (1994) 'The measurement of core beliefs and values: the development of balanced socialist/laissez faire and libertarian/authoritarian scales', *British Journal of Political Science* 24: 115–32.

Heyck, T. W. and Klecka, W. (1973), 'British radical MPs, 1874–1895: new evidence from discriminant analysis', *Journal of Interdisciplinary History* 4(2): 161–84.

Kornhauser, W. (1960) *The Politics of Mass Society*, London: Routledge and Kegan Paul.

Leece, J. and Berrington, H. B. (1977) 'Measurements of backbench attitudes by Guttman scaling of Early Day Motions: a pilot study, Labour, 1968–69', *British Journal of Political Science* 7: 529–40.

Lowell, A. L. (1919) *The Government of England*, 2nd edn, 2 Vols, New York: Macmillan.

McKenzie, R. T. and Silver, A. (1968) *Angels in Marble: Working Class Conservatives in Urban England*, London: Heinemann.

McLean, I. (1982) *Dealing in Votes*, Oxford: Martin Robertson.

——— (1989) *Democracy and New Technology*, Cambridge: Polity Press.

——— (1992), 'Rational choice and the Victorian voter', *Political Studies* 40: 496–515.

McLean, I. and Foster, Sir C. (1992), 'The political economy of regulation: interests, ideology, voters and the UK Regulation of Railways Act 1844', *Public Administration* 70: 313–31.

Miller, G. P. (1989) 'Public choice at the dawn of the special interest state: the story of butter and margarine', *California Law Review* 77: 83–151.

Ostrogorski, M. (1902) *Democracy and the Organisation of Political Parties*, 2 Vols, London: Macmillan.

Riker, W. H. (1982) *Liberalism against Populism*, San Francisco: W. H. Freeman.

Williams, P. M. (1952), 'Public opinion and the railway rates question in 1886', *English Historical Review* 67: 37–73.

9 Members of Parliament and issues of conscience

Peter Jones

The dominance of party over Parliament is a hallmark of the Westminster system. For the most part, that dominance renders parliamentary voting an insensitive and unreliable indicator of the complex patterns of opinion to be found amongst MPs. As Hugh Berrington remarked two decades ago, 'The division lists . . . reproduce the details of a ritual satisfying to the Whips but usually offer nothing of interest to the inquirer except that Labour Members have voted with the ayes and the Conservatives with the noes or vice versa' (Berrington 1973: 2). Since he wrote those words, backbenchers have shown themselves rather more willing to defy their party masters and mistresses (Norton 1975, 1980), but the party system still imposes a heavy imprint upon the parliamentary process.

Nor should we think of MPs as so many heirs of Spartacus, groaning under the lash of the whips and yearning for a new dawn when the chains of party discipline will have been broken. Most MPs for most of the time are keen to support their party and happy to be given direction; if nothing else, the whip spares them the labour of individual decision and the burden of individual responsibility. Given the complexity, technicality and sheer volume of parliamentary legislation, MPs can form genuinely independent opinions on only a few of the measures they confront. The development of party conformity amongst MPs has been, in part, a response to that practical reality (Berrington 1968: 369–70).

There are, however, some occasions when both the constraint and the security of party affiliation fall away. Those are the infrequent but significant episodes known as 'free votes'. On those occasions, MPs are permitted to vote as they individually judge best and backbench opinion moves from being influential to being decisive. The most celebrated issues that are resolved in that way are 'issues of conscience'. Something approaching a convention has developed that, on issues of conscience, MPs are entitled to a free vote – a vote dictated by their individual consciences uncompromised by party discipline. In this essay I examine that convention and consider how well founded it is. I also consider how we should conceive the role of MPs as representatives when they vote free from party obligation.

I shall focus on the use of free votes in Britain. In political systems in which parties have a less firm grip on legislative behaviour, a convention dispensing with party discipline may be less significant or simply unnecessary. Nevertheless, the use of free votes for moral issues is not peculiar to Britain. For example, in most European parliaments recent legislative decisions on abortion have been reached by free votes, the two major exceptions being the Netherlands and Norway (Lovenduski and Outshoorn 1986: 4). So the issues I consider here are not uniquely British.

The conventional distinction between issues of conscience and other issues is far from precise. For the moment, I shall simply itemise the sorts of legislative matters that have been regarded as issues of conscience. These have included capital and corporal punishment, prostitution, homosexuality and other sexual conduct, divorce, abortion, euthanasia, research involving the use of human embryos, obscenity and pornography and issues of censorship associated with them, Sunday entertainment and Sunday trading, hunting and coursing, the use of animals in research and other matters relating to the welfare of animals. This is not an exhaustive list but merely a list of leading examples of issues which, in post-war Britain, have been regarded as issues of conscience. The guiding idea is that there are some issues which are essentially moral in character and which, as such, should be decided by MPs according to their consciences (which, for some MPs, will mean according to their religious convictions).

There is clearly room for argument about which issues should be regarded as conscience issues. Some matters which would be regarded nowadays as conscience issues were subjects of fierce party political dispute a century ago – for example, the issue of the disestablishment of the Church of England. Even in more recent years, several of the issues I list above have been, on some occasions or in some respects, the official concerns of governments and parties. As I shall argue in a moment, there is reason to question the very idea that there is a narrowly circumscribed set of issues which can be distinguished from the ordinary run of political issues merely by their conscientious character. However, for ease of expression and out of deference to established usage, I shall, throughout this essay, use 'issues of conscience' and 'moral issues' to describe the catalogue of parliamentary issues that are conventionally denoted by those phrases.

While free votes are generally thought to be appropriate for issues of conscience, not every issue that is subject to a free vote is an issue of conscience. By convention MPs are entitled to free votes on private members' bills and the great majority of those bills do not concern moral issues. In fact, many private members' bills, particularly those that reach the statute book, deal with highly technical and non-contentious issues and pass through Parliament unopposed. Thus, although all private members' bills are in principle subject to free votes, many are never actually voted upon, including most of those which succeed in becoming laws (Marsh and Read 1988: 37–8). In addition, governments sometimes allow free votes on clauses in their own bills even though the concerns of those clauses are not especially 'moral' in character; for example, governments have allowed free votes on royal grants, reform of the franchise, and MPs' salaries.

A free vote is simply described – it is a vote free from the demands of the party whips. However, the circumstances that surround free votes are often far from simple. Given that most legislative proposals concerning issues of conscience come before Parliament as private members bills, they are prey to all the procedural hazards that affect those bills. Parliamentary procedure makes it far easier for MPs to impede than to promote the passage of private member's bills and, consequently, few of those bills which encounter opposition succeed.[1] The fate of a private member's bill therefore depends upon much more than its ability to secure a majority in a free vote and there are very many examples of reform proposals which have enjoyed majority support in Parliament but which have nevertheless failed to reach the statute book.[2]

The obstacles that confront a private member's bill make the government's attitude crucial to its fate. The devices that MPs can use to stymie a private member's bill are equally available to the members of a government and its supporters. In addition, since most private members' bills fail because they run out of time, a great deal depends upon whether a government is willing to make room for them in the Parliamentary timetable. In general, governments have not been generous in this respect and have become less generous in recent years (Marsh and Read 1988: 58–61), although that lack of generosity has been motivated more by governments' desires to use scarce parliamentary time for their own legislative programmes than by their hostility to private members' proposals.

When a government has made time available for the successful passage of a private member's bill, that has often been because members of the government have been sympathetic to the measure. That was true, for example, of the assistance given by the Labour Government to Sydney Silverman's bill (1964/5) abolishing the death penalty. The government committed itself in the Queen's Speech to providing time for a free vote on the issue of capital punishment and, during the passage of Silverman's bill, used the whips to combat procedural tactics employed by the bill's opponents to impede its progress (Short 1989: 79–81; Richards 1970: 52–4). The Labour Government's sympathetic attitude was also crucial to the success of measures passed during the late 1960s reforming laws on abortion, homosexuality and divorce (Richards 1970; Marsh and Read 1988: 54–6, 114–15).

However, a government may make time available not because it wants to assist in securing a particular outcome but because it recognises that an issue needs to be resolved or because it is under pressure to secure a resolution. That broadly describes the position of the Conservative government on the issue of Sunday trading in 1993. Having failed to secure the passage of its own proposals by a whipped vote in 1986, the government, in December 1993, simply placed a number of options before a committee of the whole House for decision by free vote.

Governments may affect the fate of measures subject to free votes in two other ways. First, a government or the relevant Minister, instead of remaining neutral, may express support for or opposition to a measure and that may influence how some MPs cast their votes. Second, governments often take a close interest in the precise content of private members' bills and secure their own amendments to them.[3] On some occasions it has been the government itself that has formulated the proposals on which free votes have been held.

WHY ARE FREE VOTES HELD?

My main purpose is to consider whether there is a sound basis for the notion that MPs ought to be able to vote freely on moral issues and, if so, what that is. But I want to begin by considering why, in fact, parties have taken to allowing free votes on those issues. In distinguishing between these two questions, I do not mean to suggest that the reasons why free votes *are* held are necessarily different from the reasons why they *ought* to be held; but neither are they necessarily the same.

Why, then, do parties characteristically allow their MPs free votes on moral issues? A simple answer, which I have already mentioned, is that those issues often come before Parliament in the form of private members' bills and, by tradition, private members' bills are subject to free votes. However, that simple answer is not really an answer but a reformulation of the question. Why have moral issues been treated as part of the proper domain of private members' bills with their associated free votes? Moreover, moral issues do not invariably come before Parliament in that form. Sometimes they arise as clauses in government bills or as amendments to government bills yet they are still resolved by free votes.

A major explanation is that the members of a political party are often sharply divided on issues of conscience. Typically, moral issues do not figure in the ideologies and policies which give British political parties their identities. Nor usually do those identities clearly imply a correct party view for each moral issue. Thus, being a member of the Labour Party need have no implications for one's view of abortion and being a member of the Conservative Party need have no implications for one's view of Sunday trading. Consequently, a party which formally adopted a position on a moral issue would risk precipitating a damaging split amongst its members; the simplest way for it to avoid that split is to leave the issue well alone.

Parliamentary parties are not always divided over moral issues. In recent votes on capital punishment, for example, Labour MPs have voted virtually unanimously against its reintroduction.[4] But a party has to concern itself not only with the opinions of its MPs but also with the opinions of its non-parliamentary members and with those of its actual and potential supporters amongst the electorate. Free votes are a way of avoiding division and disaffection outside as well as inside Parliament.

A related reason why parties avoid moral issues is that those issues are often hotly disputed matters on which people have strong convictions. Whatever line a party or a government takes, it is likely to incur passionate hostility and criticism from outside as well as from inside its own ranks. It can most easily avoid that hostility and criticism by forgoing any control over those issues. Thus, even when the members of a government *do* have a clear preference on a moral issue, they may have reason to secure that position by allowing a free vote which they anticipate will go the way they wish, rather than by making the issue a matter of formal government policy. Indeed, the use of free votes has sometimes been criticised for enabling governments to secure the passage of controversial measures while evading responsibility for their enactment (cf. Richards 1970: 198–9).

However, neither of these considerations taken singly nor both taken together adequately explains the use of free votes for moral issues. There are many issues on which parties have been internally divided, and which have aroused strong feelings both inside and outside Parliament, which have nevertheless become subjects of party decision and party discipline. Consider, for example, the history of the Labour Party's divisions over defence policy or more recent divisions within the Conservative Party over Europe. So why do parties feel able to divest themselves of responsibility for some issues and not others? There are three possible and related answers, though each requires some qualification.

One has to do with a party's *raison d'être*. Parties can be mobilised for all sorts of purposes and there is no reason why these should not include promoting or preventing change on moral issues. But, in recent history and for the most part, those issues have not figured in the primary policy concerns of British political parties and consequently parties *qua* parties have not had to grapple with those difficult and potentially divisive issues. Thus, while some of their individual members may have cared passionately about these issues, generally British political parties as formal organisations have not.

A second explanation concerns the role of government. There are some matters on which a party which aspires to govern must take a stand. It cannot avoid commitment on questions of economic policy or social policy or foreign policy or defence policy, however awkward some of those may be, for those policies concern the inescapable tasks of government. It is much easier for it, as government or opposition, to refrain from taking responsibility for matters such as abortion, sexual conduct and vivisection. Of course, a government may not be able to duck responsibility for seeing that 'something is done' about these issues, but it can provide for their resolution without itself taking a view on what that resolution ought to be.

A third explanation has to do with the nature of what are traditionally identified as conscience issues. Some of these are said to concern 'private morality' – they deal with matters which belong to the private sphere of people's lives and which, as such, are often thought to be properly the concerns of private individuals rather than public officials. That conception of these issues is problematic in ways that I shall explain, but the fact that it seems to be widely held makes it easier for governments and parties to refrain from committing themselves on moral issues. In addition, issues concerned with private sphere of people's lives, just because they concern that limited domain, can more easily be kept at arm's length from public policy.

In fact, not all conscience issues are focused upon the private domain. The claims of privacy can do nothing to justify a government's or a party's official agnosticism on matters such as capital punishment, embryo research and vivisection. In those cases, it is perhaps the fact that the issues are reasonably clearly bounded and easily isolated that facilitates a government's passing on the responsibility for decision to free-voting MPs.

Each of these explanations is, however, very much a matter of degree. For example, although conscience issues have not been amongst the primary concerns of British political parties, not all party members have been content with that state of affairs. Many ordinary members of the Conservative Party would dearly love to commit their parliamentary representatives to the reintroduction of capital punishment, while some members of the Labour Party have regarded its abolition as a measure rooted in the humanitarian values of the Party (Berrington 1973: 125). Again, it may not be easy for a government to avoid some moral issues. During the 1940s and 1950s, it was not easy for governments to treat capital punishment as an issue wholly separate from their own policies on law and order (Christoph 1962). A government that sees the promotion of 'family values' as crucial to its social policy, or which takes a view on the proper content of religious and sex education, may find it difficult to adopt a position of official indifference on some of the traditional conscience issues (cf. Durham 1991: 99–122). The boundaries which separate the traditional conscience issues from other issues are, at best, fuzzy.

Finally, in accounting for the use of free votes on moral issues, some weight can be given to the development of the practice itself. Obviously a convention cannot be used to explain its own existence, but once it has become established its very existence can contribute to its continuance. MPs now possess the firm conviction that certain issues are conscience issues and that they are entitled to vote according to their consciences on those issues. A party which uses the whip for those issues will have to cope with the indignation, resentment and possible rebellion of its MPs, as the Conservative government discovered in 1986 when it attempted to whip its backbenchers in support of its reform proposals on Sunday trading (Regan 1988).[5]

WHY OUGHT THERE TO BE FREE VOTES?

There are, then, a number of reasons why, on 'conscience issues', political parties refrain from imposing a collective view upon their MPs. However, partisan purpose is one thing, good parliamentary practice another. Is there anything beyond party political prudence to recommend free voting on moral issues? Many MPs clearly think so. Is their conviction justified?

Let us begin with what might seem the obvious justification: MPs ought to be able to vote freely on what are conventionally identified as 'issues of conscience' just because those are issues of conscience and because people are entitled to resolve such issues according to their consciences. Two distinct claims are involved in this 'obvious' justification. One is that, in moral matters, the consciences of individual MPs should be decisive and that, correspondingly, it would be wrong in any way to prevent or to impede their acting on their conscientiously held convictions. The other is that what have been conventionally identified as 'issues of conscience' are indeed distinguished from other political issues in requiring conscientious judgements.

Our response to these claims may depend, in part, upon what we understand by 'conscience'. Among many possible meanings, I shall distinguish only two. The first of these I shall label the 'specific' conception of conscience since it associates conscience with a particular moral theory. In this specific conception, conscience is thought of as a faculty within each individual which enables that individual to distinguish between right and wrong and to make moral judgements on particular issues. This notion of conscience might form part of an objectivist moral theory which holds that conscience speaks identically to all individuals. But, nowadays, the specific conception of conscience is more commonly associated with a degree of subjectivism – one individual's conscience may require something different from another's. It is also associated with the belief that the right thing for each individual to do is to follow his or her conscience; indeed, it is commonly claimed that individuals have 'a right' to be governed by their own consciences. That is why there is often a tension between the claims of conscience (so understood) and the claims of authority.

A second way of understanding the term conscience is more prosaic. To describe an issue as an issue of conscience may be to do no more than to identify it as a moral issue. Used in this way, 'conscience' implies no particular conception of morality or moral judgement; while it indicates that an issue is a moral issue, it leaves questions about the nature of morality untouched. I shall call this the 'non-specific' conception of conscience.

It is often impossible to discern which of these two conceptions people are using when they concern themselves with issues of conscience. However, I think it fair to say that the specific conception of conscience often infects people's supposition that the conventional issues of conscience are a distinct set of issues which are improperly subjected to party discipline. The moral theory that surrounds that specific conception is highly questionable and that means that any case for free votes that relies upon it will be no less questionable. However, I shall not conduct a critique of the specific conception of conscience here and I do not exclude the possibility that 'issues of conscience' may be understood in accordance with the non-specific conception.

Should we allow that MPs have a right to follow their own consciences? That claim of right is most readily associated with the specific conception of conscience but it might also be made in relation to the non-specific conception; that is, the claim might be that MPs have a right to follow their moral judgements whatever the nature of those moral judgements. Although the notion that individuals should be governed by their own consciences is a common one, it is also one that quickly runs into difficulties. It is most simply applied to self-regarding actions since, if those actions are entirely self-regarding, they are capable of being governed by the conscience and only by the conscience of the self that performs them. But as soon as we move into the realm of conduct which impinges upon the lives of others, the idea that each individual's conduct should be governed only by that individual's conscience becomes incoherent. My conscientiously guided conduct will impinge upon you so that your life ceases to be determined solely by your conscience, and your conscientiously guided conduct will impinge upon me so that my life ceases to be determined solely by my conscience.

When we turn to the public decisions made by legislators, pleas for the autonomy of conscience run into even greater difficulty. Legislators' decisions do not merely 'affect' the lives of others, they are designed to govern the lives of others and those others typically number in their millions. The position of the legislator is therefore quite different from that of a private citizen leading his private life in acordance with the dictates of his conscience. An MP occupies a public role and is making decisions for others rather than just for himself. Perhaps it is possible, even granted these facts, for someone still to insist that an MP has a fundamental right to act only according to his conscience and that his rights of conscience trump all other considerations that bear upon how legislative decisions should be made. Certainly, conscience is sometimes invoked in parliamentary contexts in ways which seem to give it that sort of ultimate significance. But, on reflection, it seems most implausible that the pre-eminent consideration in legislation should be the rights of those who make up the legislature. Surely the concerns of legislators should be primarily other-directed rather than self-directed; legislators should account for their actions as legislators in terms of the good or the right that their actions promote rather than in terms of what is owed to themselves.

Of course, MPs will suppose that their consciences do inform them of what is good or right; that is what conscience is about. But there is a crucial difference between claiming, on the one hand, that MPs are entitled to follow their individual consciences just because that is a right intrinsic to them as individual human beings and, on the other, that it is right for MPs to follow their consciences because and in so far as their doing so will achieve the best outcome and will best serve those on whose behalf they act. The former rules out the exercise of party authority because whipping would violate the right of each MP to act only in accordance with his conscience; but the latter provides a case against whipping only if there is reason for supposing that, all things considered, whipping would result in less good or less legitimate outcomes. The burden of my argument here is that MPs cannot plausibly demand free votes on moral issues merely by standing on their allegedly fundamental rights of conscience. If MPs do have a right to follow their consciences that right is plausible only as an instrumental right, a right which is justified by its instrumentality in promoting morally good or morally right states of affairs, rather than as a fundamental right grounded in the interests or the moral personalities of MPs themselves.

Thus, if the use of party discipline in Parliament is generally acceptable, it requires something other than the bare assertion of individual MPs' fundamental rights of conscience to explain why it should be unacceptable in the case of moral issues. We may believe, of course, that anyone who holds a public office, including an MP, should have some sort of ultimate right of dissent from decisions which he or she believes to be grossly immoral; but that 'reserve' right of conscience would provide only for exceptional circumstances. It is very different from the claim that MPs' consciences should enjoy an absolute immunity or that, for certain matters of parliamentary legislation, the consciences of MPs should be routinely decisive.

The other claim that is crucial to the 'obvious' justification of free votes on issues of conscience is that those issues are indeed distinguished by their conscientious character. Is that so? Are matters such as abortion, capital punishment and the treatment of animals distinguished by having a moral dimension that other political issues do not? Certainly, not all political decisions require moral judgements. Some may involve only strategic judgements. For example, politicians may all agree that they should strive to combine full employment with low inflation but disagree about which strategy will best achieve that goal. In that case, what is 'at issue' in economic policy will be the purely technical question of which policy will most effectively deliver what everyone agrees ought to be delivered and answering that question will require a judgement that is in no significant sense 'moral'. Other issues – such as where a new airport should be sited or whether a motorway should be widened – may call for a calculus of interests or preferences, as well as for technical judgements, and those too need involve nothing that we would ordinarily describe as a moral judgement (although just how we should take various interests and preferences into account may be morally contentious).

It is quite implausible, however, to suggest that moral judgements are confined to those matters which politicians call 'issues of conscience'. As well as requiring strategic judgements, economic policy involves normative judgements about the distribution of income, about justified forms of taxation and about how far the well-being of some members of a society may be sacrificed in order to promote the well-being of others. Welfare policy turns in part on questions of how far the members of a society should be held morally responsible for one another's condition. Defence and foreign policy notoriously raises questions of a conscientious character and capital punishment is obviously not the only moral issue that arises in the field of law and order. Of course, a specific policy matter will often call for both moral and non-moral judgements, but it is simply not plausible to suggest that politicians and legislators are obliged to confront decisions involving moral judgements only in the narrow range of cases traditionally labelled 'issues of conscience'.[6]

Could it be that the traditional 'issues of conscience' are a sub-set of moral issues which are distinguished in a way which makes them eligible for special treatment? They are often described as issues concerning 'private morality' and that might suggest that they should be dealt with differently from the moral issues which arise in a society's public life.

In fact, as I have already pointed out, not all 'conscience issues' can be described as matters of 'private' morality. Capital punishment is in no sense a private issue, and embryo research and vivisection are not private activities in any sense that is relevant here. However, some, such as divorce, abortion, sexual behaviour and how people spend their time on Sundays, may be conceived as essentially private matters. What difference would that make?

The phrase 'private morality' is ambiguous. It might signify no more than the morality which governs a sphere of life commonly described as 'private', for example, family life. If that is all that it means, nothing seems to follow about how parliamentary decisions ought to be made. Alternatively, it might be used to describe a morality which not only concerns a private sphere but which is also properly private in origin: whether a person should have an abortion or get divorced or trade on Sundays should be left to the private conscience of that person. Thus, on this understanding, private morality is 'private' not only in respect of its subject matter but also in virtue of its source.

It is this second understanding of private morality – a morality which, because it governs a private sphere, is rightfully private in origin – that seems for some people to provide the case for free votes. In fact it does nothing of the kind. For one thing, it rests upon a misleadingly simple view of moral issues as those come before Parliament. What is at issue in those cases is often the very question of whether they are properly left to the discretion of private individuals or whether they involve other entities (for example, foetuses, embryos or animals) or other interests (for example, people living in the vicinity of Sunday traders) which make them something other than the entirely private concerns of individuals. In addition, what Parliament has to decide on these matters is often not just whether something should or should not be permitted but also the terms and conditions upon which it should be permitted, for example, the grounds and the time limit for abortions, the age of consent for sexual conduct, and the grounds for, and legal consequences of, divorce.

But even if we adopt the simple private conscience view of private morality, that view contributes nothing to the argument for free votes. Its claim is that each individual's private conduct should be governed only by that individual's *own* conscience. Its thrust therefore is not that MPs should resolve issues of private morality according to *their* consciences but rather that they have no business in meddling with the private affairs of individuals: on matters of private morality, Parliament should simply pass on the right of decision to private individuals.

Thus it is not easy to find anything intrinsic to the traditional list of conscience issues which makes them rightly determined by free votes and wrongly determined by party decisions. Those issues are not unique in calling for conscientious judgements, nor can MPs convincingly claim that it is wrong, in principle, that their individual consciences should be subordinated to the collective judgements of their political parties.

We may therefore begin to wonder whether there is anything about issues of conscience which argues for free votes. Perhaps 'issues of conscience' are so-called merely because they are subject to free votes and are, as a matter of fact, resolved according to MPs' consciences. In that case, it would be the mere use of free votes that would identify issues as issues of conscience and not their independent identity as issues of conscience which would argue for free votes.[7] However, before we settle for that conclusion, there is something more to be said.

It could be that we are going at this issue the wrong way round. Perhaps there should be a presumption in favour of MPs being allowed to vote according to their own sincerely held judgements so that it is not free voting that requires justification but the imposition of party discipline. Complaints about the use of MPs as lobby fodder are long-standing and commonplace. Other things being equal, it might be said, it is better that MPs should be able to vote according to their best judgements rather than be bullied into voting for things they believe to be wrong or unwise. If we accept that proposition, its effect is to shift the onus of justification from free votes to unfree votes. Of course, that need not result in a case for a more generous use of free votes since, for the most part, other things may be reckoned unequal. We all know the textbook justifications for political parties and for party discipline within legislatures and I shall not recite those here. But, in cases where those justifications do not hold, free votes may be justified *faute de mieux*. Thus, the case for free votes on matters of conscience may be negative rather than positive in character; it may rely upon the absence of an adequate case for using party whips rather than the presence of some feature peculiar to matters of conscience which makes the imposition of party discipline positively wrongful.

However, a rather more positive case can also be made for the use of free votes for issues of conscience in current British politics. Authority needs to be licensed. Two things may be said to license a party's authority over its MPs. First, in joining a political party and accepting endorsement as one of its official representatives, an MP can be said to have placed himself under the authority and organisation of that party. He may also be said to have committed himself to supporting the party's position on a number of matters even though that position may not always be well defined. Second, whatever the constitutional niceties of the British political system, the political reality is that individuals who stand for election to Parliament under a party label are, for the most part, elected as bearers of that label and not as individual personalities. Thus, parties can claim some general democratic justification for requiring their MPs to toe the party line.

In so far as the conventional issues of conscience are kept out of party politics, neither of these justifications of party discipline applies. Although an MP in becoming a member of a party accepts the authority of that party, he need not accept that its authority is unlimited in scope. If the party has no avowed and acknowledged stance on issues of conscience, an MP can reasonably claim that he has not accepted its authority over *those* matters. Similarly, if issues of conscience do not figure in the electoral platforms of political parties, there is no electoral justification for subjecting MPs to a party whip on those issues. In saying this I do not mean, by implication, to endorse the doctrine of electoral mandate for the ordinary run of political issues; that doctrine suffers from well-known limitations. But the limited force possessed by the notion of the electoral mandate has no relevance for issues that are kept out of the electoral arena.

These, I suggest, are more plausible justifications for free votes on issues of conscience. Those issues are not distinguished by some feature which makes the imposition of party discipline intrinsically wrong or wrong in all possible circumstances. The justification for free voting is a contingent one. It is contingent upon the absence of issues of conscience from the avowed positions of political parties. If a political party were to adopt a position on an issue of conscience, there would be nothing essentially wrong in its requiring its MPs to conform to that position – or, at least, there would be nothing more wrong about the use of party discipline for that issue than for other issues.

I should make clear that my purpose has not been to argue against the use of free votes. I have no wish to see the rigours of party discipline increased. I have tried only to track down a justification of free votes that is defensible. However, it does follow from what I have argued that the consciences of MPs are not entitled to the sort of immunity that is sometimes claimed for them.

MORAL ISSUES, FREE VOTES AND REPRESENTATION

If political parties continue to allow their MPs to vote freely on moral issues, how, for those issues, should we conceive the relationship between Parliament and people? Political representation in Britain has become party representation. How then should we conceive the role of MPs as 'representatives' in the absence of party commitment? Should the right of MPs to vote freely on moral issues include their right to vote unconstrained by popular opinion as well as by party discipline?

The Burkean ideal

Perhaps the most obvious basis for a positive answer is the Burkean ideal of the MP as a trustee who is able to follow his own judgement of how the good of his electors and the interests of the nation are best promoted. For the most part, the partisan nature of twentieth-century British politics has made Burke's eighteenth-century ideal of the representative as irrelevant as it is celebrated. But, when the whips are off, MPs have a chance to reclaim that ideal.

MPs have indeed often invoked Burke's conception of representation in relation to matters of conscience. When they vote freely, MPs cannot hide behind the demands of party loyalty; they have to take full responsibility as individuals for the way in which they vote (although they can, of course, refrain from voting). They therefore become unusually vulnerable as individuals to criticism from their constituents and their constituency parties. MPs who find themselves under attack on issues of conscience frequently defend their independence by appealing to Burke's doctrine.

Yet the Burkean ideal is not without its difficulties in this context. The justification behind the ideal of the MP as an independent trustee is usually a claim that his judgement is likely to be superior to that of his constituents or, more generally, that the judgement of Parliament is likely to be superior to that of the general public (cf. Mill 1910: 315–24). But can that claim be made in respect of moral issues? Burke apparently thought so. In his *Speech to the Electors of Bristol* he declared that an MP owed his constituents not only his 'unbiased opinion' and his 'mature judgement' but also his 'enlightened conscience'. What are we to understand by an 'enlightened conscience'? There are two possibilities.

People with enlightened consciences need not be reckoned to have a better grasp of the difference between right and wrong. Their greater enlightenment may consist only in their having a better knowledge of all the relevant circumstances and considerations that surround a moral issue. They may also have a greater capacity for thinking through the significance of those circumstances and considerations. On this understanding, people with enlightened consciences are better placed to make good or right decisions not because they are morally more informed but only because they are more apprised of all the circumstances and considerations that form the contexts of particular moral judgements. For example, someone who is informed about the frequency of error in convictions for murder and who has examined evidence on the deterrent effects of a death penalty is better placed to reach an overall judgement on the use of capital punishment than someone who has not, even though the more informed person can claim no special insight into the moral propriety of using death as an instrument of punishment.

Notice that, in so far as differences of view between MPs and electors turn on these non-moral questions, those differences are not really differences of conscience. That cuts two ways. It means that MPs cannot properly enter pleas of conscience to excuse their departing from the wishes of their electors. On the other hand, for reasons I shall explain shortly, the non-moral expertise of politicians provides a more sustainable basis than simple pleas of conscience for defending Parliament's right to depart from public opinion on moral issues.[8]

While disputes over moral issues can turn on their non-moral elements, it is not plausible to hold that all differences between people and Parliament either must be or have been exclusively non-moral in origin. It seems likely for example that, in part, past conflicts of view between people and Parliament over the death penalty arose because strictly *conscientious* objections to capital punishment were more common amongst MPs than amongst the general population. If there really is that sort of dispute between Parliament and people and if we use the Burkean doctrine to defend the departure of MPs from public opinion, that really does imply a claim that MPs are morally more enlightened than those they represent.

Is that claim sustainable? That question divides into two: can there be moral experts? If so, can MPs claim moral expertise? The answer to the first question depends partly upon our understanding of the nature of morality. For example, those who subscribe to a theological morality based upon sacred texts can certainly hold that students of those texts are more morally informed than those who know little of them, whereas it is hard to see how emotivists could allow that some people's moral views are superior to those of others.[9] The specific conception of conscience that I identified earlier certainly militates against any notion of differences in moral competence, since it gives equal standing to all consciences. But even if we do not adopt the specific conception of conscience and recognise that people can operate with different conceptions of morality, politically those different conceptions are part of the problem rather than avenues to a solution. If a collective decision has to be reached amongst people who have different conceptions of morality, the simplest practical way of dealing with that state of affairs is to give each person an equal standing and an equal voice in the decision. In other words, there is reason to treat all consciences equally even when they are 'consciences' in the non-specific sense. To that extent, the vocabulary of conscience may be motivated by politics and pragmatism rather than by a specific moral theory. Either way, claims to conscientious expertise fare badly and, even if they fared well, there would be ample room for scepticism about the specifically moral expertise of politicians.

Rather than claiming that their consciences are 'better' than the consciences of those whom they represent, MPs might claim only that their consciences are their own and that they have a right to follow their own consciences. I have already explained why MPs cannot satisfactorily excuse their legislative behaviour simply by standing on their supposed rights of conscience. In addition, a mere appeal to the idea of conscience can do nothing to justify our favouring the consciences of several hundred MPs over those of several million ordinary citizens. Thus, contrary to British political mythology, the more seriously we take 'conscience' in so-called 'issues of conscience', the less we can concede to the Burkean conception of representation.

Linking parliamentary and public opinion

If, out of deference to democratic principle, we concede that there really should be some link between public opinion and parliamentary decisions on moral issues, how might that link be forged?

Perhaps we should look to pressure groups to fill the void left by parties. Pressure-group activity has been conspicuous on some moral issues, notably abortion, although on others it has been slight.

However the group process cannot be relied upon faithfully to reproduce the patchwork of public opinion on moral issues and pressure groups usually have little beyond the power of persuasion with which to make free voting MPs bend to their wishes. In this area, rather than acting as intermediaries between public and Parliament, pressure groups have often had to use public opinion as a vehicle for their own influence upon MPs (Pym 1974: 116–20).[10]

More traditional delegate theories have proposed that MPs should be tied to the populace through their constituencies. However, popular beliefs about the reality or the possibility of close links between MPs and their constituents are not well founded (Berrington 1985; Crewe 1985). Given the diverse make-up of constituencies, it has always been difficult to see how the single voice of an MP could speak for the different and conflicting voices of his constituents. Nor are there mechanisms in place through which MPs can gather reliable information on the opinions of their constituents. The constituents who are likely to be most in contact with their MP and who are best placed to 'lean' on him are his party's local activists, but they are notoriously unlikely to provide a microcosm of the whole constituency.[11]

Rather than relying on influences external to Parliament, we might focus on the composition of Parliament itself. For some theorists of representation, a legislature would ideally be a microcosm of those whom it represents. If MPs as a body were an accurate cross-section of the population as a whole, parliamentary democracy could function as a surrogate for direct democracy: decisions made by Parliament would be identical with decisions that would be made by the people were they to vote directly on issues themselves. There are obvious reasons why that sort of microcosmic Parliament would be difficult to achieve and why it might be far from desirable even if it could be achieved. Nevertheless, it does not follow that we should be wholly unconcerned about differences between the social compositions of people and Parliament or about the consequences of those differences. Different consciences speak with different voices and those different voices are not spread randomly across the population; nor are they spread randomly amongst MPs.

In his study of backbench opinion between 1945 and 1955, Hugh Berrington found a series of significant associations between the background characteristics of MPs and their opinions on political issues. In particular, he established an association between support amongst Labour MPs for the abolition of capital punishment and their occupational background, age and education; professionals, the under-fifties and graduates were more supportive of abolition than workers, the over-sixties and those who had received only elementary education (Berrington 1973: 127–30, 245-6). Amongst Conservative MPs during the early 1950s, the restoration of corporal punishment was more enthusiastically supported by non-graduates and the over-sixties than by graduates and the under-forty-ones (ibid.: 176–7). Similarly, his study with Finer and Bartholomew of backbench opinion between 1955 and 1959, revealed associations between the degree of 'humanitarianism' displayed by Labour MPs on penal issues (including the death penalty) and their age and occupational background. The under-fifty-ones were more 'humane' than the over-fifty-ones and Labour MPs coming from the professions and the 'miscellaneous' group of occupations were more 'humane' than the workers (Finer, Berrington and Bartholomew 1961: 43). Amongst Conservative MPs, graduates and younger MPs were consistently more 'humane' on capital and corporal punishment than non-graduates and older MPs (ibid.: 95–6, 129–30, 197*f.*).

Studies of parliamentary voting on moral issues during the 1960s, 1970s and early 1980s, have revealed other associations between the opinions and sociological characteristics of MPs (Richards 1970: 179–96; Hibbing and Marsh 1987; Marsh and Read 1988: 84–107). Unsurprisingly, associations have been found between religious affiliation and voting, most markedly in the case of Roman Catholics and opposition to abortion and, to a lesser degree, opposition to the liberalisation of divorce. Age has also sometimes been significant: younger MPs have generally been more liberal than older MPs, particularly on homosexuality. Educational differences seem to have had a more limited impact, although Oxbridge MPs appear to have been somewhat more liberal on abortion and homosexuality and somewhat more conservative on capital punishment than other MPs.

The extent to which these sort of characteristics determine MPs' thinking on moral issues should not be overplayed. Their impact differs from issue to issue and may vary over time. Moreover, individual MPs can and sometimes do revise their thinking and their voting on moral issues – sometimes between the second and third readings of the same bill. On the other hand, it is hardly surprising that the opinions of MPs on moral issues should bear some relation to other features of themselves and, while the relationship between backbench opinion and the background characteristics of MPs is significant for more than just free votes on moral issues, its impact is likely to be more significant for those issues since it is uninhibited by party whipping.

'It is an irony that representatives in a democracy are likely, in many respects, to be grossly unrepresentative of those who elect them' (Berrington 1973: 5). That irony need not always be a matter for regret. But, if we discover that Parliament has resolved an issue of conscience differently from the population at large and if we also discover that that difference is systematically related to the unrepresentative composition of Parliament, we need to ask some questions. For example, if the resolution of a moral issue were significantly affected by the over-representation of a religious group in Parliament, that would seem hard to defend. If it were significantly affected by the over-representation of graduates, that might be easier to defend: a better educated Parliament, it might be argued, is better equipped than the general public to make well-informed and well-considered decisions. But we should still need to be satisfied that the departure of parliamentary from public opinion really was capable of that sort of rational defence and that it was not merely a reflection of the non-rational impact of different socialisations.

The characteristic for which this is most relevant at present is gender, given the chronic under-representation of women in Parliament. In fact, existing studies of parliamentary voting on moral issues suggest that gender has so far made little difference to the pattern of MPs' voting on those issues (Richards 1970: 182; Hibbing and Marsh 1987: 284–9; Marsh and Read 1988: 90–9). On the other hand, the number of women currently in Parliament is so small that these findings may mean very little and, like other characteristics, gender may have different effects at different times and for different issues.

Nor need a concern about the composition of Parliament be tied to a wholly microcosmic ideal of representation. Even if we adopt a Burkean conception of the MP's role, we can still recognise the relevance and significance of composition. Ill-informed members of the public might be best advised to defer to well-informed Members of Parliament, but well-informed Catholic MPs may still think differently from well-informed atheist MPs, and well-informed female MPs may still think differently from well-informed male MPs.

CONCLUSION

Parliamentary representation in Britain has become so overwhelmingly party representation that it has become unclear how we should conceive the role of MPs in the absence of party. In some measure, the description of non-party moral issues as 'conscience issues' has enabled this question to be evaded. Labelling an issue 'an issue of conscience' has been a way of conflating a description of the content of the issue with a suggestion about the way in which it ought to be resolved. It has therefore been easy to suppose that it would be just wrong for a political party formally to adopt a position on a moral issue and to impose that position upon its MPs. It has also been easy to suppose that MPs should not have to subordinate their consciences to those of their electors.

I have tried to cast doubt on both of those suppositions. There is no reason why, as a matter of principle, political parties ought not to take collective views on moral issues, although, in the absence of a clearly formulated party policy, there would be reason to object to a party's subjecting its MPs to a whip. Nor is it clear that an issue's being a conscience issue should place it beyond the reach of the democratic process. In particular, the Burkean view of the MP's role becomes less rather than more convincing the more a matter is conceived as one of individual conscience. We may not like the proposition that Parliament should slavishly follow public opinion but, the more we insist that an issue is simply an issue of conscience, the harder that proposition becomes to resist.

NOTES

1 For accounts of the procedural and tactical obstacles that confront a private member's bill, see Marsh and Read (1988: 7–40), Richards (1979) and Bromhead (1956: 26–42).

2 A good example of this was the failure of successive private members' bills which tried to amend the Abortion Act 1967, even though several of them enjoyed majority support in Parliament; see Marsh and Read (1988: 111–35) and Durham (1991: 16–31). The Abortion Act 1967 was eventually amended in April 1990 during the committee stage of the Government's Human Fertilisation and Embryology Bill. The Secretary of State for Health presented MPs with a number of options on the time limit for abortions on which a series of free votes was held. The eventual outcome, by a vote of 335 to 129, was that the permitted period for abortions was reduced from twenty-eight weeks to twenty-four weeks.

3 For a case study which illustrates well the close involvement of government departments with the content of private members' bills, even when those bills deal with issues that are, in the context of British politics, relatively minor, see Sochart (1988).

4 Generally, since 1945, Labour MPs have divided less evenly than Conservative MPs in free votes on moral issues, the main exceptions being some votes on abortion and two of the three votes on Sunday trading held in December 1993. Although issues of conscience are not formally party political issues, party affiliation remains a better predictor of the pattern of MPs' voting on those issues than any other factor. See

Richards (1970: 180), Hibbing and Marsh (1987), Marsh and Read (1988: 89–105).

5 For another example – a successful rebellion of Labour backbenchers in 1969 against their government's attempt to whip them on a bill concerning divorce settlements – see Richards (1970: 151–2).

6 The history of disputes arising from the Labour Party's 'conscience clause' (exempting members from having to conform to the Party's decisions when those decisions conflict with their conscientious convictions) illustrates well the problems involved in trying to contain the scope of conscience; see Alderman (1966). One might expect the Labour Party to be more inclined than the Conservative Party to 'moralise' central questions of public policy, but the Thatcher government was keen to claim a moral basis for the whole range of its policies, including its social and economic policies (Isaac 1990).

7 Cf. Richards (1970: 213): 'In practice, a matter becomes an issue of conscience when it is convenient for the parties to treat it as such.' Sometimes the phrase 'issue of conscience' has been used to describe *any* matter which is left to the decision of individual MPs irrespective of the content of that matter.

8 In distinguishing moral from non-moral judgements, I am not suggesting that these can or should be kept entirely separate in the final decision. An overall moral judgement will have to take account of the moral significance of the findings of non-moral judgement (for example, the moral significance of the consequences that are judged likely to follow upon legal reform). Nevertheless, that does not turn non-moral judgements (for example, of probable consequences) into moral judgements.

9 By 'emotivists', I mean those who believe that moral judgements are nothing but expressions of emotion.

10 The fullest study of pressure group activity in this context is Pym (1974); see also Marsh and Chambers (1981) and Marsh and Read (1988: 62–83). Some groups have played an important part in creating or exploiting a 'moral panic' which has enabled a bill to be rushed through Parliament unopposed, when, in other circumstances, some MPs might have questioned the need for the bill or challenged its details. That tactic appears to have been used with some success for private member's bills dealing with children and pornography (McCarthy and Moodie 1981; Marsh, Gowin and Read 1986; Marsh, Read and Myers 1987). But those are exceptions. Generally, if MPs are not already inclined to conform to public opinion, pressure groups are not well placed to make them do so. In addition, the virtues claimed for the group process as a transmitter of preferences and interests may not hold good for opinions. One of those virtues is supposed to be the sensitivity of the group process to differences in people's intensities of preference but, on moral questions, it is not obviously acceptable that stronger opinions should entitle their holders to more influential voices, particularly since there need be no correlation between the strength of people's opinions and the quality of their judgements (Jones 1988).

11 On moral issues, MPs have often had to cope with considerable pressures from their constituents or constituency parties; see, for example, Nicolson (1958: 94–105). Although territorial constituencies are

unsatisfactory as vehicles for the transmission of opinion from people to Parliament, the distribution of moral opinions is not always and entirely unrelated to geography. There have been regional variations in the way MPs have voted on moral issues: on the whole MPs from the South of England have been more liberal in their views than MPs representing Scotland and Wales and the North of England (Hibbing and Marsh 1987: 284–92; Marsh and Read 1988: 89–99) and their behaviour probably mirrors similar regional variations in public opinion. There is also evidence that the larger the Roman Catholic population in a constituency, the more likely it is that the relevant MP will vote conservatively on moral issues (Hibbing and Marsh 1987: 290–2).

I am grateful to Simon Caney, Philip Daniels, Ella Ritchie and Albert Weale for their helpful comments on an earlier draft of this essay.

REFERENCES

Alderman, R. K. (1966) 'The Conscience Clause of the Parliamentary Labour Party', *Parliamentary Affairs* 19: 224–32.

Berrington, H. B. (1968) 'Partisanship and Dissidence in the Nineteenth-Century House of Commons', *Parliamentary Affairs* 21: 338–74.

—— (1973) *Backbench Opinion in the House of Commons 1945–55*, Oxford: Pergamon.

—— (1985) 'MPs and their Constituents in Britain: the History of the Relationship', in V. Bogdanor (ed.) *Representatives of the People?*, Aldershot: Gower.

Bromhead, P. A. (1956) *Private Members' Bills in the British Parliament*, London: Routledge and Kegan Paul.

Christoph, J. B. (1962) *Capital Punishment and British Politics*, London: Allen and Unwin.

Crewe, I. (1985) 'MPs and their Constituents in Britain: How Strong are the Links?', in V. Bogdanor (ed.), *Representatives of the People?*, Aldershot: Gower.

Durham, M. (1991) *Sex and Politics: the Family and Morality in the Thatcher Years*, Basingstoke: Macmillan.

Finer, S. E., Berrington, H. B. and Bartholomew, D. J. (1961) *Backbench Opinion in the House of Commons 1955–59*, Oxford: Pergamon.

Hibbing, J. R. and Marsh, D (1987) 'Accounting for the Voting Patterns of British MPs on Free Votes', *Legislative Studies Quarterly* 12: 275–98.

Isaac, J. U. (1990) 'The New Right and the Moral Society', *Parliamentary Affairs* 43: 209–26.

Jones, P. (1988) 'Intense Preferences, Strong Beliefs and Democratic Decision-making', *Political Studies* 36: 7–29.

Lovenduski, J. and Outshoorn, J. (eds) (1986) *The New Politics of Abortion*, London: Sage.

McCarthy, M. and Moodie, R. (1981) 'Parliament and Pornography: the 1978 Child Protection Act', *Parliamentary Affairs*, 34: 47–62.

Marsh, D. and Chambers, J. (1981) *Abortion Politics*, London: Junction Books.

Marsh, D., Gowin, P. and Read, M. (1986) 'Private Members Bills and Moral Panic: the Case of the Video Recordings Bill (1984)', *Parliamentary Affairs* 39: 179–96.

Marsh, D. and Read, M. (1988) *Private Members' Bills*, Cambridge: Cambridge University Press.

Marsh, D., Read, M. and Myers, B. (1987) 'Don't Panic: the Obscene Publications (Protection of Children, etc.) Amendment Bill (1985)', *Parliamentary Affairs* 40: 73–9.

Mill, J. S. (1910) *Utilitarianism; On Liberty; Representative Government*, London: Everyman.

Nicolson, N. (1958) *People and Parliament*, London: Weidenfeld and Nicolson.

Norton, P. (1975) *Dissension in the House of Commons 1945–74*, Basingstoke: Macmillan.

——— (1980) *Dissension in the House of Commons 1974–79*, Oxford: Oxford University Press.

Pym, B. (1974) *Pressure Groups and the Permissive Society*, Newton Abbot: David and Charles.

Regan, P. (1988) 'The 1986 Shops Bill', *Parliamentary Affairs* 41: 218–35.

Richards, P. G. (1970) *Parliament and Conscience*, London: Allen and Unwin.

——— (1979) 'Private Members' Legislation', in S. Walkland (ed.) *The House of Commons in the Twentieth Century*, Oxford: Clarendon.

Short, E. (1989) *Whip to Wilson*, London: MacDonald.

Sochart, E. A. (1988) 'Agenda Setting, the Role of Groups and the Legislative Process: the Prohibition of Female Circumcision in Britain', *Parliamentary Affairs* 41: 508–26.

10 Parliamentary sovereignty and public opinion[1]

W. L. Miller, A. M. Timpson and M. Lessnoff

Over the last decade there have been increasing demands from groups such as Charter 88 for a more formal, legal, constitutional framework that would protect human rights in Britain either by enacting a new British Bill of Rights or by incorporating the European Convention on Human Rights into British domestic law. But others, some with impeccable liberal credentials, argue equally strongly against the idea. Objections to such a legal framework include the following:

1 There is no problem: there is greater respect for human rights in Britain than in most other countries in the world.
2 A legal, constitutional framework would conflict with the doctrine of parliamentary sovereignty.[2]
3 It is better to rely on social and political rather than legal protections for human rights – that is, on the sense of fair play of Ministers, the vigilance of backbench and opposition MPs, and the influence of a free press.
4 A constitutional framework merely shifts powers of discretion from elected, representative and accountable members of Parliament to unelected, unrepresentative and unaccountable judges.

Those who advocate a new Bill of Rights respond that while respect for human rights in Britain compares well with the rest of the world in general, it does not compare so well with other countries with a similar culture and a similar level of economic development. The doctrine of parliamentary sovereignty is a peculiarly English doctrine that has always been contested in other parts of the United Kingdom, especially in Scotland and Ireland. To the civil rights lobby, the 'sense of fair play of ministers' is a bad joke in poor taste. But the final argument carries more weight with the left. Radicals and reformers, as well as revolutionaries, have had good reasons to view

British courts and judges with suspicion. Far too often they have given way to hysteria and acted as instruments of repression.

The political and theoretical arguments may go on for ever. We do not propose to add much to them here. But let us see whether the public believes there is a problem of human rights in Britain; whether they accept the doctrine of parliamentary sovereignty, whether they support a Bill of Rights and whether they have sufficient confidence in judges and courts to back them against our elected Parliament.

IS THERE A PROBLEM OF HUMAN RIGHTS IN BRITAIN?

The proper international comparison is not with the Third World but with other economically advanced Western democracies. So, in our public opinion survey we asked whether 'on the whole, the rights and liberties enjoyed by British citizens are [greater/less] than those enjoyed by people who live in [America/West European countries like France and Germany/Scandinavian countries like Norway, Denmark or Sweden]'. This question came in six different forms depending upon whether it used the word *greater* or *less*, and upon which of the three different international comparisons it used. The six different forms were assigned randomly to interviews and each respondent was asked simply to agree or disagree with the proposition as put to them. Interviewing was carried out by telephone and controlled by computer. We make a great deal of use of this experimental technique in our interviews. It allows us to measure the impact of using different forms of wording, some of which appear to differ much less than in this first example. In order to investigate public opinion on different levels we used two samples: a random sample of 2,060 members of the general public and a sample of 1,244 senior local government politicians (mainly leaders of party groups). The latter sample was closer to a population than a sample, including over 85 per cent of politicians in the target categories. We also used a 'booster' sample in Scotland, providing 1,255 Scottish interviews in all, but we shall make few references to Scottish peculiarities here. Interviews were spread over the period from November 1991 to August 1992.

Averaging the percentage who agreed that rights were greater in Britain with the percentage who disagreed with the proposition that they were less in Britain provides a useful comparative index of popular perceptions of Britain's respect for human rights. By this measure Britain scored well against America but badly against Scandinavia and about as well as Western Europe. Our sample of

Table 1: International comparisons

Percentage agree rights are greater in Britain (or disagree that they are less) than in:	General public	Local politicians
America	60	56
Western Europe	55	47
Scandinavia	38	31

local politicians was slightly more pessimistic than the general public about British rights and liberties.

Concern has been expressed that British rights and liberties were diminished 'during the Thatcherite decade'. We asked whether 'on balance, British governments have been [reducing/increasing] the rights and liberties of British citizens in recent years'. Again the two forms of the question were randomly assigned to interviews, and each respondent was asked merely to agree or disagree with the statement as put to them. It proved an unusually difficult question for the general public: a majority agreed with the proposition which-ever way it was put – 61 per cent agreed that British governments had been *reducing* rights and 57 per cent agreed they had been *increasing* them. Such patterns suggest the general public's perceptions of trends were unclear, weakly held, and at the mercy of their natural wish to be agreeable to our interviewers. Politicians, however, had clear views: 66 per cent agreed that British governments were reducing citizens' rights and only 38 per cent agreed that they were increasing citizens' rights.

Since the question explicitly mentioned government behaviour as well as human rights it naturally evoked a partisan response which was especially marked amongst the politicians. Labour, Liberal and Scottish Nationalist group leaders were even more critical than their voters of the government's track record on human rights while

Table 2: Perceived trends

	General public (%)	Local politicians (%)
agree British Govts are reducing citizens' rights	61	66
agree British Govts are increasing citizens' rights	57	38

Conservative group leaders applauded their government's record even more than Conservative voters. But partisanship was not everything: even amongst Conservatives a fifth of their group leaders and a third of their voters were critical of their own government's record.

One motivation for a Bill of Rights is that immigration has changed the make-up of the nation very considerably since the Second World War. As a result both new and newly mobilised groups of citizens have become more conscious of discrimination in their daily lives. We found a widespread feeling that not enough had been done to ensure equal rights in Britain. To avoid net bias in the answers we used two forms of question about equal rights assigning one or other form randomly to each interview. We asked whether 'we have [gone too far/not gone far enough] in pushing equal rights in this country'. Let us take agreement with 'not gone far enough' or disagreement with 'gone too far' as an index of support for more equal rights. On that basis three-quarters felt we should push further for equal rights in Britain. For them, there was a problem.

We tested consciousness of discrimination directly by asking whether people had personal experience of being 'discriminated against in some important matter on grounds of sex, race, ethnic background, religion, age, disability or political beliefs'. The question was designed to exclude the minor irritations of social life and focus upon significant discrimination. Just over a quarter of the general public alleged discrimination.

We asked those who felt discrimination to identify the main grounds for that discrimination and the main culprit. Obviously that question format prevents any discussion of multiple discrimination – either on multiple grounds (e.g. race and gender) or by multiple culprits (e.g. police and employers). But it has the advantage of identifying the grounds and the culprit who seemed most important to the victim. Few of the general public blamed government or its agents: most blamed employers or just 'other people' with whom they came into contact. Substantial numbers alleged discrimination on grounds of age and gender and, within Scotland, religion. Much to our surprise, political leaders claimed to have suffered more discrimination than the public at large, mainly because so many of them claimed to have suffered political discrimination and the politicians, unlike the general public, did blame government officials as well as employers and others.

Different sections of the public complained of particular forms of discrimination – women complained particularly of gender discrimination, the young and old complained particularly of age discrimina-

Table 3: Discrimination

	General public	Local politicians
Percentage agree we have not gone far enough (or disagree we have gone too far) in pushing equal rights in this country	73	75
Percentage personally felt discrimination	28	41
Discrimination was by:		
employer	58	47
police	6	2
local or national govt official	8	20
other people	28	31

tion, Catholics particularly of religious discrimination, though to a large extent one complaint substituted for another. Thus women complained very much more than men about gender discrimination but much less than men about racial, religious and political discrimination. Of course, our question format made it impossible to detect complaints of multiple discrimination.

Thus there does seem to be a degree of concern about citizens' rights but not a crisis in the relationship between citizens and government. There is a general concern about rights and some, though very much less, personal experience of discrimination. But – politicians apart – government itself is not regarded as the main culprit. That was true of personal experience of discrimination and it is true of other personal experiences as well. When people come into personal contact with government or its agents they usually find both its elected and unelected officials helpful.

We asked whether people ever personally contacted a local

Table 4: Helpful government

	General public (%)	Local politicians (%)
Found local councillor helpful	71	92
Found council offices helpful	66	95
Found MP helpful	74	81
Found govt department helpful	70	71

Note: Percentage of those who had made contact and expressed a view about helpfulness councillor, council offices, a Member of Parliament or an office of a central government department and whether 'on balance you found them helpful or unhelpful'. On average 70 per cent of the general public found such contacts helpful. Not surprisingly, over 92 per cent of senior local government politicians found contacts with other people in local government helpful, though they found central government offices no more helpful than the general public and MPs only a little more so. Perhaps governors, at whatever level, find their own government machine particularly helpful. Nonetheless the important point is that between two-thirds and three-quarters of the general public also found a variety of personal contacts with government helpful.

We tested personal experience of government a bit further with questions about the police and the National Health Service. We asked whether people had 'personally been stopped and interviewed by the police about a traffic violation or anything else' and, if so, whether on balance the police had behaved 'courteously or rudely'; whether they had 'personally ever been the victim of a crime such as having your house broken into, your car stolen, or being assaulted' and, if so, whether on balance the police had been 'helpful or unhelpful'. Similarly we inquired whether 'in the last few years you, or anyone in your household received treatment at an NHS hospital' and, if so, whether they were 'satisfied or dissatisfied' with the service provided.

Over two-thirds of the public had found the police helpful, four-fifths had found them courteous, and almost nine-tenths were satisfied with NHS treatment. The figures were even higher amongst politicians. Again this seems to show that the majority of personal contacts with government agents are satisfactory. Of course, it is also true that one-fifth of the public found the police rude and some of that fifth may have found police conduct much worse than rude. Personal

Table 5: Police and health services

	General public (%)	*Local politicians* (%)
Found police courteous	81	86
Found police helpful	68	81
Satisfied with NHS treatment	89	94
Agree police protect rather than harm liberties (or disagree police do more to harm than protect)	75	82

contact with agents of government proves helpful to the majority of the public but certainly not to everyone.

As with equal rights and personal experience of discrimination, we complemented these questions about direct personal experience with a broader question about the extent to which they felt the police either protected or harmed their liberties. We asked whether 'On the whole, the police [do more to harm our liberties than to protect them/protect our liberties more than they harm them]'. As usual, each form of words was used in a randomly selected half of the sample. In this case, the wording made little difference: roughly three-quarters of the public disagreed with the first version and agreed with the second, i.e. three-quarters felt the police did more to protect than to harm our liberties. Amongst politicians, over four-fifths felt so. General perceptions therefore mirrored personal experience – something less than complete satisfaction but not a crisis of relations between citizen and state.

THE DOCTRINE OF PARLIAMENTARY SOVEREIGNTY

Lord Hailsham has argued that the doctrine of parliamentary sovereignty is just another name for an 'elective dictatorship'. It is a distinctively English doctrine that is occasionally challenged in Scottish Courts. Few Scots, of course, have a sound grasp of constitutional law or even of Scottish history. The few who do, make the headlines and make the nation appear more distinctive than it is, but the distinctive are not the typical.

Throughout Britain there was almost universal agreement to the proposition that 'constitutional checks and balances are important to make sure that a government doesn't become too dictatorial and ignore other viewpoints'. Scots were no more in favour than the English: there was nothing distinctive about Scottish public opinion on the need for constitutional checks and balances. On the other hand, checks and balances are an American rather than an English notion, fundamentally at odds with any notion of unlimited sovereignty. Perhaps it would be more correct therefore to say that there was nothing distinctive about English public opinion and that most English people showed scant regard for their constitution or history. The surprise is not that the Scots failed to reject the notion of parliamentary sovereignty (they did reject it) but that the English also rejected it.

However, when we put the proposition the other way round we found a large majority apparently willing to support the principle of government prerogative and discretion: 79 per cent of the British public (and only slightly less in Scotland) agreed that 'it is important for a government to be able to take decisive action without looking over its shoulder all the time'. Nonetheless, there was much less than universal support for this principle, and evidence that some of that support was conditional. No one has much difficulty accepting decisive government when it acts in a way they approve. The issue only becomes acute when government does something of which they disapprove. So we asked: 'Suppose Parliament passed a law you considered unjust, immoral or cruel. Would you still be morally bound to obey it?' Those who accept the unlimited sovereignty of Parliament would have to agree. In practice many others might obey such a law under duress, fearful of the penalties of disobedience. But compliance under coercion does not signify acceptance of sovereignty.

Half, but only half, the general public agreed they would be morally bound to obey such a law. Politicians were more liberal than the public on most aspects of citizens' rights, but not on their moral duty to obey Parliament: two-thirds felt morally bound to obey unjust laws. Realistically, much might depend upon the particular nature of a law. There are degrees of injustice and immorality. No doubt the percentages who feel a moral duty to obey an unjust law would vary with their perception of the degree of injustice. Nonetheless there seems to be a large body of public opinion, though significantly less in political circles, which simply does not accept Parliament's sovereign right to pass whatever legislation it thinks fit. Support for decisive government is not support for unlimited govern-

Table 6: Parliamentary sovereignty

	General public (%)	Local politicians (%)
Agree importance of constitutional checks and balances	96	98
Agree importance of decisive government	79	70
Feel morally bound to obey unjust law passed by Parliament	51	65
Who feel important issues should be decided by referendum rather than by Parliament	64	34

ment and the principle of constitutional checks is so universal as to be part of our common culture.

Indeed public opposition to parliamentary prerogative goes further: two-thirds of the public – though only one-third of politicians – believe that important issues should be decided by the people themselves, in referenda, rather than by Parliament. We asked whether: '[Important political issues are too complex to be decided by everyone voting in a referendum and should be left to Parliament to decide / It would be better to let the people decide important political issues by everyone voting in a referendum rather than leaving them to Parliament as at present]?' Irrespective of which way the proposition was put, the public came down decisively in favour of referenda and the politicians equally decisively against. Perhaps even local politicians have a deeper understanding of the nature of political issues. Perhaps they have a sense of fellow feeling for parliamentary politicians. But this result certainly betrays a lack of deference amongst the general public towards the wisdom and authority of parliament.

ALTERNATIVE CHECKS AND BALANCES

While the American revolutionaries devised a complex system of legal and constitutional checks and balances to put restraints on arbitrary government, English traditionalists like Dicey preferred to rely upon purely informal and political mechanisms – the government's sense of fair play, the vigilance of backbench MPs, and the influence of a free press.

But unlike Dicey, the public does not trust politicians. We asked whether: 'most politicians can be trusted to do what they think is best for the country'. It was a one-sided question. If that produced any bias it should have inflated the degree of trust in politicians. The question was kind therefore – perhaps too kind – to politicians. Elsewhere in the interview we inserted another question, designed to calibrate this first one. We asked: 'Generally speaking, would you say that most people you come into contact with are trustworthy or untrustworthy?'

Although 90 per cent of the general public felt most people they met were trustworthy, only 33 per cent felt they could trust politicians. Politicians had a rosier view of human nature, or perhaps more fortunate personal experiences: 97 per cent felt most people they met were trustworthy but only 57 per cent felt they could trust (other) politicians. So even politicians were ambivalent about the trustworthiness of other politicians, and a large majority of the public

Table 7: Trust in politicians

	General public %	Local politicians %
Trust most people	90	97
Trust politicians	33	57

simply distrusted them. Dicey's view is not representative of the electorate today if, indeed, it ever was.

We can also measure the extent of public confidence in the other informal checks upon which Dicey relied. We asked respondents to give a 'mark out of ten for how much you feel citizens' rights and liberties are protected by each of the following' – and then listed seventeen different potential safeguards for citizens' liberties, including a proposed 'Bill of Rights, passed by Parliament, and enforced by the courts', 'backbench MPs in Parliament' and three elements of the press – 'tabloid newspapers like the *Sun/Daily Mirror*', 'quality newspapers like the *Telegraph/Guardian*', and 'television'. The list also included 'local government councils' which could be expected to win high marks from local politicians at least.

Amongst both public and politicians a constitutional Bill of Rights scored higher than backbench MPs or the press. Let us focus on the percentage who awarded an item more than a bare pass, i.e. at least six marks out of ten. Amongst the public, a Bill of Rights got a clear pass from 73 per cent, backbench MPs from only 54 per cent, and local government councils from only 52 per cent. Local politicians naturally had a good opinion of their own councils, but they had an even better opinion of a Bill of Rights: 83 per cent gave a clear pass to a Bill of Rights, 76 per cent to local government councils and only 72 per cent to backbench MPs. No one placed much reliance on the

Table 8: Public evaluations of alternative protectors of rights

Percentage who give six or more marks out of ten for protecting citizens' rights, to:	General public	Local politicians
A Bill of Rights	73	83
Backbench MPs	54	72
Television	64	70
The quality press	66	74
The tabloid press	24	21
Local government councils	52	76

tabloid press to defend citizens' rights and liberties. Politicians rated television and the quality press about as effective as backbenchers and local councils while the public rated them higher. But even television and the quality press got about 12 per cent less than a Bill of Rights. A century ago, Dicey may have felt that political checks were more effective than constitutional ones, but neither public nor politicians feel that now.

UNELECTED, UNREPRESENTATIVE AND UNACCOUNTABLE

The final argument against a formal, legal, constitutional framework for the protection of rights is that it would only shift power from elected, representative and accountable politicians to unelected, unrepresentative and unaccountable judges. Consequently some people may support the idea of constitutional checks and balances in the abstract, but refuse to accept it in practice because they do not trust the courts.

Despite long-standing suspicions reinforced by a series of recent miscarriages of justice, public confidence in British courts and judges was surprisingly high: 70 per cent gave British courts a clear pass mark for 'protecting citizens' rights and liberties' – far less than 100 per cent certainly, but still a comparatively good score. Rather less, particularly amongst the general public, gave judges a clear pass for 'fairness and impartiality'. That seems to indicate more public confidence in juries than judges. The right of a jury to acquit – whatever the weight of evidence in favour of the Crown – was established in a series of celebrated English 'free speech' cases during the seventeenth and eighteenth centuries[3] and juries have recently reaffirmed their role as defenders of the citizen against the state in, for example,

Table 9: Public perceptions of courts and judges

	General public (%)	Local politicians (%)
Give six or more marks out of ten for protecting citizens' rights to:		
British courts	70	70
European courts	65	75
Give six or more marks out of ten for fairness and impartiality to British judges	60	68

the 1985 Ponting case.[4] European courts were rated about the same as British courts and higher than British judges.

But such generalised perceptions of courts and judges are not quite the issue. The critical question is whether Parliament or a court should have the final say in a dispute over citizens' rights. We asked about both British and European courts. First we asked: 'Suppose we had a Constitutional Bill of Rights, as some other countries do. If Parliament passed a law but the courts said it was unconstitutional, who should have the final say, Parliament or the courts?' Although the text was not explicit, the position of this question in the interview and the implication of the wording invited comparison between Parliament and specifically British courts. Then we went on to ask: 'Suppose someone in Britain objects to a law passed by Parliament and takes the case to the European Court of Human Rights. Who should have the final say, the European Court or the British Parliament?'

A slender majority of the public would give the final say to Parliament rather than British courts, but to the European Court rather than Parliament. Politicians distinguished much more sharply between British and European courts: only 38 per cent would let a British court overrule Parliament, but 61 per cent would let the European Court do so.

Support for British courts overruling Parliament was greatest amongst those who described themselves as being 'in the centre' politically and lower amongst those who placed themselves on the right and left – especially amongst left-wing politicians, who clearly remained suspicious of British courts. But ideological differences were not great.

By contrast there were very sharp ideological differences in support for the European Court. Among the public, the European Court was backed by over twice as many on the left as on the right; among

Table 10: Should Parliament have the final say?

	General public (%)	Local politicians (%)
Percentage who say the court should overrule Parliament when the court is: a British court enforcing a Bill of Rights	48	38
European Court of Human Rights	55	61

Table 11: Ideology and parliamentary sovereignty

	General public	*Local politicians*
Percentage who would let a British court overrule Parliament amongst those who place themselves:		
on the left	47	34
in the centre	49	42
on the right	40	36
Percentage who would let the European Court overrule Parliament amongst those who place themselves:		
on the left	71	84
in the centre	57	62
on the right	33	26

politicians, it was backed by over three times as many on the left as on the right. Of course the survey took place when a right-wing government had been in power for a decade, which was bound to incline those on the left towards any system of restraint, but the left only gave strong backing to the European Court, not to British courts.

The addition of a supranational layer to government strikes at the very principle of parliamentary sovereignty. Opposition voters, and more especially opposition politicians, remain suspicious of British courts but are more willing to accept an external, supranational court – a court which is above, as well as beyond, domestic politics. It is possible that, if a British Constitutional Court were set up, public opinion would distinguish between that court and other domestic courts. But we suspect the new Constitutional Court would need to establish a track record for upholding the rights of British citizens against the British government, as the European Court has already done, before public opinion – especially opposition opinion – would accept it as anything more than a creature of British government.

SUMMARY AND CONCLUSION

At the start we outlined four of the principal objections to a more formal, legal structure for the protection of citizens' rights in Britain. The alternative is to persist with the English doctrine of parliamentary sovereignty. It is the doctrine of the 'Good Tsar', albeit an elected Tsar. It asks us to judge the system by its performance rather than by its structure.

We have found little evidence of an acute 'crisis of confidence' between British citizens and the state, but the public does not have a specially favourable view of citizens' rights in Britain when compared with other economically advanced Western countries. They judge Britain no better than Europe and worse than Scandinavia. They give lukewarm support to the basic notion of parliamentary sovereignty over its citizens; only half of the general public believe they should obey an unjust law passed by Parliament and two-thirds believe important issues should be decided by popular referendum rather than by Parliament. Almost everyone believes in the American doctrine of 'checks and balances'. Few have faith in the informal checks advocated by English theorists such as Dicey. Only a third trust politicians to do what they think is best for the country. As a protector of citizens' rights, they rate a Bill of Rights as better protection than television or the quality press, and far better than backbench MPs in Parliament. They are ambivalent about whether Parliament should have sovereignty over the judgments of courts, though both the general public and especially politicians tilt in favour of Parliament against domestic courts and in favour of European courts against Parliament.

Overall, public support for the doctrine of parliamentary sovereignty is already weak and likely to weaken still further as supranational institutions develop further. It is a doctrine of lawyers, textbooks and government propagandists, not a doctrine of the people.

NOTES

1 For a further development of this and related themes using data from our British Rights Survey, see Miller (1995).

2 The doctrine of parliamentary sovereignty, or parliamentary supremacy, is particularly associated with A. V. Dicey who made a robust restatement of this very old doctrine at the end of the last century. For a more recent summary with reference to Dicey see Wade and Bradley (1985), especially p. 64.

3 Noted in Hurwitt and Thornton (1989: 30).

4 Briefly reviewed in Ewing and Gearty (1990: 143–7).

REFERENCES

Ewing, K. D. and Gearty, C. A. (1990) *Freedom under Thatcher: Civil Liberties in Modern Britain*, Oxford: Oxford University Press.

Hurwitt, Malcolm and Thorton, Peter (1989) *Civil Liberty: The Liberty/ NCCL Guide*, London: Penguin.

Miller, W. L. (ed.) (1995) *Alternatives to Freedom: Arguments and Opinion*, London: Longman.

Wade, E. C. S. and Bradley, A. W. (1985) *Constitutional and Administrative Law*, 10th edn, London: Longman.

11 Party, personality and law
The political culture of Italian corruption

David Hine

CORRUPTION AND POLITICAL CULTURE

Modernising Italian politics

Mature liberal democracies are better protected against political corruption than most other regimes. Many of their fundamental features such as the rule of law and an independent judiciary are geared towards this end, as are their broader value systems. Nevertheless, corruption occurs even where vigorous mechanisms and deep-rooted norms are in place to check it. When it is only occasional, it is generally written off as the irregular manifestation of pathological behaviour by individuals who have not been effectively socialised into the norms and sanctions of the civic culture. However, periodic surges lead commentators to ask whether, even in liberal democracies, it is fed by particular facilitating conditions, and whether changes in political life or wider social circumstances are making societies more susceptible to it.

Western Europe is currently passing through such a phase, as cases of corruption in various countries seem to be increasing. Much the most striking case is Italy, where, even before the dramatic changes in the political and judicial climate brought by the 1992 general election, the level of political corruption was already in a class of its own. From mid-April 1992 to mid-October 1993, the Italian investigating judiciary served notices to no fewer than 247 members of the 625-seat Chamber of Deputies and 86 members of the 325-seat Senate that they were under investigation for corruption. (*Corriere della Sera* 14 October 1993: 5). The parliament elected in 1992 had within eighteen months lost all legitimacy, and fresh elections under a new electoral system were held in the spring of 1994. Many senior members of the country's business and administrative elite were also involved.

If there is a relationship between the elimination of corruption and economic and political modernisation, the high incidence of political corruption in Italy might seem to square ill with long-term post-war political developments. 'Modernisation' is of course a loose concept; it includes factors like the collective representation of social interests, the reform of public administration, the establishment of legal-rational procedures governing public life, and so on. But it is less clear whether it also includes the elimination of corruption, or whether in fact the extensive public intervention in economic and social life which comes with it actually increases the scope for corruption. Nevertheless, since united Italy's first two regimes after 1861 were in many respects unreformed and unmodernised systems of government, with high levels of corruption, and since the post-war Republic subscribed much more systematically to the rule of law, civil rights, and administrative accountability, it has often been assumed that modernisation would, over time, assist the elimination of corruption.

Certainly, many observers of Italian politics in recent years have assumed that the depolarisation of its party system and the apparently steady institutionalisation of its formal structures (the constitutional court, the balance between legislature and executive, the territorial devolution of power, etc.) were helping to modernise what was previously a polarised and unstable democracy. Moreover, at the level of political culture, the thesis of a polarised society, built upon alienation, isolation, and fragmentation (Zariski 1972: 92–116) had, for many years, been giving way to a rather different view. Revisiting its 'civic culture' qualities two decades on from Almond and Verba's classic study, Giacomo Sani not only argued that the political culture was then (1980) that of a mature democracy, but even that much of the earlier doubt cast by Almond and Verba had itself been the result of methodological shortcomings in the original approach. (Sani 1980: 273–323). By the mid-1980s, the possibility of the liberal-democratic system collapsing in some way seemed improbable. Italy was becoming a mature, 'consolidated' democracy even if the ultimate test – alternation in power between government and opposition – had still to be passed. The extent of corruption over the last decade therefore suggests that not all aspects of the political system proceed towards a state of 'modernity' at the same pace. In Italy, the relationship between modernisation and the eradication of corruption looks uncertain. Corruption seems quite systematic, and is not limited to a series of individual cases where the normal restraints of guilt, social disapproval and risk of detection have, exceptionally, failed to work. Political relationships are widely affected, as is the allocation of public resources, the representation of interests, and ultimately the attitudes of citizens towards their regime.

Interpreting corruption

Corruption is undesirable for two main reasons. It misallocates public resources and it undermines the legitimacy of the political order. The immediate beneficiary on the political side of the exchange may not be an individual acting in a private capacity; the great majority of Italian corruption seems to involve financing of parties rather than direct personal enrichment of politicians. But the distortion of the political process thereby created is no less serious. Voters support parties they might not otherwise have supported and, by occupation of office, with paid employment with power and privilege attached, those who receive bribes on behalf of their party are themselves likely to be personal beneficiaries.

Neither effect is easy to measure but it has been widely argued that the extent of corruption in Italy in recent years, as suggested by the size of scandals exposed by the judiciary, has been so great as to have had real macroeconomic effects. Side-payments (*tangenti*) to secure contracts or other forms of political favour, rising in magnitude from 5 per cent upwards, were clearly the norm for wide areas of public-sector contracting (Della Porta 1993: 98–115). This certainly constituted a substantial misallocation of public resources. Political support in the shape of campaign contributions, exchanged for various forms of political protection afforded to organised crime and to the recycling of its profits, is also highly damaging. The presence of organised crime can weaken the economic infrastructure of sizeable areas of a country and undermine confidence in its financial institutions. However, as with the study of the black economy, it is difficult to quantify precisely, and extrapolating from what is made known by successful prosecution is not easy.

Corruption is not only difficult to measure; it is also difficult to define. If the definition is couched in terms of moral imperatives, it will vary across cultures. If it is couched in terms of positive law, it will vary across legal orders. Corruption on one side, and mere dishonesty and manipulation on the other, are legally distinguishable, but in other respects similar. Governments maximise votes or party finances by tolerating low levels of productivity in public services, by allowing exploitative private monopolies to survive, by disbursing public assets to private interests at beneficial values and by introducing relaxed legislation on political financing. Whether action in these areas counts as 'corruption' depends on where the legal lines are drawn.

When it comes to the second major cost of corruption – the potential delegitimisation of the wider political order – some caution is also in order. Societies may differ considerably over time, not just in voter knowledge of how much corruption exists, but also in the tolerance shown towards it when it *is* known about. Almost all comparative literature on corruption emphasises that different types of socio-political community are likely to generate different attitudes towards various types of corrupt practice. Indeed, comparative studies of corruption are most convincing, in terms of explanatory power, when they are dealing with very broad comparisons, rather than comparisons of similar types of regime.[1]

Furthermore, the reasons why corruption is tolerated may vary over time. When there are deep ideological conflicts at issue in a society, corruption may not seem very salient to voters. They may tolerate a level of corruption from those who govern them, reckoning that to do so is better than to allow the opposition to come to power. A similar attitude may prevail among voters from particular geographical regions. They too may see the effective representation of local or regional interests as far more salient than the absence of corruption. In addition to salience there is also the question of dissonance reduction. In polarised societies, whether the polarisation is based on ideology or territory, it is probably more difficult for political opponents to exploit charges of corruption effectively, for voters are far more likely to discount them as politically biased.[2]

Understanding a society's attitude towards corruption, then, requires that we consider not only attitudes towards the law and its status held by various political actors, but also the structure of broader political conflicts, and how these may change over time. In particular, different parts of society – ideological sub-cultures or peripheral regions, for example – may take different views of corruption, especially in a society with such strong social and geographical fractures as post-war Italy.

THE SYSTEMATIC NATURE OF MODERN ITALIAN CORRUPTION

The chief purpose of this essay is to explain rather than to document. The evidence of corruption emerging in the last two years has been thoroughly documented by massive press coverage of charges and trials, and by a numerous commentaries and academic analyses.[3] However, some description is necessary before constructing an explanatory model, because what any model needs to account for is the *systematic* nature of Italian corruption. This, in turn, is related both to its role as the central mechanism for financing parties, and their internal factions, and to the complex relationships on which it was built. The latter have involved not only the usual private interests who – through contracting between private suppliers and the state and local authorities – form a ubiquitous source of funds for political corruption, but also organised crime (i.e. the southern-based mafia, *camorra* and *'ndranghetta*), and the state sector of the economy. Moreover, the extensive nature of corrupt practices appears to have been built on a system of protection which – at least at the level of national politicians – has impeded the normal mechanisms for checking, controlling, investigating, and prosecuting politicians involved in corruption. Before discussing such networks, we need at least a minimal account of how they developed.

The liberal state

Italy has a long-standing tradition of political corruption, and the ability of senior politicians to evade prosecution over a period stretching back to Italian unification has affected attitudes, institutions and procedures in a lasting way. The political scandal as a mechanism for shocking voters into punishing their political leaders was already thoroughly devalued by the end of the liberal era, during which there were few periods when one large public scandal or another was not resident in the short-term political memory. The institution of parliamentary immunity has its origins in this period. To prosecute ministers, the investigating judge had to request authorisation from parliament. Without authorisation, proceedings had to be dropped. Requests for authorisation increased from three per year in the period 1861–76 to over thirteen per year in the period 1900–19 (Cazzola 1988: 113). The percentage of such authorisations granted, though higher than the level to which it fell in republican Italy, was always low. The justification of the mechanism was that deputies and senators had to be protected against political persecution through the courts, but its abuse in the face of widely suspected corruption led inevitably to indifference and resignation among many voters.[4]

The republican state

When democracy returned after the fascist interlude, the republican state was built more explicitly on the rule of law and judicial independence than the liberal monarchy had been. However, the possibilities for political corruption were gradually much enhanced. The size of the public sector had expanded considerably with the interventionism of the fascist regime, and this continued in the 1950s and 1960s. Italy developed the usual post-war range of welfare-state services and public enterprises in transport, energy, communications and local services. But it also developed an unusually large, joint (private–public) sector known as the 'state participations' (IRI, ENI, EFIM, etc.). While in the early post-war years such agencies were in the hands of independent-minded public-sector entrepreneurs, over time they came, through a process of *lottizzazione* (literally 'political parcelling out'), to be cherished prizes in the enduring interparty struggle for political patronage. The bulk of the financial sector was also in public, and equally politicised, hands.

Political parties too were fundamentally different from their pre-fascist counterparts. With universal suffrage, they became large political machines with substantial appetites for resources. They were not only numerous (there were never fewer than eight in parliament), but also internally divided, with factions in the governing parties operating machines that devoured significant resources in their own right. Moreover, for the governing parties, these machines were certainly not built on voluntarism alone. Over time, their real numerical strength came to be rooted in the southern half of the country, where political and interest-group participation had always been low – a clear indication of the clientelist nature grass-roots' party organisation had assumed (Hine 1987: 82–6). These two sets of developments complemented one another, and provided facilitating conditions for an extension of corrupt practices in both public-sector contracting with the private sector and the syphoning of money from public-sector agencies to political parties. The formidable financial needs of Italian parties were serviced through rigged contracts, illicit payments, loans, transfers, or contributions in kind from public-sector bodies.

The quantity of evidence about how these mechanisms worked is now overwhelming. What is less clear is how rapidly the practice of corruption had been growing over time, since most of the cases brought to light dealt with relatively recent offences. Nevertheless, the way in which pressures built up in the relationship between the political class and the judiciary in the 1980s, and the gradually increasing seriousness of the scandals which did reach public consciousness, suggests that an incremental process *was* taking place. In the early post-war period, there were relatively few major *causes célèbres* and what did percolate to the surface of public consciousness was not initially connected, for the most part, with the public-sector and party finance. Even in the 1960s, the signs of corruption were still relatively sporadic: the most notable being the Trabucchi scandal, named after the finance minister alleged to have rigged private contracts in two state monopolies – bananas and tobacco – to obtain campaign contributions. Only in the 1970s did evidence of corruption begin to filter out on a more extensive scale, and to touch higher political levels. The Lockheed affair in 1974 precipitated a – largely ineffective – reform of party finance law.[5] Shortly thereafter, the collapse of Michele Sindona's private international banking empire threw up for the first time a clear connection between extensive political corruption at national level and organised crime. The violent deaths first of the liquidator of the collapsed banks, and then (allegedly by suicide in jail) of Sindona himself pointed towards a possibility that was becoming alarmingly evident: that a loose interweaving was emerging between the mafia, the security services, factions within particular governing parties and occult channels of international finance.

The clearest evidence for this emerged in the P-2 affair, which coincided with, and was connected to several others: the collapse of a second financial empire, this time Roberto Calvi's Banco Ambrosiano; the so-called petrol tax scandal, involving none other than the head of the Guardia di Finanze (the Italian national tax inspectorate); the murder of a journalist, Mino Pecorelli, while gathering information about P-2 and the petrol tax scandal; and the ENI-Petromin affair, involving extensive kickbacks on overseas oil contracts. From records obtained by the investigators, it appears that nearly 1,000 individuals including several dozen politicians, virtually all chiefs of staff of the various security services, and numerous other senior public officials, industrialists, journalists and magistrates were members of a secret organisation whose purposes, while obscure, involved numerous acts of fraud and subversion, and a high degree of mutual assistance between its members. The latter were manifestly selected for their ability to assist one another in dealings connected with high finance, security and criminal investigations, press relations and public appointments. It is unclear exactly how far such connections involved outright violence, but an extensive series of murders and terrorist attacks from the late 1970s onwards – in which subsequent investigations pointed in the direction of covert links between organised crime, terrorist groups, and the security services – certainly provide circumstantial evidence of such connections.[6]

The institutionalization of corruption and the judicial response

P-2, and the scandals to which it was linked, several of which were of prodigious financial dimensions, provided clear evidence of extensive corruption across a wide range of Italian public life. But it also set in motion a slow, initially almost imperceptible, change of outlook among voters, journalists and, most important of all, the judiciary. This change was further assisted by the much more threatening context of organised crime. The growth of the drugs trade in the late 1970s and 1980s increased the role of organised crime syndicates in Italian political life. In the south, their control of votes and funds available for party use could not be matched by voluntary activists. Gradually, they infiltrated key factions of the main governing parties, establishing an unspoken and uncomfortable *modus vivendi* at local level which leaders at national level could not easily ignore (Chubb 1982: 138–51; Gambetta 1993: 182–7).

These developments substantially increased tension between certain members of the political class and the judiciary. The tension was heightened by the ambiguity surrounding the judiciary itself. Nominally independent, it had since the 1960s been divided into different more or less explicitly political tendencies. Among its younger elements was a group reluctant to accept the political limits on judicial freedom posed by the ever-present likelihood that investigations pointing towards senior political circles would be taken over by parliament and buried in extensive investigations or thwarted by the foreclosure of parliamentary immunity. The result was an enduring battle against an allegedly 'politicised' judiciary, waged especially by the Socialist Party, which considerably impeded the task of prosecuting corrupt politicians. Matters came to a head in the middle of the decade when a referendum on the issue of the civil liability of the judiciary was pushed through under vigorous PSI sponsorship (Turone 1992: 320–30). Henceforth investigating judges could be sued personally by aggrieved citizens, and shortly thereafter a Milanese judge was successfully sued by a major property developer he had been investigating over planning consents. Admittedly, by the 1990s, public sympathy had switched decisively back towards the judiciary, and the 1987 referendum came to look like an anomaly, but the very fact that it could have been passed at all demonstrated how badly relations between politicians and judges had deteriorated, and how difficult it was to keep the judiciary out of the political sphere.

The 1980s thus brought increasing evidence of systematic corruption in Italian politics, though in comparison with what was to emerge after the 1992 election, public knowledge and understanding of the levels of corruption being practised were still minimal. In the tactical war being waged between party secretariats and the judiciary, the parties – mainly through the effective conspiracy of silence maintained by all participants in the system of illegal party finance – retained the upper hand most of the time. Occasionally, mainly at local level, things went wrong and there were municipal scandals like that which brought down the ruling coalition in Turin and exposed the local Socialist Party to much humiliation. Occasionally events erupted into violence when the multiple pressures of the system broke down. This was especially the case with organised crime in the south. The link between governing parties and individuals clearly associated with criminal organisations was often too visible for comfort. When public pressure for more effective measures built up and parliamentary commissions of inquiry demanded action leaders with such links were under pressure from both sides. A few who failed to deliver were even assassinated by their semi-detached clients in the underworld.[7] However, these pathological outbursts were in general limited to areas where organised crime had infiltrated what elsewhere were more mundane and stable systems of corruption. They created serious tensions inside the national party networks, and contributed to the re-emergence of a deep-rooted north–south psychological divide in political life. But they did not reach crisis point until 1992.

The collapse

It is not the main purpose of this essay to explain why the climate did change so dramatically in 1992. The full answer will only be known when recent events can be seen in proper perspective. Many factors brought about the change. Some operated at the political level, where the substantial shift in voting habits, first in the north, then more generally, removed the – hitherto safe – assumption that the same parties would remain in power well into the future. It disoriented local politicians and local entrepreneurs in search of contracts, who had previously been able to assume that their relationships would continue in relative safety with little danger of new parties coming into office to expose what had been going on or to renege on previously agreed arrangements. It suggested that political protection at the highest level in Rome might no longer be forthcoming and that the climate of public opinion was becoming more sensitive to the issues of good-quality, incorrupt, public services.

Other factors operated at the judicial level. A new generation of younger, independent-minded judges was clearly emerging in the 1980s and came into influential positions at around this time. The work of the so-called 'pool' led by Antonio Di Pietro in Milan, whose careful investigative work on local-authority contracting in Milan caused the initial breakthrough, is the clearest example of this. The methods employed by this new group were, to say the least, novel. Especially controversial was their employment of lengthy pre-trial detention periods while they gathered evidence and waited for their suspects to crack and confess – as many did. The extensive development of plea-bargaining was also highly controversial, but in many cities it led to something like a stampede to confess once the edifice of corruption started to crumble.

Whatever factors are judged to be the main underlying causes of the breakthrough achieved after the 1992 election, it is clear that during the 1970s and 1980s a system of carefully calibrated and quite institutionalised procedures developed for sharing these revenues out among a wide range of parties. Exposure of the affairs of local government, first in Milan, then elsewhere, has shown that kickbacks not only became the norm, but spread to wider areas of public-sector activity. The conspiracy extended not just to politically appointed senior management in public-sector firms, but to the top of private-sector companies like FIAT and Olivetti. The greatest of all was the fraud against the exchequer perpetrated by the parties through the private-sector company Feruzzi, the public-sector company ENI, and their chemicals-sector joint venture, Enimont.[8] Astonishingly, even the Northern League, a movement founded on public revulsion against political corruption, admitted taking an illicit campaign contribution from the Feruzzi network.

EXPLANATIONS OF SYSTEMATIC CORRUPTION

From what has been described above, it should be clear that there are no simple explanations of corruption in Italian politics. Imposing an explanatory framework, however sophisticated, involves a great simplification of a very complex social process. An adequate account would have to combine various levels of explanation:

- a 'developmental' account of the way in which key stages of political development, such as regime change, and the evolution and nature of party competition, have affected the incentives towards and perceptions of corruption;
- a 'macro-level' account of institutional relationships such as those between the judiciary and the political class, and between politicians and economic actors in both the public and private sector, including the internal operation of political parties, the way public agencies are managed, the mechanisms for controlling the judiciary, and so on;
- a 'micro-level' account of individual mechanisms of corruption and its concealment, covering what individuals do, with whom, for what immediate purpose, and how far and why they get away with it;
- a psychological account of the climate of public and private morality against which background the agents of corruption pursue their aims, including an account of the status and legitimacy of public institutions, the attitudes of important arbiters of morality such as the church, etc. ,

The first of these, the developmental account, must inevitably include a number of culture-specific considerations. For although we do not know exactly how far corruption in post-war Italy has *increased* over thirty or forty years, there are grounds for supposing that it has done so, and the explanation seems to lie in certain peculiar features of Italian political development stemming from the dual nature of political culture. The coexistence of social structures which, for deep-rooted historical reasons, differ greatly in economic development, social and religious habits, and styles of political relationships, has combined with a system of *national* political parties that have, until quite recently, held the political system together surprisingly effectively. As a result, over time, features of these sub-national political cultures have percolated upwards into national party networks.

What is peculiar to Italian political development, however, is that despite the considerable economic development achieved by the more 'backward' parts of the peninsula, the overall political system, including sub-national politics in the northern half of the country, seems to have acquired many of the characteristics originally most prevalent in the south. In the context of the 'modernisation' issues raised earlier, it might almost be said that political development has reversed the direction of expected causality. The economic and political development of the north has not modernised southern political relationships. Rather, in so far as corruption is closely linked with clientelistic machine-politics, requires substantial political resources and is facilitated by extensive state intervention in the economy, then such political relationships appear to have spread gradually from the south to other parts of the country. For most of the post-war period, this has been limited to the governing parties. In recent years, especially where corruption has been most systematically institutionalised, it has even spread to opposition parties as well.

Institutional incentives

Explaining *why* economic development has failed to counteract the spread of southern political practices then takes us to the second and third levels of analysis outlined above: especially the institutional relationships between the political class, the judiciary and economic actors. It requires first a complex account of the ways in which the governing parties have changed over time (in particular the growing strength of southern voters, members and leaders within them) and why it has become increasingly necessary for them to dispose of very large financial resources – only available through the state, or through systematic, largely forced, bribes from those who had to work alongside the state.

Part of that explanation lies in the understandably difficult task governing parties faced in obtaining resources through voluntary party fundraising activities, in a society where voluntarism is not well developed, and in which the governing parties have in any case been in power too long to sustain any strong sense of innovative purpose or programmatic commitment. Interestingly, looking closely at particular periods in the recent history of the two main governing parties, it is evident that the struggle for resources that has helped breed corruption has not gone uncontested by would-be reformers. There have been cycles of attempted renewal (for the example the early periods as DC party secretary, of Beniamino Zaccagnini (1975–9) and Ciriaco De Mita (1982–8)), but these efforts were largely unsuccessful. The self-conscious efforts to halt the spreading influence of organised crime and illicit funding have quickly proved counter-productive for both electoral support and party cohesion, and have been quietly dropped (Chubb 1986: 69–86).

A further part of the explanation lies in the fragmentation of the parties themselves and the proportional mentality by which all factions in the governing coalition have had to be incorporated into the distribution of power. Including everyone, even at times through package deals with the opposition, has ensured there are few whistle-blowers or protesters left on the outside (Della Porta 1993: 107–9). The system has been fed by specific formal mechanisms as well, foremost among them the preference vote in parliamentary and local elections. The latter, only finally abolished in the electoral reform of 1993, turned elections between parties into secondary contests between candidates on the same party list of candidates. The mechanism was a major incentive to factionalism. It encouraged alliances between local groups of candidates and particular regional and national leaders, and generated much electoral malpractice: most notably, interparty conspiracies to allocate on ballot papers the preferences left blank by many voters. The system made elections very expensive to fight, and encouraged parties to collude on a wider front beyond the ballot box.[9]

A final part of the explanation at this level focuses on the inherent difficulty experienced by the judiciary in prosecuting corruption. Here there were numerous factors at work. Some involved moral pressure such as constant claims by parties of political bias by investigating judges. Some involved institutional/legal pressure, such as repealing the judges' immunity from civil prosecution. Some involved outright coercion through mafia-organised assassinations of senior judicial and police figures in Sicily, or simply intimidation, as in the case of the inadequate personal protection frequently afforded members of the judiciary. However, the underlying problems were the lack of objective proof, the tightly closed communities that practised corruption, and the severe shortage of resources enjoyed by the judiciary in seeking to break these communities open. On the one hand, mechanisms of corruption left few clear traces since most formal dealings and exchanges would involve middlemen and brokers, or at best faction officials and treasurers, rather than high-profile parliamentary leaders. On the other, without clear confessions or denunciations from businessmen and others who were the co-conspirators of the political leaders, evidence was difficult to assemble. Funds accumulated through political corruption tended to be held in secret accounts, often offshore, which were virtually impossible to trace. Only a wholesale willingness of the business class to stand up against politicians and denounce them to the judiciary would have made this possible, and since so many of this class were already implicated, it was necessary to await the special conditions of 1992, explained above, to create the necessary breakthrough.

Moreover, the difficulty of prosecuting those at the top of this system of vertical exchanges was reinforced by the extensive use of parliamentary immunity. As we have seen, this mechanism had its origins in nineteenth-century Italy, but its role was enshrined in articles 68 and 96 of the republican constitution in a particularly comprehensive way. Until its reform in 1993 under the pressure of an outraged public, virtually no minister was sent by Parliament for prosecution by the constitutional court under article 96; Mario Tanassi, one of the very few who were, and who was found guilty in the Lockheed affair, had his sentence reduced to a derisory period under the 're-educative' supervision of the Rome social service department. Likewise, the judiciary was authorised to proceed with prosecution against very few members of parliament. And as observers frequently pointed out, the basis on which parliament took its decisions in this regard lacked any procedural foundation, with few rules to guide the gathering of evidence or its presentation, or even an effective time limit within which judgments should occur (Caferra 1992; 155–63).

The weakness of normative sanctions

Ultimately, the explanations mapped out above return to the major structural feature which distinguishes Italy from most other post-war European democracies: the 'blocked' and polarised nature of party competition and the absence of turnover in government. These conditions have given politicians both the assurance and the time necessary to build mechanisms of control, greatly lowering the risks of exposure and punishment. However, interpretations of corruption based on rational-actor calculations of opportunity and of the risks of detection are probably insufficient. There certainly are structural incentives to corruption, and mechanisms to check and control corruption work poorly. But liberal democracies rely on much more than procedural rules, sanctions and penalties. They need the socialisation processes of the civic culture which sustain procedural norms and values. Without a more culturally directed understanding of the attitudes of politicians and ordinary voters towards law and legality in both political life and civil society we cannot fully understand why Italy seems so vulnerable to corruption.

Studying the production and maintenance of such norms is fraught with pitfalls, and what is outlined here is little more than a framework for further analysis, but there is at least a case for arguing that in the Italian context much of the problem lies in the ambiguous status of the law and procedural norms in general, and that this has contributed to fundamental weaknesses in the socialisation processes. Certainly, actors in Italian political and business life seem to be affected by a climate of moral relativism in which the superiority of the liberal state and its laws does not go unquestioned. This stems ultimately from the lack of congruence between the formal constitutional framework and its rules, on the one side, and the realities of political power and its exercise through informal channels (parties and factions, interparty forums, outside advisers, special working parties) on the other. Precisely because it has always been acknowledged that Italian liberal democracy does not work in the way claimed by its constitutional architects, there is an expectation and almost an acceptance that the real map of power is likely to be different from the formal one.

There are numerous manifestations of this. In a sense the most comprehensive is identifiable in the early years of the Republic, in the emptying of much of the content of the 1948 constitution, over the ensuing decade, through failed implementation and failed enforcement. As many observers argued, the 'First Republic' rapidly gave way, under the political pressures of the Cold War, to a 'Second' very different in nature (Cheli 1978: 56–9). The regions, the constitutional court, judicial independence, direct democracy, and many civil rights, were simply not introduced for many years. An equally powerful mismatch between theory and reality lay in the area of administrative law. Liberal-democratic theory in Italy has always relied heavily on the notion that administrative law provides a more effective check against the misuse of executive power than do the Westminster-style virtues of parliamentary sovereignty or the more informal freedoms of voter sovereignty and press freedom. Hence the panoply of administrative checks inherent in the council of state, the regional administrative tribunals, the court of accounts, etc., and the huge body of administrative law which has grown up to surround the public service, and which puts a heavy premium on legal expertise in the profession of administration. Ironically, however, it is precisely such a framework which has contributed, in many eyes, to an undermining of the centrality of law. By making administrative law so complex, Italian government has actually encumbered policy-makers with slow, blunt and often inappropriate instruments that get in the way of policy objectives and often require special, fragmentary and frequently temporary correctives in the form of even more administrative law. Indeed, the real task of many of the most effective and imaginative senior civil servants is to find ways around, or through, the administrative law jungle for their political masters.

A third example is found in the ambiguous boundary between public and private in economic life. In so far as markedly different principles of accountability, and of welfare calculations, underlie the use of resources in the public and private spheres, then all modern states face this problem. The potential factor-misallocation and the disincentives to productivity inherent in the introduction of public intervention into areas of economic life governed largely by market principles is a long-standing source of concern for economists. The consequences of the introduction of market principles into the public sector in an effort to counter some of these tendencies is a more recent concern, but such action can also jeopardise fundamental principles of public accountability and probity. Interestingly, in Italy, the boundary between public and private has been more porous, and for longer, than in most European countries. The existence of a large mixed public–private sector, in which the state shares the ownership of banks or manufacturing concerns with private stakeholders, in businesses that compete alongside fully privatised concerns, creates a fundamental ambivalence in the purpose of such organisations. The pricing at which assets are transferred back and forth between the public and private domain (as in the notorious Enimont case), provides extensive scope for a confusion and concealment of motives and objectives, and blurs the principles guiding the behaviour of many of the actors involved.

A final example lies in the role of political parties. Italy has at one level a very strong form of party government in which parties seem to monopolise processes of political articulation and policy implementation. Yet its version of party government does not imply a close nexus between electoral choice, party or coalition programme and government output. Coalitions are not natural or cohesive in ideological or policy terms; they are not self-sufficient in parliament (the boundary between government and opposition is indistinct); nor finally can they articulate clear policy options. Moreover, though strong in organisational terms (they have large nominal membership roles and employ many party officials) parties are weak as mechanisms for making policy and rely heavily on outside experts, consultants, academics and interest groups. Thus Italian party government is built on a fundamental ambiguity: publicly, ideological and social cleavages are trumpeted in a crude form of megaphone politics; behind closed doors, policy is made through opaque bargains crossing many apparently unbridgeable boundaries.

It is not surprising, therefore, that Italian politics seems to operate in a climate of moral relativism. The constitutional map of power and its formal principles have often departed quite radically from the practical reality. Government processes at many levels are poorly institutionalised and opaque. For businesses and citizens, getting satisfactory outcomes from government has depended on linkages, personal contacts, and informal arenas which are not easily understandable, and not always dependable. But perhaps worse than this, for the prestige and supremacy of the rule of law, is the range of institutions which claim an equal, if not higher, moral status to that of the state. Foremost among these, in many eyes, is the Catholic church, which in some areas of personal and moral life offers its own moral code. The church came to terms with the secular state in Italy only very late (well into the twentieth century), and by a formal *treaty* incorporated into the 1948 constitution. Despite a subsequent revision, the treaty (the Concordat) still gives the church certain rights to moral and spiritual leadership within Italian society. Linked to this is an imprecise sense that the church, rather than the law, can guide individual consciences in areas of civil life, because the church, through its lay and political contact organisations, most notably the Christian Democrat Party, is indirectly engaged in political life, even though it would publicly deny this to be the case. One institution that has been said to have provided some evidence of this, in the shape of interesting, though inherently unverifiable journalistic investigation, is that of the confessional box, where there is evidence of high levels of tolerance towards political corruption – at least when confined to illicit party financing in the interests of the Catholic movement.[10]

The alternative sub-culture to that of the church is often said to be the collectivist/Marxist one, which has in the past expressed an even more fundamental critique of the liberal state than the Church itself. The ideological polarisation of Cold War politics set the left against the bourgeois political centre even more starkly than the triumph of the secular state set liberals against catholics in early post-war Italy. Though the gradual transformation of the Communist Party reduced this tension in later decades, many liberals blamed the Communist Party itself for being the unwitting midwife of left-wing terrorism in the 1970s. Its long-standing critique of liberal society, they argued, had contributed to an undermining of the legitimacy of the state. Like the liberal case against the Church, this argument is essentially unverifiable, but has elements of plausibility in the evidence on the socialisation processes of former terrorists, and in the persistence of a radical segment of the electorate which continues to exercise a powerful influence on the left of the former Communist Party, and in the trade unions.

Beyond these two classical sub-cultural influences there are other active social institutions which work in the same way. The pull of the local community as a source of loyalty for many Italian citizens is clearly one. The dual sense of identity has traditionally been strong in the poorer peripheral regions. The weather eye that government in Rome has to keep on the sharing out of centrally allocated benefits to local communities is regularly underlined by anomic outbursts against the state in the shape of social protest, violence, occupations and even kidnappings. The six-month period of riots in Reggio Calabria in 1970/1, when the city failed to win nomination as regional capital in the new regionalisation process, is legendary – and was rewarded with a steelworks! Even a government as market-oriented as the recent Ciampi government (1993/4) felt it prudent to mitigate the effect of a major plant closure by ENI in the face of occupations and protests in the province. Perhaps more surprising, however, has been the emergence of similar tendencies in the north. The impact of the Northern League and its associated groups has not yet led to outright social protest or violence (though tax-strikes and even a 'secession' have been threatened) but the clear message that the centralised unitary state has lost the moral authority to govern, is an unmistakeable part of the League's message and its apparent popularity.

Other social institutions challenging the authority of the state's legal order include networks of organised crime and secret elite networks such as that discovered in the P-2 case. The informal social networks, and the 'business of private protection' contained in organised crime, while not necessarily constituting alternative legal systems in their own right as some have claimed for the mafia (see Gambetta 1993: 4–7), nevertheless force the state itself to negotiate, and to recognise their existence. They also subvert at least some of the state's functions sufficiently effectively to persuade individuals to entrust themselves, albeit unwillingly, to the 'protection' of the criminal syndicate, rather than to the state.

There are, therefore, a range of agencies which erode the status of the law in modern Italy. There are also many habits and practices in ordinary social life which have the same effect, and which are themselves probably reinforced by the low prestige of the public domain. The widespread habits of absenteeism from work in the public service, and the prevalence of second (private-sector) jobs undertaken at the expense of commitment to the first (public-sector) job, are certainly manifestations of this which erode not just the productivity of the public sector, but the entire ethos of public service. The widespread willingness to cheat public insurance schemes by absenteeism from work, and by spurious claims for invalidity benefit, sustained by the connivance of the medical profession, falls into a similar mould as, at another level, does manipulation of equity markets. Finally, there are other widely practised categories of petty and not so petty crime, such as systematic flaunting of traffic regulations and extensive tax evasion. So great is the latter, in fact, that entire categories of the self-employed are taxed on imputed earnings for their trade or profession in an unashamed acknowledgement by the authorities that evasion is indeed the norm. The extent of these practices has been used in some quarters to suggest that the Italian population has, in its extensively corrupt political leadership, only got the political class its own disrespect for the law deserves.

Establishing the direction of causality, let alone assessing the overall worth of such an argument, is impossible, but the private and civil dimension to the syndrome of low levels of respect for the law cannot entirely be ignored. It is not that the low prestige of the law necessarily makes Italy a violent or otherwise inherently uncivilised place to be (though there are areas where violence is alarmingly common). On the contrary, many institutions of social cohesion work rather effectively. But the relationship between the state on the one hand, and the private citizen, the public official and the elected representative on the other, does seem to be affected by a belief that flouting the law is not to be placed in the same category as other forms of crime, and is justifiable by the low status and ineffectiveness of the state, by the 'victimless' nature of crimes against it, and by the fact that so many other politicians, officials, and ordinary citizens are acting in a nominally 'illegal' way and are regularly going unpunished.

What emerges with striking regularity from the penitent reflections of politicians and businessmen caught up in recent scandals is the extensive belief that, as far as the receipt of undeclared party finance contributions was concerned, they were only doing what everyone in the party system did; they were not doing it for their own benefit; and that if party democracy were to be effective, substantial financial resources were necessary. The last point, at least, looks contestable and there is no doubt a significant element of *ex post facto* justification in such protests. On the other hand, no less an institution than the Constitutional Court, in its judgment of 2 May 1979 in the trial of

Mario Tanassi, the minister impeached in connection with the Lockheed affair, could assert with extraordinary frankness:

> The Court is not unaware that the episode which has been brought to its attention took place before the entry into force of law n. 195 (on the financing of political parties); in a situation, therefore, in which the widespread practice of contributions, not all illegal, to political parties, could have weakened the legal and moral sensibilities of some of those found guilty.
>
> (quoted in Caferra 1992: 142)

Given that the 1974 law on party finance is universally agreed to have failed completely in its efforts to cap the growth of party appetites for finance and that unrecorded contributions to parties probably continued in the 1980s at an even faster pace, it is to be assumed that members of the political class continued to have their 'legal and moral sensibilities' weakened in this way.

CONCLUSION

There is no single explanation for the extremely high level of corruption in Italian politics exposed by judicial campaigns since the 1992 election. Despite a process of economic and political modernisation which has brought profound – and ideologically depolarising – changes to the political system over four decades, there are structural features inherent in constitutional arrangements, social structure and the shape of the party system which act as incentives to high levels of corruption. However, these factors alone do not seem adequate to account for the extent of the problem. All liberal democracies face difficulties in devising adequate procedural controls to combat corruption, and those in Italy are not, except in the absence of turnover in government, fundamentally different from those found in other European liberal democracies. To understand the systematic and extensive practices which have developed in recent years, a part of the explanation must also be sought in attitudes towards the law, its status and meaning. Many of these attitudes have themselves developed over the long run as rational responses to objective shortcomings of the state, its policies, and its procedures. In the short run, however, it is at least arguable that they have an indepedendent force in their own right on political behaviour both at mass and elite level. The test of that proposition will be the capacity of procedural improvements in protection against corruption, and increases in the probability of detection – both of which seem likely to be generated by recent events – to make a real contribution to eradicating the problem. If they do, then the status of the law may come to be seen as less significant than outlined here. If the process is a much slower one than many optimists currently hope, it will suggest that underlying normative factors really are important and independent explanatory variables.

NOTES

1　cf. Heidenheimer's distinction between kinship-based systems, client-based systems, boss-follower machine type, and 'modern civic culture' (Heidenheimer *et al.*, 1989: 149–63) and his account of different levels of and attitudes towards corruption across this range.

2　Sicilian voters appear to have done so fairly consistently. Nuncio Nasi, deputy for the Sicilian city of Trapani at the turn of the century, despite the distinction of having been impeached for syphoning off funds from teachers' pay while Minister of Education, was regularly returned to Parliament in every subsequent election (Turone 1992: 91–8). In post-war Sicily too, there is evidence that voters expect, even demand, behaviour that neutral observers would define as corrupt (Chubb 1986: 81–4).

3　A well-documented narrative is Bellu and Bonsanti (1993), which has an extensive chronology of events from late 1989 till mid-1993. The best 'confession' is probably that of Licandro and Varano (1993), tracing the mechanisms employed by a former mayor of the city of Reggio Calabria. Carlucci (1992) documents the unfolding of the evidence of the Milanese investigations in great detail. Della Porta (1992) provides a useful overall framework for understanding the micro-level mechanisms of corruption.

4　The literature, frequently polemical, on parliamentary immunity, is extensive. See, *inter alia*, Zagrebelsky (1979) and Berlinguer (1991).

5　The US Senate's Church Commission revealed that Italy was a central player, purchasing Hercules C-130 transport planes for which, it later became clear, the armed services had little use. On law n. 195, 2 May 1974, concerning party finance, see D'Orazio (1974: 407–25) and Caferra (1992: 139–43). The crucial shortcoming of the legislation was that it was not followed up, as originally intended, with further reforms to procedures governing declarations of party income and parliamentary immunity from prosecution.

6　The most notorious such case was that of General Carlo Alberto Dalla Chiesa, the special anti-mafia investigator, who was assassinated in Sicily in 1982: the first of several of his profession over the following decade. In the late 1970s and 1980s numerous politicians were also murdered or died in mysterious circumstances: Moro, Bisaglia, Lodovico, Ruffilli, Tarantelli and others. Later, in Sicily, the killing focused on senior island politicians with clear mafia connections. However, exactly which groups were involved in which outrages was rarely clear. The report of the P-2 commission is found in Camera dei deputati – Senato della Repubblica (1984).

7 'Delivery' in this context meant, for example, denying the Sicilian police and judiciary the resources necessary to work effectively, or securing the release at appeal of convicted mafia members. Many of the convictions in the so-called maxi-trials of the late 1980s – mass trials based on the testimony of supergrasses – were overturned on appeal by a Court of Appeal judge widely regarded as sympathetic to such groups.

8 When the issue of who controlled Enimont proved unresolvable, ENI, for a grossly overinflated sum, bought out the Feruzzi interest, in return for which Feruzzi then massively rewarded the political parties through private offshore bank accounts. Ironically, however, the enormous profit made by Feruzzi did not save it from the same eventual fate as the Sindona and Calvi empires. Within a couple of years it too was bankrupt, and its former president, Raul Gardini – Italy's most glamorous entrepreneur of the 1980s – had committed suicide. Other even more publicly repugnant kickbacks revealed in investigations in 1992/3 included substantial kickbacks demanded by parties from Third World countries on transfers of foreign aid and from manufacturers of pharmaceuticals to facilitate the award of product licences.

9 The preference vote became a major focus for proponents of electoral reform and the 1991 referendum limiting its use to one preference rather than three or four was a major boost to the reform campaign. See Hine, (1993: 130–1) and Pasquino (1993: 7–31, 337–58).

10 Two recently published exercises of this type are Guerri (1993) and Nicotri (1993).

REFERENCES

Barbacetto, G. and Veltri, E. (1991) *Milano degli scandali*, Roma-Bari: Laterza.

Bellu, G. M. and Bonsanti, S. (1993) *Il crollo. Andreotti, Craxi, e il loro regime*, Roma-Bari: La Terza.

Berlinguer, G. (1991) *I duplicanti politici in Italia*, Roma-Bari: Laterza.

Caferra, V.M. (1992) *Il sistema della corruzione: le ragioni, i soggetti, i luoghi* Roma-Bari: Laterza.

Camera dei deputati – Senato della Repubblica, (1984) *Relazione della Commissione parlamentare d'inchiesta sulla loggia P2* (Rel. Tina Anselmi: Comunicata alle camere 12 luglio 1984): Roma.

Carlucci, A. (1992) *Tangentomani. Storie, affari e tutti i documenti sui barbari che hanno saccheggiato Milano*, Milano: Baldini and Castoldi.

Cazzola, F. (1988) *Della corruzione. Fisiologia e patologia di un sistema politico*, Bologna: Il Mulino.

——— (1992) *L'Italia del Pizzo: Fenomenologia della tangente quotidiana*, Turin: Einaudi.

Cheli, E., (1978) *Costituzione e sviluppo delle istituzioni in Italia*, Bologna: Il Mulino.

Chubb, J., (1982) *Patronage, Power, and Poverty in Southern Italy: A Tale of Two Cities*, Cambridge: Cambridge University Press.

——— (1986) 'The Christian Democrat Party: reviving or surviving?', in R.

Leonardi and R. Y. Nanetti (eds) *Italian Politics: A Review*, Vol. 1, London: Frances Pinter.

Chubb, J. and Vannicelli, M. (1988) 'Italy: A web of scandals in a flawed democracy' in A. S. Markovits and M. Silverstein (eds) *The Politics of Scandal: Power and Process in Liberal Democracies*, New York: Holmes and Meier.

Della Porta, D. (1992) *Lo scambio occulto. Casi di corruzione politica in Italia*, Bologna: Il Mulino.

——— (1993) 'Milan: immoral capital', in S. Hellman and G. Pasquino (eds) *Italian Politics: A Review*, Vol. 8, London: Frances Pinter.

D'Orazio, G. (1974) 'Il finanziamento pubblico dei partiti', *Diritto e Società*: 407–25.

Galli, G. (1983) *L'Italia sotterranea. Storia, politica e scandali* Rome-Bari: Laterza.

Gambetta, D. (1993) *The Sicilian Mafia: The Private Business of Private Protection*, Cambridge, Mass. and London: Harvard University Press.

Guerri, G.B. (1993) *Io ti assolvo. Etica, politica, sesso: i confessori di fronte a vecchi e nuovi peccati*, Milano: Baldini and Castoldi.

Heidenheimer, A. (1989) 'Perspectives on the perception of corruption', in A. Heidenheimer, M. Johnson and V.T. LeVine (eds) *Political Corruption: a Handbook*, New Brunswick and Oxford: Transaction Books.

Hine, D. (1987) 'Italy: Parties and party government under pressure', in A. Ware (ed.) *Political Parties: Electoral Change and Structural Response*, Oxford: Basil Blackwell.

——— (1993) *Governing Italy: the Politics of Bargained Pluralism*, Oxford, Oxford University Press.

Iacopini, V. (1981) *Pecorelli-OP: storia di un agenzia giornalistico* Milano: SugarCo.

Licandro, A. and Varano, A. (1993) *La città dolente. Confessione di un sindaco corrotto*, Turin: Einaudi.

Nicotri, P. (1993) *Tangenti in confessionale: come i preti rispondano a corrotti e corrottori*, Venezia: Marsiglio.

Pasquino, G. (ed.) (1993) *Votare un candidato solo. Le conseguenze politiche della preferenza unica*, Bologna: Il Mulino.

Pizzorusso, A. (1986) 'Correnti della magistratura e politicazzione' *Quaderni della giustizia*, 62: 4–25.

Rodotà, S. and Veltri, E. (1991) *Milano degli scandali*, Roma-Bari: Laterza.

Sani, G. (1980) 'The political culture of Italy: continuity and change', in G. Almond and S. Verba (eds) *The Civic Culture Revisited*, Boston: Little Brown.

Spagnuolo, G. (1990) *I reati di illegale finanziamento dei partiti politici*, Padova.

Turone, S. (1992) *Politica ladra: storia della corruzione in Italia, 1861–1992*, Roma-Bari: Laterza.

Zagrebelsky, G. (1979) *Le immunità parlamentare. Natura e limiti di una garanzia costituzionali*, Turin: Einaudi.

Zariski, R. (1972) *Italy: the Politics of Uneven Development*, Hinsdale, Ill.: Dryden.

12 Psychology and political theory
Does personality make a difference?

Tim Gray

INTRODUCTION

Hugh Berrington's favourite teaching course has been his under-graduate option entitled 'The Psychology of Politics'. Successive cohorts of students have flocked in large numbers to this course; at one stage it was the most popular subject in the Department. In part its popularity reflected Hugh's consummate teaching style and infectious enthusiasm for the subject. But students were also attracted by the intrinsic fascination of the material itself. Whether or not they became convinced that personality does matter in politics, they found discussion of the issue compelling. It is not hard to grasp why the study of political psychology is so riveting. It focuses on a question with which everyone can identify – the linkage between personal traits and political activities – and it brings 'the great and the good' down to our level, so to speak. It also offers endless speculation about whether history would have been different if certain political leaders had not been blessed with particular personalities.

In Hugh Berrington's publications on political psychology he is careful to avoid claiming too much for the discipline, though he does insist that it possesses at least *some* explanatory value:

> It would be absurd to argue that political decisions can *only* be explained by reference to the psychology of decision-makers. It would be no less foolish to assert that the temperament of leaders never makes a significant difference to what happens.
>
> (Berrington 1989b: 89)

He points to two central questions that occupy political psychologists:

> Students of political psychology have two prime interests: (i) What sort of people, psychologically speaking, are recruited into politics? (ii) What effects does the personality of an office-holder

have on political outcomes?

(Berrington 1989b: 86)

On the first question, Hugh Berrington associates himself (albeit cautiously) with the view of Lasswell and Iremonger that 'politics draws those *lacking* in self-esteem – people who seek fame, applause and status in compensation for the psychological bruises of adult failure or an unhappy childhood' (Berrington 1989b: 86). In the case of British Prime Ministers, for example, he notes that they were 'more likely than their peers to lose a parent in childhood'; they were 'likely to feel rejected or unappreciated as children'; they 'tended to be unsociable and introspective in childhood and retained these qualities in adult life'; and above all they were isolated: 'It is lonely at the top, because it is the lonely who seek to climb there' (Berrington 1976: 234).

On the second question, Hugh Berrington argues that in certain circumstances the influence of personality on political decisions could be decisive:

> If it is easy to find instances . . . where the personality and indeed the ideology of the policy maker is of little account, it is equally easy to visualize situations in which personality has played a decisive part. Take, for example, the appointment of Churchill as Prime Minister in 1940.

(Berrington 1976: 237)

His article on Lord Cherwell demonstrates how significant were some of Cherwell's traits in determining the British policy of area bombing of Germany in 1942–3. (Berrington 1989a)

There is, however, a third question mentioned by Hugh Berrington – that of how far a politician's belief system is affected by his personality. On this underresearched topic he comments that 'A fascinating field for speculation and enquiry is open'. (Berrington 1974: 367)

It is the aim of this chapter to explore an issue similar to that raised in this third question – the issue of how far a *political theorist's* belief system is affected by his (or her) personality. More specifically, I will try to show how the political belief systems of Thomas Hobbes and Jean-Jacques Rousseau reflected their personalities. In effect this is to transpose the format of the second question from the arena of politics to the arena of political theory; that is, to consider what effect the personality of a political theorist has on his/her political ideas. The enquiry may also shed some light on an adapted form of the first question – what sort of people, psychologically speaking, are recruited into the ranks of political theorists?

THOMAS HOBBES (1588–1679)

The personality of Thomas Hobbes is much less comprehensively documented than that of Jean-Jacques Rousseau, but from his short autobiography (composed in Latin verse at the age of eighty-four) and from his young friend John Aubrey's spirited account of him in his *Brief Lives*, we have a picture of a man whose life was coloured by fear and insecurity. His very birth at Malmesbury in Wiltshire was precipitated by his mother's anxiety at the news of the sighting of the Spanish Armada off the south coast of England:

> For Fame had rumour'd, that a Fleet at Sea,
> Wou'd cause our Nations Catastrophe;
> And hereupon it was my Mother Dear
> Did bring forth Twins at once, both Me, and Fear.
> (Hobbes 1979: 2)

Hobbes's father, a failed Anglican clergyman, contributed to his son's insecurity by fleeing to London in 1603 and abandoning his family after being excommunicated by Salisbury Consistory Court for libelling and assaulting a fellow clergyman. Hobbes never saw his father again.

After graduating from Oxford at the age of nineteen, Hobbes found a post of tutor to the family of Lord Cavendish (later the Earl of Devonshire) – a post which he occupied for much of the rest of his life, interrupted only by his exile in France, 1641–52, and by a period of financial embarrassment for the Cavendish household. Although Hobbes benefited from the extensive library maintained by the Cavendishes and from the free time he had to study, the fact is that he was a retainer (or 'domestic' as he himself put it), with all the dependence and financial uncertainty that that entailed. As an impecunious tutor Hobbes was unable to marry, and therefore he never experienced the security of a family life of his own.

Hobbes was thus rather a solitary man, ploughing his own furrow, isolated from the deep ties of intimate family relationships (though he was rumoured to have fathered an illegitimate daughter). To some extent his own behaviour contributed to his isolation, in that he was rather secretive, rarely confiding in others (Rogow 1986: 11) Moreover, he was disputatious and combative in advancing his iconoclastic opinions on science, religion and politics, and he became a rather dangerous person for others to be associated with.

By all accounts Hobbes was also a fearful person, much concerned about his physical safety. He was reportedly 'afraid of the dark and kept a candle burning at night', and 'he would not be left alone in any empty house'. A contemporary described him as a 'great Coward, whose whole Life was govern'd by his Fears'. (Rogow 1986: 241) Aubrey wrote that 'I have often heard him say that he was . . . afrayd of being knockt on the head for five or ten pounds, which rogues might thinke he had in his chamber'. (Aubrey 1949: 254)

Hobbes was also anxious about political threats to his safety. For example, in 1641 he fled from England to France because he feared that the Long Parliament would imprison him in the Tower, or even seek to take his life, because he had expressed royalist views in his *Elements of Law*. With much apprehension he returned to England ten years later only because he believed that his life was in even greater danger from French priests who had been incensed by his attack on the Papacy in *Leviathan*, and who had persuaded the exiled Charles to expel him from the English Court in France.

> And they accus'd me to the King, that I
> Seem'd to approve *Cromwel's* Impiety,
> And Countenance the worst of Wickedness:
> This was believ'd, and I appear'd no less
> Than a Grand Enemy, so that I was for't
> Banish'd both the King's Presence and his Court . . .
> And stood amazed, like a poor Exile
> Encompassed with Terrour all the while . . .
> Then home I came, not sure of safety there,
> Though I cou'd not be safer any where.
> (Hobbes 1979: 11)

The later years of Hobbes's long life were also clouded by fears of parliamentary hostility. After the Great Fire of London in 1666, a Bill was introduced into the House of Commons to make heresy a criminal offence, and Hobbes's *Leviathan* was targeted in Committee. Although the Bill failed, it was repeatedly reintroduced in later years. Hobbes's evident anxiety led him to burn some of his papers (Aubrey 1949: 245).

Finally, there is evidence that Hobbes sought to prolong his life by physical exercise. 'Besides his dayly walking, he did twice or thrice a yeare play at tennis (at about seventy-five he did it); then went to bed there and was well rubbed . . . This he did believe would make him live two or three yeares the longer' (Aubrey 1949: 252). It was only when he was well into his eighties that Hobbes lost his fear of death.

> I've now Compleeted my Eighty fourth year,
> And Death approaching, prompts me not to fear.
> (Hobbes 1979: 18)

The question arises, however, why, if Hobbes was so anxious for his self-preservation, did he publish doctrines that he must have known would provoke people in positions of power to take action against him? As Rogow (1986: 175) points out, Hobbes chose 'not merely to jar or bruise but to draw blood' in attacking religious and secular prejudices.

In answer to this question, Peters suggests that in the case of religious prejudices, Hobbes could not restrain himself. 'Hobbes has the angry, aggressive style of an insecure man, and when he writes about religious organisations his furious pen seems almost to jab and lacerate the paper as if it were a Puritan or a Catholic' (Peters 1967: 28–9). But what drove Hobbes into such a rage? Why could he not restrain himself? The answer is pride – Hobbes held a very high opinion of his intellectual abilities, and felt a messianic duty to correct the errors of others. At times, the compulsion to point out the truth overrode almost any other consideration in his mind. He was embroiled in several academic disputes – notably with Bishop Bramwell and John Wallis – where 'the rather lofty tone of Hobbes's easily wounded pride' (Malcolm 1988: 49) was much in evidence.

What bearing, if any, do these personality traits of Hobbes have on his political theory? The most obvious link is between Hobbes's personality and the view of human nature expressed in *Leviathan*. Ironically, perhaps, Hobbes himself insisted that we can only understand human nature by looking into ourselves:

> to read one another . . . read thyself . . . whosoever looketh into himself, and considereth what he doth, when he does *think, opine, reason, hope, fear*, etc. and upon what grounds; he shall thereby read and know, what are the thoughts and passions of all other men upon the like occasions.
> (Hobbes 1946: 6)

In his account of human nature, Hobbes identified three causes of quarrel: 'competition', 'diffidence', and 'glory'. 'The first, maketh men invade for gain; the second, for safety; and the third, for reputation' (Hobbes 1946: 81). These three causes of quarrel led men in the state of nature to a condition of 'war . . . of every man, against every man', in which the 'life of man, [was] solitary, poor, nasty, brutish, and short' (Hobbes 1946: 82). However, Hobbes also attributed to man three 'passions' that inclined him to 'peace': 'fear of death; desire of such things as are necessary to commodious living; and a hope by their industry to obtain them' (Hobbes 1946: 84).

It is not hard to imagine that in this picture of raw humanity, Hobbes was projecting his own personality. Although (unlike his father, perhaps significantly) he was never given to 'invade' others, Hobbes was certainly competitive (in the realm of ideas), diffident (personally insecure) and vainglorious (jealous of his reputation). Moreover, he clearly suffered from a fear of death – the strongest of all the Hobbesian passions – and yearned for a settled life of leisure and study.

Three elements that are common to Hobbes and his picture of human nature deserve special attention – those of self-preservation, fear and solitariness. As we have seen, Hobbes was obsessively preoccupied with preserving himself, and in projecting this trait on to humanity at large he set the entire framework for his ideas on politics. Indeed, the *Leviathan* could be described as the political theory of self-preservation.

Second, we have seen that Hobbes was a fearful and anxious person; in attributing this characteristic to humanity at large, again he ensured that it played a critical role in his political theory. Fear was what drove men to escape from the state of nature and to form a commonwealth, and fear was also the reason why men obeyed the sovereign thereby established by their covenants.

Third, solitariness is another link between Hobbes the man and Hobbes the theorist of human nature. Given the isolation of his own life, it is not without significance that in his description of life in the state of nature – 'solitary, poor, nasty, brutish and short' – the first adjective was 'solitary'. Rogow speculates that 'we can therefore surmise that he regarded the "solitary" condition not just as a foremost evil in the state of nature and in war but also as a particularly unhappy circumstance in his own life' (Rogow 1986: 242).

There is a further feature of Hobbesian psychology that reflects Hobbes's own personality – the faculty of reason. Although he sometimes allowed his passion for the truth to lead him into danger, Hobbes was careful to formulate strategies for escaping the wrath of his antagonists. Similarly, in his analysis of the state of nature, he showed how man's capacity for reasoning provided the key to his escape from the 'war of all against all'. By reasoning, men perceived the laws of nature, which specified the mechanisms whereby they could safely relinquish their right to all things and submit to a sovereign rule which would afford them peace and security.

It may be objected, however, that there are many other features of Hobbesian man that do not bear any resemblance to the personality of Hobbes. For instance, the 'restless desire for power after power until death' (Hobbes 1946: 64) did not appear to characterise Hobbes himself, since he showed no inclination to obtain political office. However, we must remember that power was defined very broadly by Hobbes. 'The Power *of a man* . . . is his present means, to obtain some future apparent good' (Hobbes 1946: 56). And it included the power of persuasion. 'Eloquence is power; because it is seeming prudence' (Hobbes 1946: 57). There is little doubt that Hobbes was very keen to exert the power of persuasion – that is to convert both subjects and rulers to his point of view and thereby to secure a stable and peaceful state. He declared to the Duke of Newcastle that his *Elements of Law* 'would be an incomparable benefit to commonwealth, if every man held the opinions concerning law and policy here delivered' (Rogow 1986: 126). If successful, such influence would have been a form of political power.

Moreover, Hobbes's technique for maintaining his prickly self-esteem was to take the offensive in disputation, protecting himself against others' hostility by dominating them – the strategy of the pre-emptive strike. Such a strategy, which Hobbes described in *Leviathan* as 'diffidence', is characterised in Karen Horney's analysis of the strategy of the apprehensive person in terms of the precept 'If I have power, no one can hurt me'.

Alternatively, we might interpret Hobbes as subsuming or sublimating his natural desire for (political) power in his desire for intellectual power – to gain self-esteem from the pen rather than the sword. This would explain the contrast between his physical timorousness and his mental combativeness – a contrast exemplified by his use of military metaphors, as Rogow (1986: 241) notes. 'In his *Autobiography* . . . he had frequent recourse to battlefield similes and images, though he was a man who would go to almost any extreme to avoid battlefields.' Significantly, Hobbes also likened his academic disputes to military engagements. For instance, he referred to one of his opponents – the mathematician John Wallis – as 'The Army' who thought of nothing but 'Victory', and he admitted 'Liking the Combat' and responding in kind, concluding that 'These were my Wars' (Hobbes 1979: 16).

So far we have discussed the links between Hobbes's personality and his view of the human dilemma represented by the state of nature resulting from his theory of human nature. What remains to be discussed is the connection between Hobbes's personality and his solution to that dilemma – absolute sovereignty. In *Leviathan* the sovereign acquired authority as a result of a covenant entered into by the people to submit to his rule in all things save where their own lives would thereby be put in danger. As a result of this non-renegotiable covenant, the sovereign's authority was absolute: he had supreme executive, legislative, judicial, administrative, military and ecclesiastical power; none of his subjects could legitimately stand in judgement over his actions or seek to punish him; he was not bound by civil law (which he alone made); all his actions were just (since he was not a party to the covenant, he could not break it, and therefore he could not commit injustice); he could censor any opinion or doctrine which he deemed prejudicial to peace; he was the sole determiner of his subjects' property rights; and he alone had power to reward and punish subjects.

One obvious link between Hobbes's personality and this theory of sovereignty is that absolute authority was necessary to provide the physical security for which (as we saw earlier) Hobbes himself deeply yearned. He argued that unless his authority was absolute, the sovereign would lack the power to deter law breakers and other free riders.

However, it could be objected that much of Hobbes's fear for his safety was caused by action against him threatened by the state itself – notably by the Long Parliament in 1641 and by the House of Commons in 1666 – and that an increase in the power of the state was hardly likely to alleviate that fear. In reply to this objection, it is important to note that in both these situations it was not an absolute sovereign but a limited Parliament, that caused apprehension to Hobbes. In a governmental system derived from *Leviathan*, Hobbes would have no such apprehensions to face, since the absolute sovereign, whose authority Hobbes's writings strongly supported, would have no reason to suppress his views. Moreover, on the other occasion when Hobbes faced serious public danger – in 1651 when he was forced to flee back to England from France, it was not the French *state* but the French *Church* which caused him alarm, and under his prescribed form of government, the Church would be firmly subordinate to the state.

Further connections between Hobbes the man and his prescription of absolute sovereignty are more psychoanalytically based. For example, Rogow speculates that Hobbes's authoritarianism may have been rooted in Hobbes's low self-esteem. The main evidence to support this speculation is that Hobbes once referred to his birth in

demeaning terms: 'I, a poor worm, was born' (Hobbes 1979: 1).
Although Rogow admits that 'such evidence is too flimsy to establish
that Hobbes suffered from self-doubt', he does claim that 'Those
whose own instincts and impulses make them apprehensive, are apt
to call for more religion, which Hobbes did not, or for more authority,
which he did' (Rogow 1986: 247).

Pearlstein argues that Hobbes created the sovereign figure as a
father substitute, pointing out that since the absence of Hobbes
senior was due to desertion rather than death, his mother was unable
to remarry, and so Hobbes was denied a replacement. Pearlstein
claims that it is not unreasonable to conclude that at least part of
Hobbes's motive in writing *Leviathan* was to fill that void by creating
a father figure in an idealised form, endowed with authority, power
and honour. 'Indeed, Hobbes' vision of the Leviathan recalls Freud's
famous statement that " . . . all the features with which we furnish the
great man are traits of the father." Thus Hobbes, who had no real,
personal father, creates the Leviathan' (Pearlstein 1986: 321).

An alternative interpretation is that the *Leviathan* was a fantasy
projection, not of Hobbes senior, but of Hobbes himself. On this
view, the root of Hobbes's authoritarianism lay not in *low* self-
esteem, but in *high* self-esteem. Hobbes confidently believed that
he alone had discovered the true basis of governmental authority –
perhaps he alone could be entrusted with that authority? Although
there is no evidence that Hobbes ever contemplated a political career,
this does not mean that he cannot have fantasised about taking
political control.

JEAN-JACQUES ROUSSEAU (1712–78)

By contrast with Hobbes, for whom there is very little biographical
material, in the case of Rousseau there is abundant documentation.
The main source is Rousseau's astonishingly revealing autobiographical *Confessions*, together with its sequel, *Reveries of the
Solitary Walker*.

As with Hobbes, the circumstances of Rousseau's birth and
upbringing in Geneva were highly significant. After praising 'my
mother's beauty, intellect and talents', Rousseau wrote that 'I was
born a weak and ailing child; I cost my mother her life, and my birth
was the first of my misfortunes'. He added that his 'inconsolable
father believed that he saw his wife again in me, without being able to
forget that it was I who had robbed him of her' (Rousseau 1992 I: 3).
He had a brother, seven years older, who ran away from home when

Rousseau was young, and they never met again – and thus I have remained an only son' (Rousseau 1992 II: 6). Rousseau's father deserted him when Rousseau was ten years old, in a situation not unlike the desertion by Hobbes's father. Rousseau senior had a quarrel with a French Army captain which led to a court charge. To avoid this, Rousseau senior fled to Nyon in Switzerland where he got married again and settled for the rest of his life, rarely contacting his son.

Rousseau was put into the care of his Uncle Bernard, who boarded him with a Protestant Minister and his sister for two years, after which he was apprenticed to an uncouth engraver. Hating his master, Rousseau absconded from Geneva at the age of sixteen and found solace in the beauty of the natural countryside of Savoy, where he was given refuge in the idyllic rural home of Mme de Warens – Rousseau's idealised surrogate mother figure and lover, and a formative influence on his life. In Turin he renounced Protestantism to become a Catholic and he dabbled in music teaching, music copying, and tutoring (in Lyon), devised a new method of musical notation, met Diderot (in Paris) and undertook diplomatic work (in Venice), before settling down with his life-long mistress Thérèse Levasseur (they eventually married), with whom he had five children, all of whom were sent at birth to the Foundling Hospital (conduct that attracted Burke's deadly jibe that Rousseau, a self-proclaimed lover of his kind – humanity – was a hater of his kindred).

In 1750 Rousseau's first major work, the *Discourse on the Arts and Sciences*, won the Dijon Academy prize, and he began to make his name as an *enfant terrible*. Nearly all his most important writings were published during the next twelve years. He contributed articles to Diderot's *Encyclopedia*, despite the fact that his first discourse denounced culture for enslaving humanity, thereby implicitly attacking enlightenment ideas of progress. He had an opera, *The Village Soothsayer*, produced before King Louis XV at Fontainebleu, and a play, *Narcissus*, performed at the Théâtre Français in Paris, though he also provoked uproar in Parisian musical circles by adversely comparing French music with the Italian style. He visited Geneva, returning to the Protestant faith, and in 1755 he published his second discourse – on the *Origin of Inequality* – savagely indicting modern society for its injustice and dehumanisation. His sentimental novel, *Julie ou La Nouvelle Heloise*, appeared in 1761, and the following year saw the publication of both his most important work on politics – *The Social Contract* – and also his most controversial work – *Emile* – his treatise on education, which contained free-thinking religious ideas that so outraged the authorities in France that it was denounced by Parlement.

For the rest of his life Rousseau was pilloried and persecuted for his views, and his books were periodically banned and sometimes publicly burned. Threatened with arrest, he was forced to flee from France to Switzerland in 1762. Three years later he was stoned at Motiers and driven out of his beloved island retreat at Saint-Pierre in the middle of Lake Geneva. *Emile* was burnt in Geneva, where another warrant for Rousseau's arrest was issued.

> These two decrees gave the signal for the cry of execration which went up against me throughout Europe with unexampled fury. All the newspapers, journals and pamphlets sounded a most terrible note of alarm . . . I was called an infidel, an atheist, a lunatic, a madman, a wild beast, a wolf.
>
> (Rousseau 1992 II: 230)

He was 'taken for a monster, a poisoner, an assassin . . . the horror of the human race, the laughing stock of the rabble' (Rousseau 1979: 27–8). After a brief visit to England where he antagonised his host, David Hume, Rousseau returned to France to live precariously under the protection of the Prince de Conti, and later, back in Paris, he was forbidden from giving readings of his *Confessions*.

As a result of these oppressions Rousseau developed a paranoid streak, suspecting a conspiratorial league against him. He quarrelled with almost all his erstwhile friends and collaborators, including Diderot. He died one month after Voltaire, one of his most virulent critics.

This sketch of Rousseau's life suggests four personality traits that are highly relevant to his political theory – uncompromising independent-mindedness, close affinity with nature, chronic insecurity and a passionate temperament. The first two traits lie at the root of one of the two visions of Rousseau's political theory – that represented by his first two *Discourses* – the *Discourse on the Arts and Sciences* and the *Discourse on the Origins of Inequality*. The last two traits lie at the root of the second of the two visions of Rousseau's political theory – that represented by his *Social Contract* and his third *Discourse* – the *Discourse on Political Economy*.

Let us begin with his uncompromising independent-mindedness. Rousseau found it difficult to tolerate obstacles to his will. He referred to 'my unfitness for submitting to any yoke' and declared that 'I was born to love independence' and 'I worship freedom; I abhor restraint, trouble, dependence' (Rousseau 1992 II: 278; I: 110, 32).

This fierce independent-mindedness was partly instinctive – like his noble savage, Rousseau simply could not bear restraint. 'he was a Protestant among Catholics and a Catholic among Protestants' (Malkin 1974: 68). But it was also instrumental – to protect his integrity and authenticity. For example, Rousseau refused to compromise his freedom to write what he liked (Rousseau 1992 II: 53). He also declined to accept gifts – 'I know no slavery more cruel and degrading than that' – and refused a pension from the King – 'I escaped the yoke which it would have imposed upon me . . . I could only flatter or keep my mouth closed if I accepted this pension' (Rousseau 1992 II: 19, 31).

Rousseau's desire to distance himself from society – his need for solitude – is the link between his independent-mindedness and his affinity with nature. He yearned for isolation, describing his 'total renunciation of the world and the great love of solitude which has never since left me' (Rousseau 1979: 52). This was partly because he felt ill at ease in society (Rousseau 1992 I: 104) – a feeling that increased with age – and partly due to his contempt for social rituals (Rousseau 1992 I: 141). He was a private not a public man (Rousseau 1992 II: 288), and he had an aversion to society: 'as soon as I feel the yoke of . . . human society I become rebellious' (Rousseau 1979: 103).

Rousseau infinitely preferred nature to society. By contrast to his severe criticism of society, he had nothing but praise for nature (Rousseau 1992 II: 281). His feelings were ravished by the sight of mountains and lakes, and his mind was captivated by the complexity of flora and fauna (he was a talented botanist). 'I feel transports of joy and inexpressible raptures in becoming fused as it were with the great system of beings and identifying myself with the whole of nature' (Rousseau 1979: 111). Accordingly, he preferred to live in the country – closer to nature – than in the town (Rousseau 1992 II: 52).

It may be asked, however, why was Rousseau so independently minded, and why did he develop this close affinity with nature? The answers to these questions are connected; Rousseau's independent-mindedness and his nature worship both arose from the same root – his inability to form satisfactory long-term relationships with members of the same sex. His early relationships with males were unfulfilling; he failed to bond with his errant father, partly because he felt guilt for his mother's death – which also clouded his relationship with his brother, whom he knew for only a short period; his uncle was a remote figure; his master was a tyrant; he was led astray by a number of unstable young men; and a close encounter with a homosexually inclined religious novice filled him with revulsion. In later life, Rousseau quarrelled with nearly all his male friends and associates, though he did retain an affectionate if obsequious regard for a few venerable acquaintances (for example the Duke of Luxemburg). Kligerman (1951: 243) attributes to Rousseau an 'intense dread of accepting anything from men for fear of being pushed into the passive, masochistic, castrated role'.

Rousseau's independent-mindedness may therefore be seen as a form of compensation for his failed personal relationships with men – he withdrew into himself, falling back on his own resources. Crocker suggests that Rousseau's independent-mindedness was a reaction formation.

> It was because he was so dependent, and longed for infantile dependence, that guilt and shame made him yearn for independence. Independence was a 'reaction formation' to dependence ... a way both of compensating for his dependency and of avenging his failure to integrate into a normal state of interdependence.
>
> (Crocker 1973: 190)

Rousseau's nature-worship may be seen as another kind of compensation – recoiling from human (male) company, he turned to the natural world and to the countryside for solace. If he could not relate to men, he could relate to nature; nature did not seek to coerce or threaten him. And in his countryside retreat he could have Thérèse with him.

As we shall see, these two personality traits of Rousseau – uncompromising independent-mindedness and close affinity with nature – are the keys to the political ideas in his first two *Discourses*. Let us now turn to the remaining two personality traits of Rousseau identified above – chronic insecurity and a passionate temperament – which I will argue provide the keys to the political ideas of his *Social Contract* and his third *Discourse*.

That Rousseau was deeply insecure seems evident from his *Confessions*. It is hardly surprising that someone who lost his mother at birth, was abandoned by his father at ten, and drifted around the countryside for years with only his wits to support him, would feel insecure. The full extent of Rousseau's feelings of insecurity were, however, revealed only at the later stages of his life, when he suffered from a persecution complex.

In his mid-forties Rousseau developed a paranoid suspicion of other people that gripped him for the rest of his life. Although his experiences of public execration and governmental warrants fuelled this paranoia, the main focus of it was the systematic treachery that he detected in the actions of his erstwhile friends and associates. His friends turned against him not because they envied his literary success, but because they felt threatened by his renunciation of fashionable society (Rousseau 1992 II: 14). He claimed that 'No sooner have I brought together separate friends of my own than they have infallibly combined against me' (Rousseau 1992 II: 48). The subsequent alienation from others left Rousseau an isolated figure. 'So now I am alone in the world, with no brother, neighbour, or friend, nor any company left me but my own' (Rousseau 1979: 27).

As we shall see, this persecution mania, and the chronic insecurity of which it was a symptom, are connected to Rousseau's *Social Contract* and third *Discourse*, in that the ideal state was designed to put an end to all divisions which were the source of such conspiracies, and to draw people together in a spirit of genuine unity. In such a state Rousseau believed he would have found the security so lacking in his own nomadic and haunted life. Hence Rousseau's insecurity provides one of the two keys to the political ideas in his *Social Contract* and third *Discourse*. The other key lies in Rousseau's passionate nature, which made him yearn for a total relationship with a woman. Let me now explain this second key.

Unlike Hobbes, Rousseau was a man of passion rather than of reason. 'I felt before I thought . . . I am a man of very strong passions, and, while I am stirred by them, nothing can equal my impetuosity' (Rousseau 1992 I: 4, 30). His passions gave him a tortured life: 'My passions have made me live, and my passions have killed me' (Rousseau 1992 I: 200).

Rousseau's deepest passion was for a female soulmate.

> The first, the greatest, the most powerful, the most irrepressible of all my needs was entirely in my heart; it was the need of a companionship as intimate as was possible; it was for that purpose especially that I needed a woman rather than a man.
>
> (Rousseau 1992 II: 64)

The only woman ever to fulfil that need was Mme de Warens, and when that relationship – described by Kligerman (1951: 244) as Rousseau's 'regression to infantile dependence' – foundered, Rousseau in his mid-twenties was cast into a void from which he never fully recovered. 'Destiny had deprived me of, or, at least in part, alienated me from, that heart for which Nature had formed me.

From that moment I was alone; for with me it has always been everything or nothing' (Rousseau 1992 I: 304).

At one stage Rousseau thought that Thérèse might fill the emotional void, but he realised eventually that she could not commit herself totally to him, even when they were living together in their countryside retreat. 'This singular want was such, that the most intimate corporal union had been unable to satisfy it; I should have wanted two souls in the same body; without that, I was always conscious of a void' (Rousseau 1992 II: 65).

Hence Rousseau's deepest need remained frustrated (Rousseau 1992 II: 70–1, 74, 75). He explained how this frustration made him turn away from the real world and to create a fantasy world – in his novel, *Julie* (1761).

> The impossibility of grasping realities threw me into the land of chimeras, and, seeing nothing in existence which was worthy of my enthusiasm, I sought nourishment for it in an ideal world, which my fertile imagination soon peopled with beings after my own heart . . . I entirely forgot the human race, and created for myself societies of perfect beings, heavenly alike in their beauties and virtues; trusty, tender, and loyal friends such as I never found in this world below.
>
> (Rousseau 1992 II: 77)

It is the central argument of my interpretation of Rousseau that one year later in his *Social Contract* he created a similarly artificial world – the male-dominated world of politics – designed to satisfy his cravings for a political utopia (just as *Julie* was designed to satisfy his cravings for a female-dominated domestic utopia) in which the closest possible union would be forged between citizens. In this sense, *Social Contract* is the political sublimation of Rousseau's frustrated search for perfect love.

In answer to the questions of why Rousseau felt so chronically insecure, and why he suffered from frustrated passion, we may speculate that the explanation in both cases lies in his overexpectation in his relationships, especially with women. Rousseau may have overdramatised the effect of the loss of his mother at his birth, but he spent the rest of his life vainly searching for someone who could take her place. Since he demanded impossibly high qualities in the successful candidate – idealisations of his mother's qualities – unsurprisingly he was frustrated, and he never found security.

We are now in a position to turn to the two visions in Rousseau's political theory (the one expressed in his first two *Discourses*, and the other expressed in his *Social Contract* and third *Discourse*), in order to demonstrate how they respectively reflect the two sets of personality traits described above (his independent-mindedness and nature-worship on the one hand; and his chronic insecurity and frustrated passion on the other). Let us begin with the *Discourse on the Arts and Sciences* (the first *Discourse*).

Rousseau's first *Discourse* was a sustained attack on the artificiality and conformism of modern society. The arts had destroyed the natural basis of morality in the human heart (Rousseau 1973: 6). As for the sciences, they had undermined 'that happy state of ignorance, in which the wisdom of providence had placed us', corrupting the 'simplicity which prevailed in the earliest times . . . when men were innocent and virtuous' (Rousseau 1973: 14, 20).

These sentiments reflect both Rousseau's independent-mindedness and his nature worship. In denouncing the 'servile conformity' of modern society, he was giving vent to his personal anguish at the controls over his own conduct which were imposed by others. In attacking science, he was defending his beloved nature from exploitation.

In his second *Discourse*, the *Discourse on the Origins of Inequality*, Rousseau broadened this attack on the pernicious effect of the arts and sciences to an attack on the pernicious effect of society itself. In Part I, he sketched a powerful if hypothetical portrait of pre-social or natural man – the noble savage – as 'an animal . . . satisfying his hunger at the first oak . . . slaking his thirst at the first brook, finding his bed at the foot of the tree which afforded him a repast; and with that all his wants supplied' (Rousseau 1973: 52). Natural man had insufficient imagination to think of other needs – such as the psychic need for glory which Hobbes had attributed to him. And he had no reasoning capacity at all – unlike Hobbesian man. 'a state of reflection is one contrary to nature . . . the man who meditates is a depraved animal' (Rousseau 1973: 56).

In Rousseau's state of nature, there were no arts, sciences, agriculture, industry or private property, not because human conflict made them impossible to sustain, as Hobbes had claimed, but because natural man had neither the desire for the benefits they conferred nor the intelligence to invent them. There would not be conflict between men in the state of nature because the simple needs of each would be satisfied without contact between them. Indeed, there were no mutual relations sustained enough to constitute either peace or war. Natural man was good; there was no original sin in humanity. The first impulses of nature were always right, and the noble savage was driven by the twin impulses of concern for his own survival (not to be confused with Hobbesian competitive egoism), and concern for others (compassion or sympathy).

Clearly this picture of the natural condition expressed both Rousseau's independent-mindedness and his personal attachment to nature. He identified both with the noble savage's freedom to roam without restriction in the forests and pastures, and with his simple lifestyle and diet. Natural man was enacting Rousseau's fantasy of both total independence and complete oneness with nature – albeit at an unconscious level (natural man *enjoyed* but did not *worship* nature) (Rousseau 1979: 101).

This personal investment in the noble savage became even more explicit in Part II of the second *Discourse* where Rousseau traced the stages of humanity's descent from this hypothetical Garden of Eden to the present-day Hell on Earth which constituted so-called civilised society. Deterioration set in as humans began to develop self-consciousness of their superiority both over other animals and over each other; as their increased leisure stimulated their desire for creature comforts; and as technological advances gave rise to a thorough-going institution of private property, which made people dependent on each other. 'Each became in some degree a slave even in becoming the master of other men: if rich, they stood in need of the services of others; if poor, of their assistance' (Rousseau 1973: 95). It also spawned inequality, avarice and rivalry between people, degenerating into a 'horrible state of war', and 'perpetual conflicts' between 'the title of the strongest and that of the first occupier' which 'never ended but in battles and bloodshed' (Rousseau 1973: 97). So, significantly, the features which Hobbes attributed to the state of nature Rousseau attributed to the corruption of the state of nature.

The penultimate stage of this process of degeneration described by Rousseau was that of the fraudulent contract of government (not to be confused with the social contract). This was a device cunningly used by the rich to seduce the poor into accepting a legitimation of their enslavement (Rousseau 1973: 99). In the final condition – despotism – everyone was enslaved; subjects were enslaved to the despot; the despot was enslaved to his passions. Moreover, 'the despot is master only so long as he remains the strongest' (Rousseau 1973: 114).

Clearly, in these first two *Discourses*, there is evidence of considerable psychological investment on Rousseau's part. First, his uncompromising independent-mindedness is reflected in the natural savage's proud refusal to submit to any artificial yoke. Rousseau liked to portray himself in a similar way, for example, by nobly declining to be manipulated or bought by patrons. The class analysis which deepened his attack on the coercion in contemporary society, mirrors Rousseau's personal aversion to property and the trappings of wealth. In turn this may be a reaction formation on his part for his failure to accumulate riches or it may express his apprehension (even terror) of taking on the responsibility for any form of dependence. Alternatively, in the stark picture he painted of his contemporary society, he may have been retaliating against it for the damage it had inflicted upon him.

Second, Rousseau's personal attraction towards nature is strongly reflected in his highly romanticised picture of natural man who was perfectly at one with the natural environment – indeed simply a part of that environment. He clearly saw himself as the ideal prototype of natural man (and Thérèse as the ideal prototype of natural woman). Conversely, in the stark picture he painted of his contemporary society as the antithesis of the natural order in which he would have thrived, he was revenging himself for being prevented from living in accordance with nature.

We must now turn, finally, to Rousseau's most important work in political theory – his *Social Contract*, together with his third *Discourse*. Here he offered an entirely different vision of politics from that conveyed in his first two *Discourses* – a vision which rejected both independence and nature, and embraced instead interdependence and social identity. This new vision, I will argue, arose out of Rousseau's chronic insecurity and passionate temperament.

By contrast to the first two *Discourses*, which were diatribes against the existing order in favour of the natural order, Rousseau's *Social Contract* and third *Discourse* were diatribes against *both* the existing order *and* the natural order. What Rousseau set out in these diatribes was a new social order, in which all traces of both existing social man and hypothetical natural man were eliminated, and in their stead was a new ideal social man. Taking for granted that although man might be 'born free', he was, and would always remain, 'everywhere . . . in chains', Rousseau saw his task as prescribing legitimate chains (Rousseau 1973: 181). That prescription took the form of a unique kind of social contract, 'in which each, while uniting himself with all, may still obey himself alone, and remain as free as before' (Rousseau 1973: 191).

What Rousseau meant by this statement, was not that man retained the liberty he enjoyed in the state of nature, but that he exchanged one form of liberty (what Berlin has called 'negative' freedom) for another, more valuable form ('positive' freedom). He gave up *natural* liberty to gain *civil* and *moral* liberty. What man lost in entering this political society was his 'natural liberty'; what he gained was both 'civil liberty' and more importantly 'moral liberty which alone makes him truly master of himself; for the mere impulse of appetite is slavery, while obedience to a law which we prescribe to ourselves is liberty' (Rousseau 1973: 196).

This exchange was, however, very demanding. It required, wrote Rousseau, 'the total alienation of each associate, together with all his rights, to the whole community'. Although he added that 'each man, in giving himself to all, gives himself to nobody', what this meant was that '*Each of us puts his person and all his power in common under the supreme direction of the general will*' (Rousseau 1973: 192).

This identification by Rousseau of the will of a person with the general will lay at the heart of the *Social Contract*. It entailed a distinction between a person's *particular* or natural and self-interested will on the one hand, and his *general* will on the other (Rousseau 1973: 194). Where the two came into conflict, Rousseau was quite unequivocal; the general will had to prevail, by force if necessary. 'whoever refuses to obey the general will shall be compelled to do so by the whole body. This means nothing less than that he will be forced to be free' (Rousseau 1973: 195).

Rousseau spelled out the full implications of the general will in his third *Discourse* – the *Discourse on Political Economy*. It was a means of

> making men free by making them subject; of using in the service of the State the properties, the persons, and even the lives of all its members, without constraining and without consulting them; of confining their will by their own admission; of overcoming their refusal by that consent, and forcing them to punish themselves when they act against their own will.
>
> (Rousseau 1973: 135–6)

Being forced to be free was not something that was entirely unwelcome to Rousseau's own nature. He was not averse to giving up his precious independence if that was the price that he had to pay for the unity with another that he so dearly desired. Indeed he was prepared to undergo the most abject self-renunciation in pursuit of this objective. 'To lie at the feet of an imperious mistress, to obey her commands, to ask her forgiveness – this was for me a sweet enjoyment' (Rousseau 1992 I: 13). Hence the appropriateness of Kligerman's remark that 'The General Will is an expression of identification of the members of the group with the mother' (Kligerman 1951: 251).

Similarly, Rousseau was willing to be forced to live the rest of his life on the island of Saint-Pierre.

> It is little enough that I am permitted to live here. I could wish to be condemned, to be forced to remain in this island . . . I at last came to wish, with incredible eagerness, that instead of merely tolerating my stay in the island, my persecutors would assign it to me as a prison for life.
>
> (Rousseau 1992 II: 284)

So in Rousseau's *Social Contract* and third *Discourse*, the independent-mindedness that was so much a feature of the two discourses, was replaced by an emphasis on *interdependence* – the total integration of subjects into a united whole. Belonging to such a political whole represented compensation for Rousseau for his failure to achieve fulfilment in his personal relationships with women. The other feature of the two discourses – the emphasis upon the natural – was also absent from the *Social Contract* and the third *Disourse*. Rousseau made it clear that his ideal society was one for which natural man would have to be completely transformed – that is, denaturalised. The 'Legislator' was charged with responsibility for 'changing human nature', by 'taking away from man his own resources' and giving him 'instead new ones alien to him' (Rousseau 1973: 214).

It seems, therefore, that Rousseau offered us two quite distinct political visions in his writings, and that each vision reflected a different aspect of his complex personality. The first vision, presented in his first two *Discourses – On the Arts and Sciences* and *On the Origins of Inequality* – looked backward to an imaginary state of nature before society had ruined the free and independent life of the noble savage. This vision clearly reflected Rousseau's defensive independent-mindedness and escapist love of things natural. The second vision, presented in his *Social Contract* and *Discourse on Political Economy*, looked forward to an ideal state which was the antithesis of the natural condition, in that it prescribed a highly integrated political order in which the denaturalised individuals were totally subjected to the general will, which they participated in expressing. This vision was sublimated compensation for Rousseau's personal insecurity and frustrated emotions. The one thing that these two political visions shared in common was their rejection of existing society.

Does this psychological analysis give us a better understanding of Rousseau's political theory? I suggest that in one respect it does; it helps us to understand why he produced his two different visions – the anti-political vision of the first two *Discourses*, and the highly politicised vision of the *Social Contract*. These two visions represented two contrasting sides of Rousseau's personality – the defensive and escapist side on the one hand, leading him to avoid commitments; and the paranoid and frustrated side on the other side, making him yearn for commitments. The first side lent itself easily to libertarian anarchism; the second side lent itself readily to totalitarian democracy. If we are willing to accept this explanation, we might cease trying to find a way of rendering Rousseau's two political visions intellectually consistent. Rousseau's political writings were no more consistent than was his personality.

However, Crocker, following Talmon (1960), claims that there is a deeper unity behind these contradictions. 'They are seen not simply as a basic contradiction or split, but rather as a dynamic tension of polarities which constitute the organic unity of his personality' (Crocker 1973: 196). This 'organic unity' lies in Rousseau's 'authoritarian personality', which includes the following characteristics: intolerance of ambiguity; defensiveness; respect for military virtues such as order, security and certainty; ethnocentrism, nationalism and in-group exclusiveness; gender differences; latent homosexuality; evasion; compulsive behaviour; obsession with secrecy and duplicity; desire for unity and harmony; snobbery; and a conspiratorial conception of history in which a mythical golden age has been destroyed by the enemy (Crocker 1973: 193–5).

However, illuminating though Crocker's argument is, the authoritarian elements that he identifies in Rousseau's personality are nearly all related exclusively to the second of the two visions – totalitarian democracy – and cast little light on the first vision – libertarian anarchism. The contrast between the two visions, therefore, seems to remain a reflection of unresolved tensions in Rousseau's personality.

CONCLUSION

This study has suggested that some illumination may be cast on the political ideas of Hobbes and Rousseau by an analysis of their respective personalities. We may also draw some comparative conclusions. For example, I would suggest that the reason why Hobbes chose an authoritarian regime, whereas Rousseau chose a totalitarian (albeit democratic) regime, can be explained by reference to their respective personalities. In both cases their choice of regime was dictated by insecurity, but for Hobbes the insecurity was physical (he feared imprisonment or even death), whereas for Rousseau the insecurity was psychological (he feared failure in his personal relationships). Accordingly, Hobbes's goal was a regime which would maintain physical stability, whereas Rousseau's goal was a regime that would produce psychological integration.

As to whether the political theory of Hobbes was more, or less, influenced by his personality than was Rousseau's by his personality, I do not think we can produce a definitive answer. Still less can we draw the conclusion that every political theorists's ideas *must* be influenced by their personalities; whether they are or not, depends upon the evidence in each case. For this reason I do not endorse the sweeping view expressed by Emile Faguet that 'Often, if not always, while expressing his ideas, a philosopher merely analyzes his own character. Often, if not always, the philosopher's starting point is his own feelings' (Quoted in Pearlstein 1986: 310–11).

On the question of recruitment – that is, of whether political theorists tend to be people who manifest particular personality traits such as insecurity – even less can be confidently asserted in advance of further evidence. It may prove significant, however, that both Hobbes and Rousseau *were* insecure; that both suffered parental loss early in life; that both were introspective and isolated; and that both were timorous yet aggressive and vainglorious in their writing.

Finally, it should be noted that none of this implies that the strength of an argument adduced in the political theories of either Hobbes or Rousseau is necessarily weakened by a psychological explanation of its origin. The strength of an argument in political theory depends exclusively upon its intellectual merits, not upon the personality of its advocate. In this respect, the sphere of political theory diverges from the sphere of political activity, where the question of who is the advocate of a policy may be more important than the coherence of the policy itself.

On the other hand, our understanding of the psychological reasons why a political theorist presented a particular argument may help us to interpret the theorist's work more effectively. For example, knowledge of Rousseau's divided personality shows us that the search for a philosophically coherent interpretation of his political theory may be misplaced. Moreover, there is a contextual consideration to be borne in mind. If we are interested in the historical question of why a political theory was expressed, then part of our answer to that question may be psychologically based; the personality of a theorist may be a relevant matter of historical fact. Of course we may never be able fully to grasp a political thinker's personality – perhaps as in Hobbes's case because of lack of evidence, and in Rousseau's case because of his psychological complexity – but this does not mean that psychological factors should be entirely overlooked by students of political thought. To quote Hugh Berrington out of context, in this area of research 'a fascinating field for speculation and enquiry is open' (Berrington 1974: 367).

NOTE

I am grategul to Peter Jones for many helpful comments on an earlier draft of this chapter, and to Pam Finlay for her research assistance.

REFERENCES

Aubrey, J. (1949) *Brief Lives and Other Selected Writings*, London, The Cresset Press, ed. A. Powell.

Berrington, H. B. (1974) 'The Fiery Chariot: British Prime Ministers and the search for love', *British Journal of Political Science* 4: 345–69.

—— (1976) 'Personality studies and politics', *Teaching Politics* 5: 231–43.

—— (1989a) 'When does personality make a difference? Lord Cherwell and the area bombing of Germany', *International Political Science Review* 10(1): 9–34.

—— (1989b) 'Politics and leadership: does personality make a difference?', *Social Studies Review*, Jan.: 86–9.

Crocker, L. G. (1973) *Jean-Jacques Rousseau: The Prophetic Voice, 1758–1778*, Vol. 2, London: Macmillan.

Hobbes, T. (1946) *Leviathan*, Oxford: Blackwell, ed. M. Oakeshott.

—— (1979) *The Life of Mr Thomas Hobbes of Malmesbury*, Exeter: The Rota, University of Exeter.

Kligerman, C. (1951) 'The Character of Jean Jacques Rousseau', *Psychoanalytic Quarterly* 20: 237–52.

Malcolm, N. (1988) 'Hobbes and the Royal Society', in G. A. J. Rogers and A. Ryan (eds) *Perspectives on Thomas Hobbes*, Oxford: Clarendon.

Malkin, E. E. (1974) 'Reich and Rousseau: an essay in psycho-history', *American Journal of Psychoanalysis* 34(1): 63–72.

Pearlstein, R. M. (1986) 'Of fear, uncertainty, and boldness: the life and thought of Thomas Hobbes', *Journal of Psychohistory* 13(3) Winter: 309–24

Peters, R. (1967) *Hobbes*, London: Penguin.

Rogow, A. A. (1986) *Thomas Hobbes – Radical in the Service of Reaction*, New York: W. W. Norton.

Rousseau, J-J. (1973) *The Social Contract and Discourses*, London: Dent, ed. J. H. Brumfitt and J. C. Hall.
—––––– (1979) *Reveries of the Solitary Walker*, London: Penguin, ed. P. France.
—––––– (1992) *Confessions*, London: D. Campbell, ed. P. N. Furbank.
Talmon, J. L. (1960) *The Rise of Totalitarian Democracy*, New York: Praeger.

Bibliography of Hugh Berrington's writings

(This bibliography does not include reviews or newspaper articles.)

BOOKS

Backbench Opinion in the House of Commons 1955–59 (with S. E. Finer and
D. J. Bartholomew), Oxford: Pergamon, 1961.
How Nations are Governed, London: Pitman, 1964.
Backbench Opinion in the House of Commons 1945–55, Oxford: Pergamon,
1973.
Change in British Politics (ed.), London: Frank Cass, 1984.

ARTICLES AND CHAPTERS

'The campaign in the constituencies: Banbury', in D. E. Butler (ed.) *The
British General Election of 1955*, London: Macmillan, 1955.
'What happened?' (analysis of the 1959 election results), in *Where?*, Fabian
Tract 320, London: Fabian Society, 1959.
'Socialisme devant la société modern' (with Jean Blondel), *Cahiers de la
République*, 1960, (27): 45–56.
'The future of the Liberal Party', *The Listener*, 6 October 1960, 64(1645):
550–1, 560.
'The Parliamentary profession in Britain' (with S. E. Finer), *International
Social Science Journal*, 1961, 13: 600–19. Revised and reprinted in
Decisions and Decision-Makers in the Modern State, Paris: Unesco.
'The Conservative Party: revolts and pressures, 1955–61', *Political Quar-
terly*, October/ December 1961, 32: 363–73.
'Local election results: their relevance to a general election', *Aspect*, May
1963: 48–54.
'Local Elections: the electoral drama', *Aspect*, January 1964: 12–18.
'The General Election of 1964', *Swinton Journal*, 1965, 10(2): 5–11.
'The General Election of 1964', *Journal of the Royal Statistical Society,
Series A, General*, 1965, 128:17–51, 60–6.
'Television and politics: the larger issues', *Journal of the Society of Film and
Television Arts*, 1965, 19: 13–15.

'Where will all the Liberals go?', *New Society*, 10 March 1966: 10–12.

'The General Election of 1966: an analysis of the results', *Swinton Journal*, 1966, 12(2): 3–10.

'Partisanship and dissidence in the nineteenth-century House of Commons', *Parliamentary Affairs*, 1968, 21: 338–74. Reprinted in abridged form in J. D. Lees and R. Kimber (eds.) *Political Parties in Modern Britain*, London: Routledge and Kegan Paul, 1972.

'Local swings and national roundabouts', *Swinton Journal*, 1972, 18(3): 27–33.

Appendix 3, 'Turn-out and the opinion poll predictions', and Appendix 4, 'Voting intention and actual vote', *Public Opinion Polling in the 1970 Election*, London: Market Research Society, 1972.

'The Fiery Chariot: British Prime Ministers and the search for love', *British Journal of Political Science*, 1974, 4: 345–69. Reprinted in abridged form in R. S. Albert (ed.) *Genius and Eminence: The Social Psychology of Creativity and Exceptional Achievement*, Oxford: Pergamon, 1983 reprinted 1992.

'The election of February 1974' (with Trevor Bedeman), *Parliamentary Affairs*, 1974, 27: 317–32.

'Electoral reform and national government' and 'Summary of electoral systems and formulae', in S. E. Finer (ed.) *Adversary Politics and Electoral Reform*, London: Antony Wigram, 1975.

'Personality studies and politics', *Teaching Politics*, 1976, 5: 231–43.

'Measurement of backbench attitudes by Guttman scaling of early day motions: a pilot study, Labour 1968–69' (with John Leece), *British Journal of Political Science*, 1977, 7: 529–41.

'Dangerous corner?', in M. Kolinsky (ed.) *Regional Assertion and European Integration*, Manchester: Manchester University Press, 1977.

'Towards a multi-party Britain', *West European Politics*, 1979, 2: 31–52.

'The Labour left in Parliament: maintenance, erosion and renewal', in D. Kavanagh (ed.) *The Politics of the Labour Party*, London: Allen and Unwin, 1982.

'The British General Election of 1983', *Electoral Studies*, 1983, 2: 263–9.

'Change in British politics: an introduction', in H. Berrington (ed.) *Change in British Politics*, London: Frank Cass, 1984.

'British government: the paradox of strength', in D. Kavanagh and G. Peele (eds) *Comparative Government and Politics: Essays in Honour of S. E. Finer*, London: Heinemann, 1984.

'Centre–periphery conflict in Britain', in Y. Meny and V. Wright (eds) *Centre–Periphery Conflict in Europe*, London: Allen and Unwin, 1985.

'MPs and their constituents in Britain: the history of the relationship', in V. Bogdanor (ed.) *Representatives of the People?*, London: Gower, 1985.

'New parties in Britain: why some live and most die', *International Political Science Review*, 1985, 6: 441–61.

'La stabilité institutionelle masque-t-elle une société en crise?', *Pouvoirs*, 1986, 37: 9–22.

'The changing party system', *Teaching Politics*, 1986, 15: 219–37. Reprinted in L. Robins (ed.) *Political Institutions in Britain*, London: Longman, 1987.

'Deference', 'Political behaviour', 'Political psychology', and 'Roll call analysis', in V. Bogdanor (ed.) *Blackwell's Encyclopaedia of Political Institutions*, Oxford: Blackwell, 1987.

'Political studies in the eighties' (with Pippa Norris), Political Studies Association of the UK, 1987.

'The British General Election of 1987: have we been here before?', *West European Politics*, 1988, 11: 116–21.

'The literature on parties and pressure groups', *Contemporary Record*, Spring 1988, 2(1): 26–8.

'United Kingdom: recent history and politics', in *Western Europe*, London: Europa, 1988.

'Does personality make a difference?', *Social Studies Review*, 1989, 4: 86–9.

'When does personality make a difference: Lord Cherwell and the area bombing of Germany', *International Political Science Review*, 1989, 10: 9–34.

'British public opinion and nuclear weapons' in C. Marsh and C. Fraser (eds) *Public Opinion and Nuclear Weapons*, Basingstoke: Macmillan, 1989.

'Dialogue of the deaf: the elite and the electorate in mid-century Britain', in D. Kavanagh (ed.) *Electoral Politics*, Oxford: Clarendon Press, 1992.

'United Kingdom: recent history and politics', *Western Europe: A Political and Economic Survey*, London: Europa Publications, 1993 (revised edn).

SELECTED UNPUBLISHED PAPERS

'Public opinion polls, British politics, and the 1970 General Election', 1972.

'Public opinion and the Common Market', 1975.

'Backbench attitudes in the House of Commons 1959-76: work in progress', 1979.

'The Common Market and the British Parliamentary parties, 1971: tendencies, issue groups . . . and factionalism', 1980.

'Parliamentary dissension: attitudes and sources', 1981.

Index